Living in Anticipation of the End-Time

BOOKS BY EDWIN ZACKRISON

Melvin Campbell and Edwin Zackrison. *Interactive Readings for Christian Worship.* (Lincoln, NE: iUniverse, Inc., 2003).
———. *Readers Theatre for Christian Worship; Biblical Stories of Courage and Faith.* (Lincoln, NE.: iUniverse, Inc., 2003).

Edwin Zackrison. *In the Loins of Adam; A Historical Study of Original Sin in Adventist Theology.* (Lincoln, NE.: iUniverse, Inc., 2004).
———. *The First Temptation; Seventh-day Adventists and Original Sin.* (Bloomington, IN: iUniverse, Inc., 2015).
———. *About Tomorrow, Let God Worry; The Place of Time.* (Bloomington, IN: iUniverse, Inc., 2019).
———. *God's Camelot; The Security of the Kingdom.* (Bloomington, IN: iUniverse, Inc., 2019).
———. *Christians Are Recovering Human Beings; Returning to God's Reality.* (Bloomington, IN: iUniverse, Inc., 2019).
———. *People Under Construction; Life is a Journey.* (Pittsburgh, PA: Dorrance Publishing Co., 2020).
———. *Profile of a Religious Man: Confessions of a Religion Addict.* (Eugene, OR: Resource Publications, 2020).
———. *For the Love of the World: For God So Loved.* (Eugene, OR: Resource Publications, 2021).

Living in Anticipation of the End-Time

The Conflict between Good and Evil

EDWIN ZACKRISON

Foreword by Florence Young

RESOURCE *Publications* · Eugene, Oregon

LIVING IN ANTICIPATION OF THE END-TIME
The Conflict between Good and Evil

Copyright © 2022 Edwin Zackrison. All rights reserved. Except for brief quotations in critical publications or reviews, no part of this book may be reproduced in any manner without prior written permission from the publisher. Write: Permissions, Wipf and Stock Publishers, 199 W. 8th Ave., Suite 3, Eugene, OR 97401.

Resource Publications
An Imprint of Wipf and Stock Publishers
199 W. 8th Ave., Suite 3
Eugene, OR 97401

www.wipfandstock.com

PAPERBACK ISBN: 978-1-6667-4553-5
HARDCOVER ISBN: 978-1-6667-4554-2
EBOOK ISBN: 978-1-6667-4555-9

06/20/22

All Biblical quotations, unless otherwise indicated, are from the Revised Standard Version of the Bible. Copyright 1946, 1952, 1971, 1973 by the Division of Christian Education of the National Council of the Churches of Christ in the United States of America.

Quotations appearing at the beginning of each chapter are taken from Ted Goodman (ed), The Forbes Book of Business Quotations (New York: Black Dog and Leventhal Publishers, 1997); and Laurence J. Peter, Peter's Quotations: Ideas for our Time (New York: Bantam Books, 1980).

To Darold Simms, Ph.D.

A long-time friend, and brilliant scholar.
Few friendships go as far back as ours.
We grew up together.
No one can understand what
an inspiration he has been to me.
We played sports, we camped, we built
hot rods and we talked at length and still do.
We learned life together.
And we pursued academic disciplines together.
He is my brother.

Contents

Foreword by Florence Young | ix
Preface | xiii
Abbreviations | xvii

CHAPTER 1	LIVING IN ANTICIPATION OF THE END-TIME	1
CHAPTER 2	SALVATION IN THE NEW TESTAMENT	11
CHAPTER 3	DOES HELL BURN FOREVER?	18
CHAPTER 4	GLORY FOR ME	29
CHAPTER 5	WHEN LEGALISM FINALLY DROPS AWAY	32
CHAPTER 6	ON THE ORDINATION OF WOMEN	37
CHAPTER 7	WHAT DO TEENAGERS NEED?	46
CHAPTER 8	THE SHOCKABILITY FACTOR	52
CHAPTER 9	GRACE UNDER FIRE	60
CHAPTER 10	"PATIENT ENDURANCE" IN THE END-TIME	63
CHAPTER 11	GOD'S PROMISE OF QUALITY TIME	67
CHAPTER 12	THE SMOKE OF THEIR TORMENT	81
CHAPTER 13	UNCONDITIONAL LOVE	84
CHAPTER 14	WHAT DOES "THE LATTER RAIN" MEAN TODAY?	87
CHAPTER 15	SAUL THE MONARCH TESTED	91

CHAPTER 16	THE HALL OF SHAME	97
CHAPTER 17	WITH EMOTIONS MIXED	101
CHAPTER 18	EAST OF EDEN	107
CHAPTER 19	THE INFLUENCE OF A TEACHER	111
CHAPTER 20	A JESUS-MODEL OF COMMUNICATION	122

NICODEMUS AT NIGHT | 127

CHAPTER 21	IMPROVING YOUR CHURCH'S RESPONSIVE READINGS	130
CHAPTER 22	A WEEK OF VIOLENCE	149
CHAPTER 23	TOGETHERNESS IN COMMUNITY	155
CHAPTER 24	THE MIDDLE RAIN	163
CHAPTER 25	WHEN ORTHODOXY COSTS TOO MUCH	169
CHAPTER 26	ENHANCING THE PREACHING OF THE PAROUSIA	179
CHAPTER 27	WHO SINGS LOUDER THAN ANGELS?	188
CHAPTER 28	SOME THOUGHTS ON FORGIVENESS	198
CHAPTER 29	COMMUNICATION, INTEGRITY AND MORAL CONFLICT	205
CHAPTER 30	BEWARE OF FALSE TEACHERS	218
CHAPTER 31	I HAVE THE JOY DOWN IN MY HEART	227
CHAPTER 32	MARKED FOR ETERNITY	237

About the Author | 243
Bibliography | 245

Foreword

THE TITLE OF THIS book brings to mind the frantic preparation of the need to "get ready" for the Lord's imminent return. You will not find such a need in this book. You will find, instead, gentle discussions aimed at making life richer in a plethora of circumstances. You will learn of the importance of internalizing the divine principles of the gospel's solution to a life that waits in eager anticipation of the "end time." You will come to understand that you can look forward to finishing your life, no matter your current age, walking with God. Considering your need for true quality time will take on a more significant meaning than the dangerously ho-hum time.

Sin is serious. If God simply pardoned us he could be charged with ignoring that seriousness. So, God has provided principles to guide us through all our years of life, no matter what the number. We have no way of knowing exactly when that time will come.

You have likely heard of those who continue to live life on their own terms until laws are passed or some other earth-shaking event determines that the end is approaching. Such an attitude can completely deprive a person of the joy of walking with God now. A walk with God overcomes much uncertainty in life. Here you will read about examples for our current lives, Dr. Frank Knittel and Dr. Edward Heppenstall, who help us understand the value of living for God.

You will learn about the necessity of truly listening to a teenager, of how the danger of simply earning a living that so easily puts growing children and their needs on the backburner. The years fly by and the toddler is suddenly an adult. Where were you when that toddler has become a teen-ager, needed a listening ear? Rearing children is a time-consuming project. It is the job of a parent to spend that time wisely and profitably. Adult children will thank you.

Is there a place for women in the ordained ministry of the church? This presents a problem in many churches while others outright forbid the presence of women among the ordained. You will discover that the scriptures present no definite answer for either accepting or forbidding women to join that special group. And you will discover that those who oppose women in the ordained ministry usually exaggerate their defense claiming it to be from scripture.

You will be reminded, as you read, that only two ways of life are open to you. You can either walk with God or not. Only two possibilities as life ends—eternal life or eternal death. You will make the choice.

God will care for you, but he will not make your decisions for you. You will learn that eternal death is exactly that. Popular belief suggests an eternally burning hell. *Forever* describes it. But forever lasts only as long as it is needed. Jeremiah spoke of his mother's womb that enlarged forever. Expectant mothers can feel like that as the time for the birth of the baby seems like it will last forever. But the usefulness of that period of time ends just as the time for hell to burn lasts only until there is nothing left to be burned.

As you read about the *hall of shame,* determine that you will not allow circumstances to mold you into something useless to God or to yourself and others. Walk with God who will bring you to live a life useful to yourself and others. You may know difficult times, but you will learn, that God is as near as you allow him to be. Difficult times will eventually become history. You need not walk alone. Patient endurance will play its part during such times.

Living to the glory of God results in the understanding that God has only your best interest in mind. Run your thoughts through God's commands, especially those that focus on the treatment of others. Because you are aware of the love that God shows you, you can accept others regardless of the unacceptable ways in which they treat you. Avenging will eventually be rejected on your list of behaviors. Because we are loved in Jesus we can afford to love others regardless of how they may treat us. At the tough, rough times created by others the apostle Paul reminds us not to avenge ourselves. God has not stopped loving us at such times.

Jesus' conversations were always directional, always creating a desire to change. Jesus taught us as "one who had authority." If you are among the worship leaders in your church you will be reminded that your reason for being is to make the scriptures meaningful in the lives of your listeners. As you listen and learn you will discover the joy in the harmony of a community. The congregation is your community. You will treat the members of your community with dignity. As you are, so they are children bought by God.

You will consider a combination of topics as you read *Living in Anticipation of the End Time*. Living today, in the advance of the "end time," does not have to be a time of fearful watching but can become a time for walking joyously with God as you live out your time on earth, the reality of eternal life.

Florence Young, Ed.D.
Dean of Women, Retired
Loma Linda University
Loma Linda, CA
May 2022

Preface

These post-modern days have changed fast and significantly. Not long ago those who wrote about the "end-time" were preachers—the more fundamentalist, the more extreme by most standards. The end is coming soon, they said, and cartoons were rampant with guys carrying placards captioned by "The end is near." From the time of Christ, whose noncritical predictions included such inspiration for the placards—the religious prophets could not resist continual emphasis on such topics.

Today things are different. The "scientists" and "politicians" make the predictions. "Twelve more years" is what we hear from the latter. But they don't attack with scriptural texts or religious terms. They talk the time in the context of "climate change," and "global warming." They do not agree on how to interpret the evidence, but the religionists also had trouble with agreement. Strange interpretations of biblical texts have now gone the way of so-called science. Various elucidations carry one thing in common: *none gain consensus.* And science is not determined by consensus. So, the arguments continue.

Some enter discussions by censoring those who disagree with them. The opponents are not allowed to speak. They must remain silent. They are called nasty names and unfair methods are used to punish them. They try to stop the incongruous from speaking at all. If you disagree with the communicating powers, your products must be boycotted and punished by destroying your business or terminating your career. The use of social media makes it easier to accomplish this. The religionists declared you destined for *hell*; the politicians attempt more current devastation.

I grew up in a conservative, Christian home. My connection with the "end-time" was from my denomination's understanding of the literal hermeneutics of Scripture. Historically, we watched our views being critically attacked as thought leaders in society attended worldly universities. Then some of us went to those universities or were warned about them in our denominational universities and we had to struggle as well.

My doctoral studies centered in the study of soteriology (salvation) and eschatology (end-times). The former is the examination of salvation history and is clearly an area of faith connected to philosophy. Eschatology is the study of "the last things" and deals with the kingdom of God—still in the areas of faith and religion but more relevant now that the scientific world has taken on "the last things."

My approach in this book is not going to give you a series of charts, something that is often involved when dealing with biblical prophecy. Here I will emphasize the study of salvation. How does soteriology deal with eschatology? The tradition I grew up in had connections inherited from the European Reformation of the sixteenth century and the New England theology of the nineteenth century. New England was involved in the modern era but the twentieth and twenty-first centuries have moved to the post-modern era.

The Industrial Revolution introduced us to a movement of more radical change. Our minds deal today with a different set of concerns. In Martin Luther's day no one talked about humans effecting "climate change." Now such talk is convenient for those who are naturalists or agnostics and make little or no room in their philosophies for the involvement of a supreme being. They do not see natural law as something coming from God. Yet America was founded on a recognition of God and today many are offended if you take that seriously. That is considered outdated, out-moted, and unscientific. It fits into the study of mythology. In their offense they attack the believers in such philosophy.

But something has *not* changed: *We still die.*

Thanks to drugs, prescriptions, modern medical science many have postponed death a bit. We've got penicillin and Salk vaccine and that has taken away some of the fears of my childhood. We are struggling with alleged attempts to cause another world war without nuclear bombs—but the human drive is still there, perhaps this time in the form of biological warfare. The challenges are here even though we entertained the thought that they were gone. How many people do you read about in the news who say that what is happening today is a "judgment of God?" If they are heard at all they are usually depicted as weird since it is not considered normal to think this way.

I don't plan to pursue in this book the approaches of the early Christians from what has become the "eschatological approach" to faith as commonly understood. I rather move from my other half of doctoral studies—developmental psychology. This is not a psychology book, but I am aware of psychological realities, and perhaps more of my readers will identify with me from there than in the theological framework.

Regardless of where you may be in this post-modern age, you are probably struggling with a lot of beliefs your grandparents did not struggle with in the same way. I taught dramatic arts for ten years and that introduced me to discipline that I had not received in Seminary or graduate school. Suddenly I had to create characters on stage who were believable people. These people were from all walks of life and it affected my thinking with sociological understanding. My theatre teachers unfolded simple observations of human behavior that Seminary professors only touched on from a theological position. Each discipline widened my understanding of life.

I hope you will find this book different than any "end-time" book you may have ever read. I will evaluate teaching, education, drama, religion, thought-patterning, behavior, and other developmental aspects of human life.

As you have looked and thought about your life, you may have noticed that little has ended up much like you planned it so long ago. I notice that every day. That doesn't have to be discouraging. *That is life* if you have advanced beyond toddlerhood. Enjoy it and grow into having evidence that God knows what is going on. When I get depressed I am able to recall *"I have read the book, and God wins!"*

Edwin Zackrison, Ph.D., M.B.A.
Professor of Theology and Ministry, Retired
La Sierra University, Riverside, CA
May 2022

ABBREVIATIONS

SCRIPTURE ABBREVIATIONS

Hebrew Bible / Old Testament

Gen	Judg	Neh	Song	Hos	Neh
Exod	Ruth	Esth	Isa	Joel	Hab
Lev	1–2 Sam	Job	Jer	Amos	Zeph
Num	1–2 Kgs	Ps (*pl.*Pss)	Lam	Obad	Hag
Deut	1–2 Chr	Prov	Ezek	Jonah	Zeck
Josh	Ezra	Eccl (or Qob)	Dan	Mic	Mal

New Testament

Matt	Acts	Eph	1–2 Tim	HEB	1-2-3 John
Mark	Rom	Phil	Titus	Jas	Jude
Luke	1–2 Cor	Col	Phlm	1–2 Pet	Rev
John	Gal	1–2 Thess			

CHAPTER ONE

LIVING IN ANTICIPATION OF THE END-TIME

> "I have lived a long time, and I have seen history repeat itself again and again. Be as brave as your fathers before you. Have faith. Go forward."
>
> —THOMAS EDISON

2 CORINTHIANS 4:1–6

¹ Therefore, having this ministry by the mercy of God, we do not lose heart. ² We have renounced disgraceful, underhanded ways; we refuse to practice cunning or to tamper with God's word, but by the open statement of the truth we would commend ourselves to every man's conscience in the sight of God. ³ And even if our gospel is veiled, it is veiled only to those who are perishing. ⁴ In their case the god of this world has blinded the minds of the unbelievers, to keep them from seeing the light of the gospel of the glory of Christ, who is the likeness of God.

⁵ For what we preach is not ourselves, but Jesus Christ as Lord, with ourselves as your servants for Jesus' sake. ⁶ For it is the God who said, "Let light shine out of darkness," who has shone in our hearts to give the light of the knowledge of the glory of God in the face of Christ.

CHRISTIAN OPTIMISM ABOUT THE FUTURE

Where will you be a million years from now? "That's an absurd question," cries the existentialist. "It is illogical and meaningless," thinks the rationalist. "I plan to have been reincarnated a myriad of times," postulates the guru. "Who knows?" questions the agnostic. "Who cares?" queries the cynic. "Dead!" concludes the empiricist.

The Christian's answer is unlike all the rest. "By God's grace I will be alive and enjoying the presence and fellowship of God," the Christian confidently asserts. "I will be on an earth finally cleansed from all sin. Things will be back to normal—like God intended all along."

Christian optimism about the future has always turned some people off. It is no longer popular to be looking constantly on the bright side of life. But it is surely fair to ask which of the above answers we will accept and which of them will bring us the most peace. After all, if God exists and eternity is real, why be satisfied with living only a speck of time in an endless forever?

THE MODERN MIND

The modern mind has incredible difficulty with this question of being around a million years from now. There was a time when people not only believed in eternal life but planned for it. But today there are a thousand gadgets and thought patterns that effectively force hope to flee from us. Many live merely mindful of death, thinking only from day to day, despite their awareness that this narcissistic approach often makes them feel boxed in a prison cell without windows. On the brink of despair, cognizant of the ever-present meaninglessness of life, they would simply cry out: "Why would anyone want to be around a million years from now?" Life is too burdensome to saddle myself with it for that long a time.

One young man told me that he was planning to have a death-bed conversion. "I, for one," he said, "would like to be around a million years from now. I want to live forever," he candidly admitted, "but first I want to live!" The "Christian life," as he had come to perceive it by way of his family, preachers, the religious media, and what he called "church people," was clearly not a delectable example of true living. He saw no correspondence between Jesus' notion of "the abundant life" and his own concept of such a life.

Yet the thought of eternal life and everlasting death, or separation from life, and the sheer fear of annihilation made him shudder. Consequently, he sought to scheme his future, and his answer was, "I will live as I please. I will have my 'fun,' and when I am old I will ask God to forgive me and take me to heaven, just in case Christians are right." It was a fascinating rationale.

LIVING IN THE FACE OF DEATH

Such a scheme is, of course, hopelessly naïve. Even as I wrote this chapter, the clean-up crew was working to collect the rubble and remains of plane and passengers on a major airline disaster a few hundred miles away. Only minutes before this plane crash hundreds of kisses were exchanged, and, at the other end, scores of relatives began planning for a Los Angeles arrival that, unknown to them, would never take place. Death knows no age or time.

Our modern world has produced a generation of people who live constantly in the presence of unexpected death. You can retreat, but you cannot escape; you are going to die. While we have defeated diseases that killed our forefathers, we have in turn created a host of new destroyers that haunt our steps. They are every bit as swift and sure as the plagues of the past. No longer does the "threescore and ten" model of life seem to present a safe guide.

So, the question arises as how to handle such dismal knowledge. The language of modern philosophers and scientists is often couched in words of despair and pessimism, leaving one to wonder whether there is anything today about which one can be legitimately cheerful.

THE ABSURDITY OF LIFE

But planning a death-bed conversion is absurd for an even more serious reason than the expectation of death. If living in fellowship with God now was so torturous here, why did my friend want to live in fellowship with God in heaven forever? He apparently thought that God would perform some sort of miracle to change his hostile attitudes. And if the Christian outlook or lifestyle was a bundle of restrictions and cramps on his style, what made heaven the least bit attractive to him in the first place? He was oblivious to the fact that he viewed heaven as simply an eternal life-support system devoid of fulfillment.

Because present life has become so empty, many no longer seriously want it on extended terms. "I can stand sixty years, but eternity would be too much," they might say. And if life is absurd and devoid of meaning, perhaps they have a point. But must it be absurd? Christ offers us a realistic optimism in his promise to return to earth. His coming says more to us than just escape from hell fire. It also tells us something about living a fulfilling life, both now and then.

Jesus did not present his prophecies of the end-time in the language of despair and pessimism as modern philosophers and scientists tend to do. He always offered a way of escape from both the impending disaster of annihilation and the hopeless despair of meaninglessness. Jesus and his prophets indicated that those who believe in God live in this world as strangers passing through a foreign land, as pilgrims on their way to something better and as refugees whose country has been cruelly wrested from them by a deceitful, lying enemy.

"Rejoice!" they are encouraged, for God has redeemed the earth through Jesus Christ and has annexed it back into the territory of his dominion. Hence their optimism. We can know the happy life of heaven now, and it is for those who have chosen to live it that Jesus is returning. Soon the realization will be a seen fact in the re-creation of heaven and earth.

> [5] Hallelujah! For the Lord our God the Almighty reigns. (Revelation 19:5)

> [5] Behold, I make all things new. (Revelation 21:5)

THE BIBLE MESSAGE

The Bible message explains that long-ago humans lost possession of this earth—that God sent angels to drive them out of the paradise he had created for them, and that Satan won temporary possession by default. In Adam they joined the rebel forces of evil and teamed up against God.

> [24] He drove out the man; and at the east of the garden of Eden he placed the cherubim, and a flaming sword which turned every way, to guard the way to the tree of life. (Genesis 3:24)

> ⁴ In their case the god of this world has blinded the minds of the unbelievers, to keep them from seeing the light of the gospel of the glory of Christ, who is the likeness of God. (2 Corinthians 4:4)

The roots of selfishness grew into the display of irrational evil we witness today. However, in the beginning we did not realize where we were going. The enemy deceived us into thinking life could be more attractive without God. When Adam saw that this was not to be the case at all, and that God was the only source of meaningful life, he wanted back. He did not plan a death-bed conversion, he pleaded for immediate reinstatement. He realized that sin was not to be played with but rather to be avoided and escaped.

God took Adam back, but not into paradise right away. Rather, he promised a Redeemer who would demonstrate both God's love and God's way of life. We would have to live our lives on this earth in the self-regard we had chosen, for our race was now under the temporary dominion of Satan.

Once sin was introduced, God chose to allow us to witness firsthand the deadliness of sin's malignancy. Consequently, as we live on this earth anticipating how things could and will be, we can become eternally convinced of the wisdom of God. Whatever hope we can have, is rooted in the message that the Bible calls "the gospel," or the good news. It is God's solution to the sin problem.

THE GREAT WAR BETWEEN GOD AND EVIL

Nestled in the heart of the Bible[1] is a short story that demonstrates in cameo form the heart of the great war between good and evil, God and Satan, over human beings. A man, Joshua, is seen standing "before the angel of the Lord," and Satan, the accused at Joshua's right side, claiming authority over him.

> ¹ Then he showed me Joshua the high priest standing before the angel of the LORD, and Satan standing at his right hand to accuse him, ² And the LORD said to Satan, "The LORD rebuke you, O Satan! The LORD who has chosen Jerusalem rebuke you! Is not this a brand plucked from the fire?"
>
> ³ Now Joshua was standing before the angel, clothed with filthy garments. ⁴ And the angel said to those who were standing

---

1. Zech 3.

before him, "Remove the filthy garments from him." And to him he said, "Behold, I have taken your iniquity away from you, and I will clothe you with rich apparel." ⁵ And I said, "Let them put a clean turban on his head." So they put a clean turban on his head and clothed him with garments; and the angel of the Lord was standing by.

⁶ And the angel of the Lord enjoined Joshua, ⁷ "Thus says the Lord of hosts: If you will walk in my ways and keep my charge, then you shall rule my house and have charge of my courts, and I will give you the right of access among those who are standing here. ⁸ Hear now, O Joshua the high priest, you and your friends who sit before you, for they are men of good omen: behold, I will bring my servant the Branch. ⁹ For behold, upon the stone which I have set before Joshua, upon a single stone with seven facets, I will engrave its inscription, says the Lord of hosts, and I will remove the guilt of this land in a single day. ¹⁰ In that day, says the Lord of hosts, every one of you will invite his neighbor under his vine and under his fig tree." (Zechariah 3:1–10)

Every attempt of God to get to human beings with truth and life is met with a block attempt by Satan through accusation. "Look at these miserable people. They say they want you but look at their lives—they disobey you; they are sinners, they are mine," he claims. And he throws up their living, or lifestyle, as evidence that they are his disciples.

Joshua stands there in "filthy garments"[2] the evidence of Satan's accusation. He is undone, sinful.[3] But the story ends on a hopeful note when the angel commands,

> ⁴ And the angel said to those who were standing before him, "Remove the filthy garments from him." And to him he said, "Behold, I have taken your iniquity away from you, and I will clothe you with rich apparel." ⁵ And I said, "Let them put a clean turban on his head." So they put a clean turban on his head and clothed him with garments; and the angel of the Lord was standing by. (Zechariah 3:4, 5)

Then he commands Joshua to walk in God's ways.

Here is a simple presentation of the gospel. We all stand with Joshua when we come to God and plead for forgiveness and meaning for our lives. We come in the filthy garments of our own selfishness and despair.

---

2. Zech 3:3.
3. Isa 64:6; Matt 22:1ff.

We have nothing to offer God in terms of payment, right doing, or perfect love. We find ourselves unable to live in harmony. We are rebels. And we can be sure that Satan, "the accuser of our brethren"[4] has sent out criminal records ahead of us to the hearing.

THE SECOND ADAM

Jesus, a member of the Godhead, became a human being, lived among us as we live, and became "the last Adam,"[5] that is, he succeeded where Adam failed as the representative of our human race. He refused to yield himself to Satan's dominion as Adam had. Since he was sinless, he died illegally, for only sinners deserved death in God's universe. So, his death became the currency of eternal life for sinners, to be spent by those who have no claim on life due to their rebellion. The good news of God's solution is that Christ's death on the cross became a substitutionary death, and his righteous life became a vicarious life to stand in the place of our failure through Adam.

Zechariah shows us this picture: The "angel of the Lord" [Jesus?] clothes us with the righteousness that saves, and we are pronounced just and free of the charges that would condemn us. The "garment" represents the sacrifice and character of Christ. We add nothing to his covering. We do not, by our obedience to God, improve on that "garment." Our living in harmony with God is the delightful result of the pronouncement that we are "clean," that the removal of the filthy garments has taken place.

LIVING IN THE FACE OF THE SECOND COMING

A miracle takes place when one accepts the gospel solution. His great crippler has been guilt. Our whole race suffered when Adam participated in that first sin in Eden. God never intended that we sin, because he knew that the only knowledge we would obtain from the tree of the knowledge of good and evil would be the *knowledge of guilt*. Guilt is what one experiences when one's relationship with God is fractured. And we have felt the terrifying effects of Adam's guilt ever since his act of sin.

Immediately upon sinning, Adam experienced the unsettledness of guilt. His psycho-social makeup was disarranged. He blamed Eve for his

---

4. Rev 12:10.
5. 1 Cor 15:45.

sin.[6] He sensed his need for a "garment," and he hid from God.[7] When we are not in a right relationship with people we have loved, we want to avoid them. We blame others for our problems and often blame God for the big problems. But when there is rightness, there is nothing to hide or to run from—there is completeness and welling up of joy.

If we were free of the guilt of sin, we would have no qualms about wanting to live forever in God's presence, for only sin separates us from him. Life without guilt is a thrilling, fulfilling, happy life and the opportunities for wholesome relationships are unlimited. So, here is the tie-in between the gospel and the second coming of Christ. Jesus is returning for those who have, like Joshua, stood before God in filthy garments and asked for clean ones.

They have endured Satan's accusing them for their uncleanness and wickedness. They have admitted they deserve to die, and they have pleaded for the mercy promised them by way of Christ's atoning work for them. It has been granted. They have been delivered from the message of despair that the modern world mouths. They have experienced forgiveness and Christ's character has been credited to them. So, they are free of the crippler guilt, and their human relationships take on a new potential. Their lives change. When our life with God is right, our pilgrimage here on earth is affected.

This life is lived in anticipation of Christ's return. It includes a hope that is infinitely more optimistic, yet not one whit less realistic than that of those who live simply in anticipation of death. Living in the presence of the second coming, knowing that your Lord will soon return, does not mean you must become consciously or mechanically sinless. It does not imply that a person will make no more mistakes or that he will be "otherworldly." Rather, it means that he will be cognizant of the work of Jesus on his behalf, and that his awareness of this fact will cause him to order his life and attitudes toward God and people differently. He will seek to shun sin but to attract sinners to the promises of God.

TRUE AND FALSE MODELING

My young friend may have been naïve about the death-bed conversion, but he was partially the unfortunate victim of "church people" who had left the

6. Gen 3:12.
7. Gen 3:8–10.

impression that Christians living in anticipation of the second coming were not happy or free. Rather, they were burdened down with a terrible load on their way to the kingdom. Jesus demonstrated the difference between the true and the false by a short story in which he pictured a very religious man who was quite proud of his "good works" and a wicked man who admitted this separation from God and cast his whole burden on the Lord. He sincerely asked for deliverance.

> [9] He also told this parable to some who trusted in themselves that they were righteous and despised others: [10] "Two men went up into the temple to pray, one a Pharisee and the other a tax collector. [11] The Pharisee stood and prayed thus with himself, 'God, I thank thee that I am not like other men, extortioners, unjust, adulterers, or even like this tax collector. [12] I fast twice a week, I give tithes of all that I get.' [13] But the tax collector, standing far off, would not even lift up his eyes to heaven, but beat his breast, saying, 'God, be merciful to me a sinner!' [14] I tell you, this man went down to his house justified rather than the other; for every one who exalts himself will be humbled, but he who humbles himself will be exalted." (Luke 18:9–14)

Does living the holy life mean that one's acts are "spiritual?" Or does it mean that one is not a spiritual fraud? Does it mean that one is unreal, superhuman, incredibly detached from reality? Or does it mean that one willingly, humbly repents when he fails? Does it mean one parades his perfection? Or does it mean he admits his shortcomings with true humility?

Some have suggested that the Watergate president will be remembered in history, not for the great things he did in office but for his inability to admit that he was wrong. This suggests the difference between those who want to live *eternally* and those who want to *live* eternally.

Those who live in anticipation of the second coming have an entirely different goal in life. They recognize that sin is a deadly disease, an infinite pool of quicksand, a strangling serpent. They recognize that sin is the mother of despair, the father of pessimism, the child of rebellion; that no one has escaped it but Jesus, and that no one can who refuses him.

A HEALTHY RESPECT FOR THE SINFULNESS OF SIN

Those who live in anticipation of the Lord's coming have a healthy respect for the sinfulness of sin. They know it would ultimately destroy God if it could, even as Christ's antagonists demonstrated at the cross. They hate sin. They live to avoid it in act, to invade it in their nature by a gradual transformation of character ushered in by the "new birth."

So, you need not live in practical despair, and you may start planning what you will be doing a million years from now if you accept the life of Jesus to cover you. Then you will experience what Christ meant when he taught that eternal life begins on this earth for God's pilgrims. And you can know the optimism that comes by living in anticipation of Christ's coming.

> [28] So Christ, having been offered once to bear the sins of many, will appear a second time, not to deal with sin but to save those who are *eagerly* waiting for him. (Hebrews 9:28. Emphasis supplied)

CHAPTER TWO

Salvation in the New Testament

> "If you're looking for perfection, look in the mirror.
> If you find it there, expect it elsewhere."
>
> —Malcolm Forbes

ROMANS 3:20–26

[20] For no human being will be justified in his sight by works of the law, since through the law comes knowledge of sin.

[21] But now the righteousness of God has been manifested apart from law, although the law and the prophets bear witness to it, [22] the righteousness of God through faith in Jesus Christ for all who believe. For there is no distinction; [23] since all have sinned and fall short of the glory of God, [24] they are justified by his grace as a gift, through the redemption which is in Christ Jesus, [25] whom God put forward as an expiation by his blood, to be received by faith. This was to show God's righteousness, because in his divine forbearance he had passed over former sins; [26] it was to prove at the present time that he himself is righteous and that he justifies him who has faith in Jesus.

EXAMINING THE MEANING OF JUSTIFICATION

In the New Testament, believers are described as being (1) Justified by grace;[1] *(2) Justified by blood;*[2] *(3) Justified by faith;*[3] *and (4) Justified by works.*[4] How are we to understand such statements? What are the implications of such language?

Our purpose here is to investigate the meaning of each of these ideas as they relate to the grand work of the gospel and to notice what they say to us about the relationship between justification and sanctification.

JUSTIFIED *BY GRACE*

That justification comes by grace is clear in a number of New Testament references.

> [5] Through him [Christ] we have received grace. (Romans 1:5)

> [16] In order that the promise may rest on grace and be guaranteed to all his descendants. (Romans 4:16)

> [15] The grace of God and the free gift in the grace of that one man Jesus Christ abounded for men. (Romans 5:15)

Sanctification is also presented as flowing from God's grace.

> [14] Sin will have no dominion over you, for you are not under law but under grace. (Romans 6:14)

Grace has to do with the loving nature of God—it describes his attitude toward sinners that results in their salvation. Because of this quality of his nature, justification is possible. Justification originates in God's graciousness. The thought is rooted in Old Testament concepts of God's holiness and righteousness. The grace of God is the only source out of which human beings have any reason to hope for deliverance.

---

1. Rom 3:24.
2. Rom 5:9.
3. Rom 5:1.
4. Jas 2:24.

JUSTIFIED *BY BLOOD*

If God simply pardoned us he could be charged with overlooking or ignoring the seriousness of sin. To balance an economy, one does not print money to pay off one's debts. There must be a more serious treatment of the problem which preserves the reality of justice. To demonstrate this perspective of justification the New Testament speaks of justification "by his blood."

> [9] Since, therefore, we are now justified by his blood, much more shall we be saved by him from the wrath of God. (Romans 5:9)

The atonement of Christ is the currency of justification—the cash payment. The "blood of Christ" is his atoning death. What Paul means is that salvation is procured only with heavenly payment. Only "in his blood" is a person just before God. It is thus a holy justification, one based on full satisfaction of human indebtedness, obtained without divine graft or legal fiction. "In Christ," "in him," "in the Lord" are phrases used by Paul 164 times. In Christ, the believer is a new creation. Whereas in Adam all became dead, in Christ all may become alive.

The church must ever keep its gaze fixed on the atonement as a guard against falling into subjectivism. It is not enough to spruce up our characters, nor is it enough to say "let bygones be bygones" when it comes to solving the sin problem. There is a principle of *justice* at stake in God's universe.

The security of the universe rests on what God has done in righteousness. This is not to say that a Christian has no personal relationship with God. But the only relationship that God accepts is that which is based solely on the atoning work of Christ completed once for all.[5] The New Testament stress on Christ's blood preserves an objective nature in justification that keeps us from putting our own piety in place of Christ's sacrifice as the ground of our acceptance with God.

Theologian Adolf Köberle wrote squarely to this issue:

> If the faith of justification is endangered when the gift of sanctification is not exercised, so the sanctification will still more surely enter into false paths if it is not based on justification and guided by it. We might sum it up in two statements: (1) Without the continual return to justification, sanctification falls into Pharisaism and the wildest exaggeration. (2) When, however, we

---

5. Rom 6:10.

hold fast to the condemning and pardoning work of forgiveness, sanctification receives its true modesty and its true vitality.[6]

No less than God's grace, Christ's death is also connected to sanctification.

> [2] How can we who died in sin [in the death of Christ][7] still live in it? (Romans 6:2)

> [4] Likewise, my brethren, you have died to the law through the body of Christ, so that you may belong to another, to him who has been raised from the dead in order that we may bear fruit for God. (Romans 7:4)

JUSTIFIED *BY FAITH*

Paul describes another dimension of salvation in Romans 5:1—we are justified "by faith." When the New Testament speaks of faith it means the instrument by which salvation is appropriated or received. Just as God's grace is the SOURCE of salvation and Christ's death is the MEANS by which it is purchased, faith is the INSTRUMENT by which it is received.

> [23] Since all have sinned and fall short of the glory of God, [24] they are justified by his grace as a gift [source], through the redemption which is in Christ Jesus, [25] whom God put forward as an expiation by his blood [means], to be received by faith [instrument]. This was to show God's righteousness, because in his divine forbearance he had passed over former sins. (Romans 3:23–25)

We must never think that faith is either the source or the meritorious cause of our salvation. Faith is the hand which receives salvation, the eye which sees it, but not the fountainhead, which produces it or the price that buys it.

Charles H. Spurgeon wrote,

> Still, I again remind you that faith is only the channel or aqueduct, and not the foundation head, and we must not look so much to it as to exalt it above the divine source of all blessing which lies in the grace of God. Never make a Christ out of your faith, nor think of it as if it were the independent source of your

---

6. Köberle, *Quest for Holiness*. 250.
7. Rom 6:3–11.

salvation. Our life is found in "looking unto Jesus," not in looking to our own faith. By faith all things become possible to us; yet the power is not in the faith, but in the God upon whom faith relies. Grace is the powerful engine, and faith is the chain by which the carriage of the soul is attached to the great motive power.[8]

Only two alternatives are open to one who is seeking salvation. He may try to obtain it (1) by works of law (as a human legal payment), or (2) by faith in what Christ has done (as a divine legal payment). Paul argues strongly for the latter. This does not mean that works are unimportant, but it nullifies the value of works of law as having any merit in gaining salvation.

Faith is related to sanctification as well as justification, although not in the same sense. While justification is always passive on a human's part, sanctification is not. True sanctification is not "letting go and letting God." By virtue of divine forgiveness and liberation from sin, it is active, aggressive, and spontaneous.

Having been justified by faith, humans in their freedom cooperate within the sphere of their new fellowship with God. This is borne out in many passages that command personal sanctification. In this setting we can also find comprehensible notions as being "sanctified by the truth"[9] and "working out our salvation."[10] Truth separates the believer from error, and the result is a progressive change into Christ's image.

JUSTIFIED *BY WORKS*

Perhaps the most crucial area of our discussion, so far as experience is concerned, is in understanding the relation between faith and works. How does the obedience of the believer relate to what the apostle Paul says elsewhere about a salvation that is based on faith in Christ apart from works?

Paul never presents Christians as being saved because of their obedience. He always presents them as saved by grace, through faith in Christ's blood. But those who are redeemed from sin's bondage are no longer the slaves to sin.

> [12] Let not sin therefore reign in your mortal bodies, to make you obey their passions. [13] Do not yield your members to sin as instruments of wickedness, but yield yourselves to God as men

---

8. Spurgeon, *All of Grace*. 63–65.
9. John 17:17.
10. Phil 2:12.

> who have been brought from death to life, and your members to God as instruments of righteousness. [14] For sin will have no dominion over you, since you are not under law but under grace.
>
> [15] What then? Are we to sin because we are not under law but under grace? By no means! [16] Do you not know that if you yield yourselves to any one as obedient slaves, you are slaves of the one whom you obey, either of sin, which leads to death, or of obedience, which leads to righteousness? [17] But thanks be to God, that you who were once slaves of sin have become obedient from the heart to the standard of teaching to which you were committed, [18] and, having been set free from sin, have become slaves of righteousness.
>
> [19] I am speaking in human terms, because of your natural limitations. For just as you once yielded your members to impurity and to greater and greater iniquity, so now yield your members to righteousness for sanctification.
>
> [20] When you were slaves of sin, you were free in regard to righteousness. [21] But then what return did you get from the things of which you are now ashamed? The end of those things is death. [22] But now that you have been set free from sin and have become slaves of God, the return you get is sanctification and its end, eternal life. [23] For the wages of sin is death, but the free gift of God is eternal life in Christ Jesus our Lord. (Romans 6:12–23)

Hence obedience becomes evidence of the work of God and the fact that divine principles are internalized in the life. These are not "works of the law" in Paul's technical meaning of meritorious effort; they are "works of faith," or faith that manifests itself in WORKS. This is the ordinary response of one who has been sanctified (set apart), as an adopted son of the king. In harmony with this Pauline concept the apostle James polemicizes that faith and works cannot be legitimately separated, for faith that is genuine will transform the character.[11]

The important point here is that nowhere do we find the least hint that ethical behavior is meritorious in producing salvation. Just as a person is justified by faith, he lives in sanctification. With the acceptance of forgiveness comes both responsibility and strength. In the power of God, the believer straightens his life. The final judgment will be according to works. Works will not justify on the day of judgment any more than they justify

---

11. Jas 2:16–26.

now. They only testify to the genuineness of the disciple's faith. The way we treat others will prove whether we ourselves appreciate God's mercy.

PERSPECTIVES ON SALVATION

These New Testament perspectives on salvation can be summarized as follows.

Justification by grace means that salvation originates in God's own initiative.

Justification by blood indicates that the atonement of Christ is the all-sufficient payment of the penalty for humanity's sin.

Justification by faith describes how salvation is applied through the instrument of faith.

Justification by works means that all true faith will manifest itself in works of faith.

CHAPTER THREE

Does Hell Burn Forever?

> "The more people who believe something, the more apt it is to be wrong. The person who's right often has to stand alone."
>
> —Søren Kierkegaard

2 THESSALONIANS 2:3–8

³ Let no one deceive you in any way; for that day will not come, unless the rebellion comes first, and the man of lawlessness is revealed, the son of perdition, ⁴ who opposes and exalts himself against every so-called god or object of worship, so that he takes his seat in the temple of God, proclaiming himself to be God.
⁵ Do you not remember that when I was still with you I told you this? ⁶ And you know what is restraining him now so that he may be revealed in his time. ⁷ For the mystery of lawlessness is already at work; only he who now restrains it will do so until he is out of the way. ⁸ And then the lawless one will be revealed, and the Lord Jesus will slay him with the breath of his mouth and destroy him by his appearing and his coming.

THE MEANING OF "HELL"

According to the dictionary, the word "hell" possesses several different meanings: (1) a place for the spirits of the dead—identified with Sheol and Hades; (2) a place where the devil lives and to which various sinners and unbelievers are doomed to eternal punishment after death; (3) any place or condition of evil, pain, disorder, cruelty, etc.; (4) a slang term for any extremely disagreeable, unsettling, or punishing treatment or experience.

In the Bible "hell" is more than a slang word and a far more significant subject than the dictionary meanings might lead you to believe. It is one of those terms that describes a reality far beyond that observable to the sight of the naked eye.

Who has been to hell and back? Who has discovered the horrors of hell that have been so freely written up over the past two millennia? And more important, perhaps, where does such a concept fit into a modern frame of thinking? These questions are meaningful because the Christian insists that his knowledge of hell is founded on revelation, not empirical data. For that very reason we can carefully allow the revelation of scripture to speak if we are going to have a balanced view of its teaching on this subject.

MEDIEVAL HORROR SHOW

The pictures of hell produced by the creative imaginations of many well-intending minds of the past and present have generated nightmares and emotional trauma. Descriptions of people somehow kept alive through all eternity in order to endure the pain of unquenchable fire have penetrated the sensitive mind with superstitious fear. Only the imagination has limited some writers as they have described these horrendous scenes. One wrote,

> Now look at that body, lying on the bed of fire. All the body is salted with fire. The fire burns through every bone and every muscle. Every nerve is trembling and quivering with the sharp fire. The fire rages inside and the skull, it shoots out through the eyes, it drops out through the ears, it roars in the throat as it roars up a chimney....
> But, listen; there is a sound just like that of a kettle boiling? Is it really a kettle which is boiling? No; then what is it? Hear what it is. The blood is boiling in the scalded veins of that boy.

> The brain is boiling and bubbling in his head. The marrow is boiling in his bones! ... When he was alive, his blood boiled to do very wicked things, and he did them, and it was for that he went to dancing houses, public houses, and theaters.... There is a just and a terrible God. He is terrible to sinners in Hell—but He is just!"[1]

Such vivid and horrible depictions were thought to be deterrents for human rebels struggling with the temptations of the flesh. Such a lurid medieval horror show should scare the "hell" out of the children who were contemplating a path to perdition.[2] Perhaps no other doctrine of the Christian church has been used for more questionable negative motivational suggestions than the doctrine of hell.

POSITIVE EFFECTS

Positive effects have not always been forthcoming. The preaching of hellfire has had little measurable effect on the overall morals of any country. Early America was treated to a great emphasis on the fires of hell and their effects, but did it produce a superior morality?

In a sermon entitled "Future Punishment of the Wicked" the great Calvinist theologian and hellfire preacher Jonathan Edwards exhorted:

> To help your conception, imagine yourself to be cast into a fiery oven, ... or of a great furnace, where your pain would be as much greater than that occasioned by accidentally touching a coal of fire, as the heat is greater. Imagine also that your body were to lie there for a quarter of an hour, full of fire, ... all the while full of quick sense; what horror would you feel at the entrance of such a furnace! And how long would that quarter of an hour seem to you! ...
>
> And how much greater would be the effect, if you knew you must endure it for a whole year; and how vastly greater still, if you knew you must endure it for a thousand years! O then, how would your heart sink, if you thought, if you knew, that you must bear it forever and ever! That there would be no end!

---

1. Furniss, *The Sight of Hell.*

2. The official statement regarding the appropriateness of John Furniss' book on hell was written by William Meagher, Vicar General, Dublin, on December 14, 1855: "I have carefully read over this Little Volume for Children and have found nothing whatsoever in it contrary to the doctrine of Holy Faith; but, on the contrary, a great deal to charm, instruct and edify our youthful classes, for whose benefit it has been written."

> That after millions of millions of ages, your torment would be no nearer to an end, than ever it was; and that you never, never should be delivered![3]

Here was a variation of a longstanding medieval theme finding its most vivid description in the pictures of Dante's *Inferno*. Such visualizations were thought to be effective in controlling certain aspects of human behavior, curbing unacceptable activity, and finally winning control over the sinful pursuits of humans.

An imaginary story illustrated the length of this horror: imagine a ball of metal the size of the moon. Every 10,000 years a dove will fly by and flick the edge of the ball with the tip of her wing feathers. Conceive that after a time the ball will begin to wear away through continued flicks. Picture how long it will take for the ball to be reduced to powder, remembering that the dove flies by only every 10,000 years and touches it only lightly each time. Here is the length of eternity. When the ball is ground to powder, eternity will still be going on. And the message was clearly conveyed: If you are in hell you will still be burning even after the ball is gone.

One modern fundamentalist writer has declared that "the real key [to revival] is a return to good old-fashioned preaching of the holiness of God, his hatred for sin, and a revival of some good fire-and-brimstone preaching for sinners." Such a declaration is reminiscent of Gamaliel Bradford's poem decrying the "exit" of God (as evidenced by the silence of pulpits on the subject of hell):

> Of old our fathers' God was real,
> Something they almost saw,
> Which kept them to a stern ideal
> And scourged them into awe.
>
> They walked the narrow path of right,
> Most vigilantly well,
> Because they feared eternal night
> And boiling depths of Hell.
>
> Now Hell has wholly boiled away
> And God become a shade.
> There is no place for him to stay
> In all the world He made.

---

3. Quoted in Miall, *Can It Be True?* 5–6.

> I sometimes wish that God were back
> In this dark world and wide;
> For though some virtues he might lack,
> He had his pleasant side.[4]

THE NEEDS OF THE PEOPLE

Does such preaching meet the needs of people? Do humans change when brought to view with what one writer has called "the great fry in the sky by and by"? Is human behavior effectively transformed through a fearful appeal to the horrors of hell?

In his *Introduction to the Psychology of Religion,* Robert H. Thouless has suggested that behavior demonstrates to a large degree how hellfire preaching has affected the pew.

> Instead of being influenced by suggestion . . . [he is] showing the effect of 'habituation'; the stimulus which initially would have produced a behavior response has, by its habitual occurrence, ceased to produce any response. The forcible methods of the revival preacher are an attempt to use the forces of suggestion in a new way which will overcome his habituation. In the end, of course, the individual may be habituated also to the situation of revival services. He may go to them frequently and enjoy them and undergo the emotional crisis which leads to the act of surrender, but only as part of his habitual religious life without any radical redirection.[5]

Thouless then goes on to show that hellfire-and-brimstone preaching has often produced the opposite effect from the one desired. Emotional disorders, hysteria, contortions, speech automatisms (many times interpreted as the coming of the Holy Spirit), erratic dancing—these may simply be emotional reactions to a supposed reality that the human mind cannot handle.[6] Behaviorally, over the long haul of life, such an emotional peak cannot be maintained, and eventually such a person may throw off religion altogether or at least greatly modify his view of hell.

It is little wonder then that a large-scale reinterpretation of this doctrine has occurred in modern times. Scores of millions of modern

---

4. Bradford, "Exit God," 80.
5. Thouless, *Introduction to the Psychology of Religion,* 3d ed., 26.
6. Thouless, *Introduction to the Psychology of Religion,* 28.

Christians no longer believe in Dante's *Inferno* depiction of hell. Such modern views play down the idea of eternal punishing in favor of a more realistic view of justice or an emphasis on heaven and love. More modern views tend to emphasize God as a lover rather than a punisher. It is in this great emphasis on God's mercy that the proverbial baby may get thrown out with the bath water. Is there no such thing as hell just because modern man cannot handle the medieval horror show?

THE BIBLICAL DOCTRINE

In attempting to arrive at and maintain a biblical teaching on hell we must consider three basic questions: (1) How is one to understand the biblical words for hell? (2) What does the Bible teach about justice and mercy? and (3) What kind of God must God be in order for us truly to worship him? Perhaps the answers we give to these questions will affect our life radically.

The words translated "hell" in the English Bible are (1) *she'ol* (Hebrew), meaning "the unseen state," or "the place of the dead," and translated "hell" (31 times), "grave" (31 times), and "pit" (3 times); (2) *hades*, the Greek equivalent of *she'ol*, translated "hell" (10 times) and "grave" (1 time); (3) *geenna*, a Greek word meaning "Valley of Hinnom," translated "hell" (9 times) and "hell fire" (3 times); and (4) *tartaroo* a Greek place name indicating where rebellious angels are thrown, translated "hell" (1 time).

How one understands the New Testament meaning of hell is largely conditioned by how one understands the Old Testament view of *she'ol*. For the Greeks, the dead were conscious in death, but for the Old Testament Hebrews, death meant the dead were unconscious in the grave. This is indicated numerous times by the concept of the soul as a unity of breath and body,[7] the depiction of the body returning to the dust,[8] the picture of the breath going forth at death,[9] the picture of unconsciousness.[10] and the biblical description of death as a "sleep."[11]

---

7. Gen 2:7.
8. Eccl 3:20; 12:7; Gen 3:19.
9. Ps 146:4.
10. Eccl 9:5, 6, 10; Ps 146:4.
11. Ps 13:3.

If one accepts the Old Testament view of death as a state of inactivity, sleep, or unconsciousness, then the "place of the death"—that is, hell—is the grave.

CONCEPTS OF DEATH

The major question one must ask when approaching the biblical teaching of hell is: Did the New Testament writers presuppose a Jewish background on human nature, or did they write out of a Greek philosophical background? For the Greeks, the human soul was conscious in death and separable from the body. *Hades* was the place of "the dead," but that was a place of activity and life for the Greek mind; quite different from the Hebrew concept of a place of unconsciousness.

What complicates matters is that in the New Testament the words translated "hell" are sometimes linked up with the idea of final judgment. *Geena,* for example—the valley along the south and west edge of the hill on which Jerusalem was built—was a city dump, where fires raged, and it provided Jesus with ready illustrations of what would finally happen to sin and those who espoused it so firmly as to become identified with it.

> [29] If your right eye causes you to sin, pluck it out and throw it away; it is better that you lose one of your members than that your whole body be thrown into hell. [30] And if your right hand causes you to sin, cut it off and throw it away; it is better that you lose one of your members than that your whole body go into hell. (Matthew 5:29–30)

The picture of hell is thus complicated when we bring our preconceived ideas of Dante's *Inferno* to the teachings of Jesus.

ETERNAL FIRE?

Next comes the concept of "eternal," "everlasting," and "forever" fire.[12] When put together with the texts on "unquenchable fire" and a preconceived idea regarding the Greek notion of human consciousness after death, all seem to jell into the doctrine of a medieval horror show.

---

12. Matt 25:41; Jude 7; Rev 14:11.

> [12] His winnowing fork is in his hand, and he will clear his threshing floor and gather his wheat into the granary, but the chaff *he will burn with unquenchable fire*. (Matthew 3:12. Emphasis supplied)

> [42] Whoever causes one of these little ones who believe in me to sin, it would be better for him if a great millstone were hung round his neck and he were thrown into the sea. [43] And if your hand causes you to sin, cut it off; it is better for you to enter life maimed than with two hands to go *to hell, to the unquenchable fire*. (Mark 9:42–43. Emphasis supplied)

However, the Hebrew and Greek words for "everlasting" and "eternal" are terms that are defined by the nature of that which they are describing. Those words in the original languages mean "age" or "eon." In other words, those who burn in "eternal fire," "forever" will burn until they have reached their "age" (limit). If a man's age is immortality he will burn forever in the sense of never-endingly. If, on the other hand, humans are by nature mortal, or capable of dying, they will burn only until they are burned up. Such is the relative meaning of "eternal" in the original languages of the Bible.

When one has this latter understanding, it is simple to see why the fires of Sodom and Gomorrah are not burning today, even though the scriptures describe them as being burned with "eternal fire."

> [6] And the angels that did not keep their own position but left their proper dwelling have been kept by him in eternal chains in the nether gloom until the judgment of the great day; [7] just as Sodom and Gomorrah and the surrounding cities, which likewise acted immorally and indulged in unnatural lust, serve as an example *by undergoing a punishment of eternal fire*. (Jude 6–7. Emphasis supplied)

These eternal fires burned up the cities. But since these were not eternal cities, the fires burned only as long as anything remained of the cities that would burn. Likewise, if humans are mortal, as the Old Testament teaches, then the wicked will burn up. They will suffer eternal punish*ment*, but not eternal punish*ing*.

"Unquenchable fire" is fire that cannot be put out. Any professional firefighter can describe the horrors of unquenchable fire. Some electrical and fossil-fuel fires are just that. They can only be controlled until they burn out for lack of fuel. Jerusalem was burned with such unquenchable fire.

> **27** But if you do not listen to me, to keep the sabbath day holy, and not to bear a burden and enter by the gates of Jerusalem on the sabbath day, then I will kindle a fire in its gates, and it shall devour the palaces of Jerusalem and *shall not be quenched.* (Jeremiah 17:27. Emphasis supplied)

The city is not still burning. Since it was not made of eternal materials, the city burned until the unquenchable *fire* went out.

So, to understand the New Testament teaching on hell depends on how you understand those words for hell and everlasting fire. And it depends on what you understand the nature of man to be. If, indeed, the Old Testament gives the correct (inspired) view of our constituent makeup and God's punishment, then the New Testament merely builds upon that divine revelation to the prophets.

On the other hand, if you impregnate those New Testament words with ancient pagan and Greek philosophy notions such as the immortality of the soul or the separability of the soul and body or the consciousness of disembodied spirits, then you end up with something entirely different.

IS GOD JUST?

This brings us to our last two basic questions, which deal with our concept of God in the biblical framework. Some have suggested that everlasting hell—that is, Dante's *Inferno*—is imperative to prove and maintain the justice of God. But is it really? The Bible says,

> [4] The soul that sinneth shall die. (Ezekiel 18:4)

The biblical writers understood death to be the opposite of life. This text says nothing about fire—if it did it should read that the wicked shall burn. But rather it says they will die. Paul taught the same:

> [23] The wages of sin is death. (Romans 6:23)

Yet, as popularly taught, hell is pictured as eternal *life*—a conscious life in fire.

Nonetheless, there is a more serious question of God's justice involved here. Human sense of justice has varied through the centuries with the philosophies of political leaders and the moral thinking of the times. But the ultimate penalty of justice has always been the forfeiture of life. Some of the crueler arbiters of the past have used torture, but men of good will have always spoken out sharply against such methods. Will God now model for the universe the greatest sense of cruelty imaginable by keeping sinners alive in Dante's *Inferno*? To scream and cry by torture throughout eternity? Whether this is just should be given serious consideration.

Some well-meaning Christians have said, if the Bible teaches Dante's *Inferno* I accept it—if God does it, it must be just, and that's enough for me. Yet it is not the Christian that evangelism is concerned with—it is the non-Christian. How many infidels have been produced by this doctrine, one will never know, but the prospects of turning away sincere and questioning minds are infinitely greater if the justice of God is perceived as more primitive than modern man's sense of fairness.

Someone once told me, "I can see where God might punish a sinner for acts of sin equally, maybe sixty-five years of burning for sixty-five years of sinning [though he had trouble even with that]. But how could God ever be conceived of as just by meting out eternal punish*ing* as the penalty for sixty-five years of sinning?" A modern man characterized by a sharp sense of justice has difficulty with fire as a form of punishment, but he has an even harder time preserving a sense of justice in an eternal fiery punish*ing* for a few years of rebellion.

It is little wonder, then, that the traditional understanding of hell as Dante's *Inferno* has laid claim to the production of agnostics. When God is depicted as so unjust, one finally finds it impossible to respect him, much less worship him from love. Why should a person serve a God whose sense of justice is perceived as being lower than that of Herod the Great, Hitler, Mao, or Stalin? Justice inspires mercy and love. Injustice inspires cynicism, hatred, and finally hostile behavior.

HELL, A BIBLICAL CONCEPT

No one should argue that hell is not a biblical concept. But a more meaningful question is this: Is *your view* of hell a biblical concept. Many Christians strenuously object to the traditional doctrine of hell, with all its pagan Greek philosophical presuppositions. Scripture perceives of a God who loves this world so much that he sends his Son to this planet to carry out a rescue mission of the human race, lost through Adam's sin. He assumes the form of a man, produces a life of obedience, vindicates the law of God, and dies the death of an innocent victim of sin—a demonstration of the injustice of sin.

This God sends his Son to die for humankind that all might not have to die. His life and death therefore become a substitute, and those who accept him will escape the "fires" of "hell" by being saved in him, where the fires cannot reach. But notice again that the penalty for sin is death,[13] not fire. If it were fire, then Jesus never suffered the penalty for mankind's sin, for he never burned forever in hell, nor is he now burning in hell (this would be required if the penalty involved eternal-burning fire). Mankind escapes eternal punishment by accepting the death he died in our place.

When the wicked finally die the just death for their rejection, it will not be because God is trying to get even. It will be because they have refused life. They made that choice, not God. They will have destroyed themselves. Just as a small radio speaker blows up when one thousand watts of power are fed into it, so the wicked will be matter changed into energy when God reveals himself fully, for to sin and sinners "God is a consuming fire."[14]

That need not be anyone's fate. Salvation is offered freely for the accepting. No one needs to suffer eternal death when eternal life is offered. It is simply a matter of the choice one makes. To make such a choice when God has been depicted in such a cruel way as to make serving him a work of fear, rather than excitement and love, makes the understanding of the gospel as good news difficult to grasp.

---

13. Rom 6:23.
14. Heb 23:39; 2 Thess 2:8.

CHAPTER FOUR

GLORY FOR ME

> "Perhaps love is the process of my leading you gently back to yourself."
> —ANTOINE DE SAINT-EXUPERY

ISAIAH 43:5–7

⁵ Fear not, for I am with you;
I will bring your offspring from the east,
    and from the west I will gather you;
⁶ I will say to the north, Give up,
    and to the south, Do not withhold;
        bring my sons from afar
        and my daughters from the end of the earth,
⁷ every one who is called by my name,
    whom I created for my glory,
    whom I formed and made."

GLORY FOR ME?

In church school we used to sing a song entitled "The Glory Song."

When all my labors and trials are o'er,
And I am safe on that beautiful shore,
Just to be near the dear Lord I adore,
Will through the ages be glory for me.

Refrain:
Oh, that will be glory for me,
Glory for me, glory for me,
When by His grace I shall look on His face,
That will be glory, be glory for me.[1]

By the time one has finished singing all the stanzas of Charles Gabriel's "Glory Song" one will have repeated "glory for me" twenty-seven times. Am I to conclude from this that I get to heaven for my glory and therefore I will be strutting about the place telling all how "glorious" I am?

Of course, this was never the intent of the composer and writer Gabriel. He meant to portray the spontaneity and the purity of the saints' hymn of praise to God. He did not write, "that will be glory *to* me." These words carry the message of an important Christian truth: that living to the glory of God results unavoidably in a glorious experience for me.

CREATED FOR GOD'S GLORY

God once gave this message to Isaiah for his people.

> [5] Fear not, for I am with you; I will bring your offspring from the east, and from the west I will gather you . . . [7] every one who is called by my name, whom I created for my glory, whom I formed and made. (Isaiah 43:5, 7)

While this is primarily a promise of reward for faithfulness, it also reveals our fundamental purpose for existence: We were created for God's glory.

At first reading one might wonder that such a concept sounds selfish on God's part. I have known parents who felt their children were brought into the world for their glory. A man who had planned to be a physician, but had not made it past the MCAT, determines that his son will achieve where he failed, thinking that this will make up for the disappointment. A woman who believes she fell short of her goals attempts to relive her life through her daughter. In each case are these parents not creating offspring for their glory?

Such examples fall far afield of understanding "for God's glory," since each is set in the economy of sin, and sin is the perversion of good. Lucifer did not create anything when he thought up sin and turned himself into a devil. He merely took the things of God and "perverted" them. By

---

1. Gabriel (1856–1932), "The Glory Song," 349–54.

that I mean he used them for other than their intended use. Everything he touched became defiled by self-centeredness (including himself).

Seeking himself ahead of God became such a nasty habit that his whole personality changed. Refusing to accept the universal, eternal principle that nothing in God's creation lives wholly unto itself, Lucifer taught that pleasure is the only meaningful end to seek to the glory of oneself. Hence we tend to look at "glory" as perverted pleasure.

GLORY FOR ME!

When God created humanity for his own glory, however, he did not do so for some personal, perverted pleasure. This can be seen by making your own comparisons. Take your choice: Does it make more sense to live to your own glory or to the glory of another?

Which results in the fulfilling, satisfying life? One who tries it will testify that living to the glory of God results in the understanding that God has only another's best interests in mind throughout all his commands and promises. Thus, accepting our place in God's creation "for his glory" can only result in "glory for me."

CHAPTER FIVE

WHEN LEGALISM FINALLY DROPS AWAY

> "There is no way under the sun of making a man worthy of love, except by loving him."
>
> —THOMAS MERTON

ROMANS 13:8–10

> [8] Owe no one anything, except to love one another; for he who loves his neighbor has fulfilled the law. [9] The commandments, "You shall not commit adultery, You shall not kill, You shall not steal, You shall not covet," and any other commandment, are summed up in this sentence, "You shall love your neighbor as yourself." [10] Love does no wrong to a neighbor; therefore love is the fulfilling of the law.

GIVE ME FREEDOM FROM THE LAW

Love is the fulfilling of the law.[1] Occasionally one hears a Christian appeal to the New Testament with words something like, "Don't give me the old

---

1. Rom 13:10.

Ten Commandment legalism of Moses! I want the new covenant freedom of Paul!"

Such sentiments undoubtedly have in mind Pauline statements such as:

> [14] For sin will have no dominion over you, since *you are not under law but under grace.* [15] What then? Are we to sin because *we are not under law but under grace?* By no means! (Romans 6:14–15. Emphasis supplied)

> [12] "All things are lawful for me," but not all things are helpful. "All things are lawful for me," but I will not be enslaved by anything. (1 Corinthians 6:12)

> [23] "All things are lawful," but not all things are helpful. "All things are lawful," but not all things build up. (1 Corinthians 10:23)

But did Paul really give less ethical counsel or advice than Moses? And is it possible to be just as "legalistic" over Paul as it is to be over Moses?

ROOTED IN THE GIVER

The question of legalism is rooted in the hearer of ethical law rather than the giver. That is why the author of Hebrews could insist that the old covenant failed because God's people did not continue with him. So, whether it is Paul or Moses who gives the counsel it is possible to read and follow an author from one's own background to the extent that one never hears the author or his meaning.

Legalism is the attempt to make one righteous through the keeping of the law. Anyone who seriously tries this will fail, no matter how hard one tries, no matter how long one works at it. As James illustrated, the law is like a mirror—it only informs the face of its dirtiness, it cannot clean it.

> [22] But be doers of the word, and not hearers only, deceiving yourselves. [23] For if any one is a hearer of the word and not a doer, he is like a man who observes his natural face in a mirror; [24] for he observes himself and goes away and at once forgets what he was like. [25] But he who looks into the perfect law, the law of liberty, and perseveres, being no hearer that forgets but a doer that acts, he shall be blessed in his doing. (James 1:22–25)

So, when we study a chapter like Romans 13 we need to understand that in Paul, as in Moses, there are two kinds of instruction: (1) Revelation of God's activity for human salvation, and (2) Revelation of human duty once we accept that activity. If the duty precedes God's activity in thinking or perception of the Christian then what was meant to be response becomes legalism.

AN ETHICAL CHARGE

Romans 13 is an ethics chapter. It is part of a larger section that begins in chapter 12 and continues through chapter 15. In keeping with this context, it is packed with imperatives—twelve, in fact, in just fourteen verses. One might even call it the chapter of Twelve Commandments. Notice:

> Be subject to the governing authorities. (v. 1)
> Do what is good. (v. 3)
> Be afraid if you do wrong. (v. 4)
> Pay all government officials their dues—taxes, revenues, respect, and honor. (v. 7)
> Owe no one anything except love. (v. 8)
> Do not commit adultery. (v. 9)
> Do not kill. (v. 9)
> Do not steal. (v. 9)
> Do not covet. (v. 9)
> Love your neighbor as yourself. (v. 9)
> Put on the Lord Jesus Christ. (v. 14)
> Make no provision to gratify the desires of the flesh. (v. 14)

These are ethical concerns. They have to do with actions and attitudes toward God and other people. But then, so did the Ten Commandments. Could Christians make the same mistakes as the Jews of Jesus' day made and turn ethical concerns into legalism? That question is only answered in the realm of motivation. Legalism is a kind of response to God that sells God short. It does not understand the bigness, depth, and magnanimity of God. Nor does it appreciate his love.

Paul is trying to stress in the last few chapters of Romans that a Christian gives evidence of what he is by what he does. Here is why he acts like he does: he has been made into something, he has been adopted and his status is different. A loving person, a person who has accepted the love of God in Christ Jesus, is therefore discernible in society, not just because he has weird dress or refrains from common habits and games, but because his life is ruled by the principles of sonship.

A Christian is a predictable creature. Christian behavior can actually be forecast where principle is involved. During the Roman persecution of the second century, Pliny the young, governor of Bithynia, could write to the emperor Trajan regarding certain forbidden activities set up as tests by which to ferret out Christians.

> Those who denied that they were or had been Christians, when they invoked the gods in words dictated by me, offered prayer with incense and wine to your image, which I had ordered to be brought for this purpose together with statues of the gods, and moreover cursed Christ—none of which those who are really Christians, it is said, can be forced to do—these I thought should be discharged. Others named by the informer declared that they were Christians, but then denied it, asserting that they had been but had ceased to be, some three years before, others many years, some as much as twenty-five years. They all worshipped your image and the statues of the gods, and cursed Christ.[2]

THE ETHICAL STRUCTURE OF CHRISTIANITY

The ethical structure or fabric of the Christian's life was so sure that Pliny could predict the outcome on the Christian's own recognizance. He could know they were Christians because they acted in accordance with what they were. Since they were children of God, they could not be made to confess another father. And because of it they went to the flames, the beasts, the stakes, and the circus. The Christian was his own *witness* ("martyr" in Greek). The love of Christ so gripped the hearts of the early Christians that their *doing* followed as a matter of course.

Paul, after giving several chapters of revelation on the gospel of God in Jesus Christ and its restorative power, outlines the Christian's duty to government and to one another in this chapter. Authority is divinely ordained, he writes. But, of course, if a person does not love God why should he care? It is an adopted son of God who cares. Thus, Paul can appeal to a dimension that is lacking in the legalist.

As a citizen the Christian is one who lives in subjection to authority because authority is a microcosm of the universe. Principle: there could

2. Pliny the Younger, *Letters*, 10.96–97.

be no government without authority. So, the Christian citizen pays taxes, keeps up to date on paying bills, supports the officials of due appointment, even obeys the civil laws such as speed limits on the highway. That is part of the Christian witness. To be a Christian is impressed on the world through acting like one.

A Higher Principle

There is a higher principle—we ought to obey God rather than human structures—thus some Christians died in civil disobedience. But that is not Paul's primary concern in this chapter. Obeying authority is a demonstration of obeying God, for others can see that God is God or order by observing Christians who are orderly.

So, Paul concludes that at the heart of all Christian action is the principle of love. It is both the substance and the motivation of action. Legalism drops away when one knows he is loved. Love becomes the *fulfilling* of the law—not *talk* about fulfilling the law. The Christians are those who keep the commandments of God, not those who talk about how they should (or how others should).

Because we are loved in Jesus Christ we can afford to love, regardless of how we are treated, misrepresented, abused, or hated. Some of Paul's readers were soon to be tortured by the very authority God had told them to obey, pay taxes to, and support. But herein the church will be the powerful force it was meant to be:

> [17] Those who keep the commandments of God. (Revelation 12:17)

> [34] A new commandment I leave you: That you love one another. (John 13:34)

CHAPTER SIX

ON THE ORDINATION OF WOMEN[1]

"The first time Adam had a chance, he laid the blame on women."

—NANCY ASTOR

ROMANS 16:1-10

[1] I commend to you our sister Phoebe, a deaconess of the church at Cenchreae, [2] that you may receive her in the Lord as befits the saints, and help her in whatever she may require from you, for she has been a helper of many and of myself as well.
[3] Greet Prisca and Aquila, my fellow workers in Christ Jesus, [4] who risked their necks for my life, to whom not only I but also all the churches of the Gentiles give thanks; [5] greet also the church in their house. Greet my beloved Epaenetus, who was the first convert in Asia for Christ. [6] Greet Mary, who has worked hard among you. [7] Greet Andronicus and Junias, my kinsmen and my

---

1. This chapter was originally a radio commentary given by the present writer on WSMC-FM, Collegedale, TN, in the 1970s. Later it was revised and submitted to *These Times*, an Adventist periodical where the present writer was a contributing editor. It was rejected by the journal editors because it did not represent Adventist thinking or theology on the place of women in the church. As of this printing the issue is still being debated in the church. The statistics in this chapter have been updated to 2010 estimates. Updates and revisions have been made.

fellow prisoners; they are men of note among the apostles, and they were in Christ before me. ⁸ Greet Ampliatus, my beloved in the Lord. ⁹ Greet Uranus, our fellow worker in Christ, and my beloved Stacy's. ¹⁰ Greet Apelles, who is approved in Christ. Greet those who belong to the family of Aristobulus.

A LOGICAL SERMON OF CHALLENGE

Recently I attended the evensong service at the Washington National Cathedral. After enjoying the great choir and the magnificent organ recital, I anticipated the sermon, which would be delivered from the stately pulpit of ornately carved limestone.

To my surprise the minister who emerged to present the evening message was a woman. I assumed she was one of the officiants of the cathedral and that she was one ordained to the task. Her topic was "The Will of God," and the sermon was refreshing. She brought to the pulpit a perspective that was biblical, logical, challenging, and thought-provoking. Her descriptions and illustrations of life and crises were delivered with a pathos that was rare.

A NEW PERSPECTIVE

One experience should not change one's opinion on this question. It is just as possible that I could have heard a wretched sermon and therefore confirmed myself against ever taking seriously the quest of some women to have a greater part in the preaching and ministry of the church. But hearing a sermon well-prepared and delivered helped me receive a revelation concerning some of my own, perhaps unfounded, prejudices in the issue.

Being a mainline, traditional church, the Episcopal Church with which the Washington National Cathedral is affiliated, did not find it easy to accept the new concept of ordained women clergy. LaVonne Neff, an Episcopalian, tells of two ordained deacons, both female, who were asked to help two bishops serve communion. Part of their duties involved the administering of the rite to some young priests who were members of the large congregation.

The first communicant knelt before the male bishop and received the communion wafer on his tongue, and then moved over a few feet and knelt again as a female deacon held out to him the communal wine cup.

The young priest suddenly reached for the cup and tried to grab it away from her hissing, "Go to blazes! You're ruining the church!" Remaining calm she said to him, "I can't, I'm busy." The other female deacon had her troubles too. One male priest dug his fingernails into her hand until tears came to her eyes as she administered the wine. To finish off his protest he whispered to her, "I hope you burn in Hell!"[2]

NOT A NEW PRACTICE

Statistics regarding female ordination are not easy to be sure of. About 12% of churches in North America ordain women into pastoral positions. Evangelical churches' percentages are lower. The higher rates belong to Unitarian-Universalist Association (30%), United Church of Christ (25%), Presbyterian Church U.S.A (19%), Christian Church (Disciples of Christ) (18%), and United Methodist Church (15%). The Southern Baptist Convention, the largest evangelical church in America is around 4%.[3]

The enrollment of the nation's seminaries is now approximately 50% women, many of whom are anticipating entering newly opening clergy positions. Of course, even if "everybody's doing it" does not make a practice biblically sound. But renewed interest in understanding the biblical teaching on this subject, together with the figures and facts just cited makes the question of the ordination of women an issue that non-participating churches cannot forever escape.

WHY CHURCHES SAY NO

Some churches have simply put their foot down and said, "No!" Some appeal to the conditions of society—"the church is not ready for it" or "our church is a missionary church and the people in the third world, where women may hold lower status, would never understand." Other churches opt for tradition—"we've never done that; therefore, we could not do

---

2. Neff, "The Ordination of Women," *Adventist Review*.

3. Hartford Institute for Religion Research. Hartford, CT: Hartford Seminary. "The *Faith Communities Today 2010* national survey of a fully representative, multi-faith sample of 11,000 American congregations found that 12% of all congregations in the United States had a female as their senior or sole ordained leader. For Old-line Protestant congregations this jumps to 24%, and for Evangelical congregations it drops to 9%."

that." Still another group appeals to scripture, as the basis for their position of exclusion of women from their ranks of clergy.

Particularly in some fundamentalist churches the arguments go something like this: The Bible presents different roles for men and women. Men are to be in the role of initiator, women in the role of follower. Thus, men are to be in the authority roles while women are to assist men. It is not for women to be administrators in the church though this may work in secular business.

Another argument suggests that it is imperative to recognize the difference scripture makes between the sexes—not one of sex superiority but one of sex nature. Man is in his true nature as he plans and risks. Dr. George Sweeting wrote,

> Woman is made to reach her greatest potential when she rests on man's provision and supports him in his efforts.[4]

A third argument has said, the Bible's views on sex roles in the church are to be seen as eternal principles, not in any way historically conditioned. That is to say, Paul's admonitions about women were divine revelations from God and stand for this generation as firmly and literally as they did for the first century.

Such arguments are being dismissed by many women (and men) as thinly disguised sexism and the church is often seen as one of the last bastions of sex discrimination in our society today.

THE MOST POPULAR OBJECTIONS

The most popular objections to women's ordination make appeal to the apostle Paul. Statements are brought forth that sound as though there can be little question left in the mind of any questioner.

> [11] *Let a woman learn in silence with all submissiveness.* [12] I permit no woman to teach or to have authority over men; she is to keep silent. (1 Timothy 2:11–12. Emphasis supplied)

> [3] But I want you to understand that *the head of every man is Christ,* the head of a woman is her husband, and the head of Christ is God. (1 Corinthians 11:3. Emphasis supplied)

---

4. Sweeting, "Is the Church Unfair to Women," 77.

> [8] For man was not made from woman, but woman from man. [9] *Neither was man created for woman, but woman for man.* (1 Corinthians 11:8-9. Emphasis supplied)

> [34] *The women should keep silence in the churches.* For they are not permitted to speak, but should be subordinate, as even the law says. [35] If there is anything they desire to know, *let them ask their husbands at home.* For it is shameful for a woman to speak in church. (1 Corinthians 14:34-35. Emphasis supplied)

> [21] Be subject to one another out of reverence for Christ. [22] *Wives, be subject to your husbands, as to the Lord.* [23] For the husband is the head of the wife as Christ is the head of the church, his body, and is himself its Savior. [24] As the church is subject to Christ, so *let wives also be subject in everything to their husbands.* (Ephesians 5:21-24. Emphasis supplied)

> [2] Now a bishop must be above reproach, *the husband of one wife,* temperate, sensible, dignified, hospitable, an apt teacher. (1 Timothy 3:2. Emphasis supplied)[5]

Surely these Pauline counsels end all discussion—right? Wrong! There is a great diversity of opinion on how to interpret these texts—many of which are quite ambiguous when read in their immediate context, the broader context of God's being no respecter of persons, and in the original Greek language. Jack Buckley, a professor with the evangelical Covenant Circle in Berkeley, California, has compared fifteen books, all written by evangelicals, about women's church roles. He found a great degree of disagreement.[6]

SEXISM IN BIBLE TRANSLATIONS

In an article in Christianity Today, *Berkeley and Alvera Mickelsen,*[7] *a husband and wife team from the teaching faculty of Bethel Theological Seminary (now Bethel University) in Arden Hills, Minnesota, asked the question, "Does male dominance tarnish our translations (of the Scriptures)?"* In

---

5. And then there is the objection that seems steeped in wooden literalism—how can a woman be "the husband of one wife?" (Referring to this qualification of the Bishop in Paul's Epistle to Timothy).

6. Buckley, "Paul, Women and the Church," 30-35.

7. Berkeley Mickelsen, Professor of Greek, Hebrew, and Theology at Bethel Theological Seminary, Alvera Mickelsen, Professor of Journalism at Bethel College.

each case those translations done by committees tended to be closer to the original ambiguity in the Greek text. But where individual men had translated the version there was a tendency to interpret these passages on the side of male dominance.

One example the Mickelsens cite is the case of 1 Corinthians 11:3, which can be interpreted several ways. Literally it reads, "The head of every woman is the man." This text may mean that the man is "the original source" of the woman, that is, she was taken from him originally, or that the woman is in some way answerable to him, or simply that she is his helper. *The Living Bible*, a version of scripture paraphrased by Kenneth Taylor, interprets the text: "a wife is responsible to her husband," using words that are not in the original and making it sound far more certain than it is. The *Good News Version*, the work of Robert G. Bratcher, translates the text, "the husband is supreme over his wife."[8]

The Mickelsens stressed that such interpretations from an ambiguous original text are clearly signs of male bias. They concluded:

> Christians now trying to work through the actual teachings of the Bible on the strategically important issue of men-women relationships are thrown off course by translations that may reflect more of the translator's interpretation and biases than the actual words of the Bible.[9]

SOCIAL AND SCRIPTURAL MYTHS

In addition to these interpretive translations that tend to mislead, there are several social and "scriptural" myths that still circulate. These myths make it hard for women to break into traditionally male-dominated (and higher paying) religious roles.

There is the social myth that sexuality is somehow evil and "that female sexuality is more debased than that of the male."[10] In the mind of some men a woman is a sex object and is only complete if she is married or connected in some meaningful commitment to a man. Ironically, the same myth allows for a man to be complete in himself. This inherent devaluation of women provides for a related notion that in seeking fulfillment a woman must fill a role of constant temptation to man.

8. Berkeley and Alvera Mickelsen, "Does Male Dominance Tarnish?" 23ff.
9. Mickelsen, "Does Male Dominance Tarnish?" 25.
10. Howe, "The Positive Case for the Ordination of Women," 268.

This myth was dramatically demonstrated in a mid-western court case where the judge threw out a rape charge because, in his opinion, the woman in the case was asking to be raped by the way she dressed. She was to blame because she was tempting the man and he fell. Such a myth casts woman in the role of a temptress—as one enticing men from their holy living to the pursuit of sensual pleasure. As Margaret Howe explained, "If the male is overcome by her charm she must bear the guilt."[11]

Here is a note of encouragement for women—to accent the fact that social consciousness is revolting against this myth, the people in the judge's district impeached him for his sexist decision, though his response was that he was suffering persecution for his "convictions."

One myth that stems from a misunderstanding of scripture is that God created "man" in his image; a not-so-subtle suggestion that males alone can be truly God-like or representative of God. But such a position stands on a reading of only half the text:

> [27] God created man in his image, male and female made he them. (Genesis 1:27)

A reading of the whole text clearly shows the intention of scripture to be God created humanity in his image—both male and female.

A similar myth insists that God is "a man." Biblical depictions of God as the "Father" and Jesus as the "Son" seem to confirm this view. Some in the women's movement would re-educate us with the flip side of this record and substitute for Jesus' words in the Lord's Prayer, "Our mother who art in heaven." No one I know has seriously suggested that we begin looking at Jesus as the "only-begotten daughter" of God. However, such discussions miss the scriptural point completely.

God is God—neither male nor female. God is pictured as a "Father" not to reveal sexuality but to describe relationship in a way understandable to us.

> [13] As a father pities his children, so the LORD pities those who fear him. (Psalm 103:13)

Such texts care nothing about proving the masculinity of God—it is concerned with our heart response to the pleadings of the Godhead.

Furthermore, scripture does not confine itself to illustrations of masculine inference. Jesus looked over Jerusalem as it plotted to kill him and cried,

---

11. Howe, "The Positive Case," 268.

> ³⁷ O Jerusalem, Jerusalem, killing the prophets and stoning those who are sent to you! How often would I have gathered your children together *as a hen gathers her brood* under her wings, and you would not! (Matthew 23:37. Emphasis supplied)

WAS PHOEBE A "MINISTER?"

The suggestion is sometimes made that the New Testament gives no record that a woman was ever ordained to the ministry. Such a position seems to stand if all you have is an English Bible. But if you read it in Greek the case is not that convincing. It is curious to note that in the case of Phoebe, "the deaconess,"[12] the word in Greek is *diakonos*. It appears here in the feminine gender as required by the Greek noun rules.

In the King James Version of the New Testament the word is translated "servant."

> 1 I commend unto you Phebe our sister, which is a servant of the church which is at Cenchrea. (Romans 16:1, KJV)

In the Revised Standard Version of the New Testament the word is translated "deaconess."

> ¹ I commend to you our sister Phoebe, a *deaconess* of the church at Cenchreae. (Romans 16:1. Emphasis supplied)

For a helpful perspective it should be recognized that the church has no office called "servant" and has usually made a distinction between "deacons" and "deaconesses." Church tradition has often dictated that deacons are ordained, deaconesses are not. So, what was Phoebe? A *servant* or a *deaconess*? It makes little difference since neither carries ordination authority. Does this mean that just because a word must appear in the feminine gender in the original language that a woman can never be ordained as a deacon? There is no word in Greek that carries the connotation that "deaconess" has come to carry in Christian churches.

To complicate matters further, in every other occurrence of this word in Paul's writings, the word here translated "deaconess" is translated in the King James Version as "minister." And, perhaps coincidentally, all those other occurrences are referring to men. One can fairly inquire, Why does a scholar translate "minister" for a man's role in the church, and "deaconess" for women, when the word is the same?

12. Rom 16:1.

RELEVANCE

All of this may seem quite academic to the church member in general. But if you belong to a church that does not ordain women but does believe in education as opposed to indoctrination, it is a general announcement that you will not be able to look at it as academic forever.

Too long have women suffered the effects of male dominance in our society. They have suffered the pain of submissiveness and subservience by doing as much church work as the men, but receiving little, less, or no pay for it because the Bible allegedly makes no allowance for women to be ordained to those jobs that pay or carry real authority.

Women are waking up to male-dominance, which is thinly disguised with biblical trappings. They are beginning to believe that without women the whole church would have folded a long time ago. They are recognizing that in many cases the real issue may be financial and sexist, and perhaps not so biblical after all; that what we may be facing is a difficulty on the part of both men and women to face the shock of cultural adjustment. Like a man once said, "I'm not sure I could adjust to a pregnant pastor." Perhaps he was on to a root of the issue.

> Some *good* Christians insist that to *ordain* women to professional, ecclesiastical leadership position would be a violation of Scripture mandates. They cite Scripture for their position. Upon careful examination, such a conclusion appears to be influenced by present cultural mores.
>
> On the other hand, to see the Christian gospel influencing our organized attempts to spread the gospel, in what we have called *horizontal* redemption, or the full meaning of *redemption* is very impressive. God is not only interested in our experiencing release from human custom in heaven, but in *enlivening* the Spirit here and now. Being able to fulfill their full calling to professional ministry and being able to experience the kind of equality that would require, will be a new experience for women.
>
> All of us can work for a common cause. All of us can work without recognition and appreciation. But there is nothing quite so satisfying as being recognized and affirmed as *an equal.* That is the legacy of the gospel. We need to do this.[13]

---

13. Zackrison, Chapter 7: "Inclusive Redemption." In Habada and Brillhart, *The Welcome Table.* 175–76.

CHAPTER SEVEN

WHAT DO TEENAGERS NEED?

> "A child is a person who is going to carry on what you have started... the fate of humanity is in his hands."
>
> —ABRAHAM LINCOLN

EPHESIANS 6:1-4

> [1] Children, obey your parents in the Lord, for this is right. [2] "Honor your father and mother" (this is the first commandment with a promise), [3] "that it may be well with you and that you may live long on the earth." [4] Fathers, do not provoke your children to anger, but bring them up in the discipline and instruction of the Lord.

CHILDREN IN DEVELOPMENT

When I first became a parent, everyone wanted to hold my kids. People even brought them toys, candy, and presents. But now my babies are teenagers, and these days not many adults come around to make over them. In fact, all who come to see my teenagers are other teenagers. And they don't particularly want the rest of us around. They will even sit outside in the cold rather than risk a room full of adults or children.

Nobody really minds teenagers as long as they don't act like teenagers. Adults, in fact, really enjoy teenagers when they act like adults. I know, my youngest just turned fifteen! Adults even appreciate teenagers when they act like children. But when teenagers act like teenagers—self-conscious, rebellious, sometimes grotesque, or obnoxious, and continually challenging our most cherished beliefs—people are nervous and resist.

Did a parent ever honestly believe that his sweet infant would someday become a teenager? Well, beware—having a child puts into motion an awesome example of cause and effect. I warn those of you with bouncing babies: somewhere in that growing mass of tissue a will is developing and getting ready to meet you around age thirteen. You wonder how the number thirteen became known as unlucky?

PROVOKING TEENAGERS TO ANGER

A father observed, "My children are at the perfect age—too old to cry at night, and too young to borrow the car." Another said, "God is considerate; He gives us twelve years to develop a love for our children before turning them into teenagers." I suspect that many adults—even many church members—are afraid of teenagers. As a result, teenagers are often ignored, exploited, overlooked, snubbed, or patronized. And their only great sin is that we perceive them to be teenagers.

In working my way through the mine field of adult-teen relations, I have found helpful counsel in the words of the apostle Paul: "Fathers, do not provoke your children to anger."[1] So now the big question is: How do we provoke teenagers to anger?

NOT CARING TO UNDERSTAND

We provoke teenagers to anger by not caring to understand them. Adolescence used to be a period of life when a teenager, still in the home, prepared for work in society. During this time society joined with parents to protect the vulnerable season of adolescence. An unwritten pact between media, church, school, home, industry, and government marked off the importance of adolescence and guarded the developing adult.

---

1. Eph 6:4.

Today this is no longer true. Adolescence is a stage in name only. The media no longer protects adolescents, but thrusts upon them all its arts of persuasion and sexual innuendo. Parents, largely committed to their own middle-age crises, often fail to give their teenagers the time they need. An average American father's quality time with his children amounts to six minutes a week. With his teenager it may be less.

Our failure to care to understand the pressure and stress society has thrust upon our teenagers may be the most serious way in which we provoke them to anger. When is the last time you read a book on teenagers, adolescence, or adolescent behavior? It's time we take time to understand.

NOT RECOGNIZING AND MEETING NEEDS

We provoke teenagers to anger by not recognizing and meeting their needs. A man who lost his daughter in an accident told me of a conversation he had with her shortly before her death. "Now that you are grown, married, and planning a family," he said to her, "what would you have done differently if you had been me raising you?" "Not much," she carefully and thoughtfully replied. "But when I got to be a teenager you quit hugging me. You didn't understand that I still needed to be hugged."

What else do teenagers need?

SAFE OPPORTUNITIES TO QUESTION. Adolescence is a period of testing and trying. If you have given your children a value system, then expect them to question it. Teenagers will almost definitely interpret denial of the right to question your value system as a weakness in those values. Such action on your part could lead to the very thing you hoped to prevent—their rejection of your values.

UNDERSTANDING ACCEPTANCE. Teenagers are narcissistic and often not very altruistic, but they do respond to acceptance of what they are, not just of what you would like them to be.

PARENTS. This may sound silly, but teenagers need parents who are parents, not parents who are trying to become teenagers. Parents can help their teens best by remaining clearly defined parents. The same goes for teachers, youth pastors, and concerned church members.

REASONABLE LIMITS. This area generates anxiety for many parents. In our fear of teenagers, we sometimes fail to offer them responsible limits. Teenagers are not yet what they will become, and the failure of significant adults can have a negative effect on their future.

SECURITY. Teenagers can have it if the significant adults in their lives offer them understanding acceptance, loving treatment, and reasonable limits.

MISUSING RELIGION

We provoke teenagers to anger by misusing religion. In my church of origin, the latest research on teenagers shows a low hostility level toward religion. At the same time, teens indicate a rather high rate of hostility toward the church organization. This is a result of their perception of how religion is used to control them.

Consider the following. One church school punished its naughtiest student of the day by making that child give closing prayer. Another church school punished students by requiring them to copy pages of authoritative church literature. As a church high school student, I wrote a few term papers assigned by well-meaning teachers in retribution for my misbehavior. In every case they required me to research the denomination's prophet. The notion "God will get you if you're not good" is at best an immature, naïve view of God. Even our theology can erode God's love when we misunderstand then misrepresent it.

Religion deals with the deepest emotions of the human being. When we exploit a component of human nature as basic as religion to control and intimidate, we provoke to anger.

CONFUSING SCHOOL POLICIES WITH SPIRITUALITY

We provoke teenagers to anger by confusing school policies with spirituality. Students often think about school policy in this way. If I attend class at the public high school, it is because the state says I must go to class and be there on time; but if I attend class on time at a parochial school, it is because Jesus wants me to be punctual. Adults are largely responsible for promoting this pressure.

Schools must operate according to policies. But sometimes we integrate faith and learning too closely. Dress codes, attendance rules, social order, and discipline may have little to do with God directly. But too often we look for extra leverage to enforce rules by bringing God into the picture. So, the students reprimanded for dress-code infractions may feel a loss of favor with God. And being expelled means "God no longer finds me acceptable." Parents who leave the church or quit paying tithe because of a "raw deal" at school often validate the teenager's suspicion that school policies really are a definition of God.

DISSONANCE BETWEEN MODELING AND IDEALS

We provoke teenagers to anger by presenting role models that do not model our ideals of religion. Teenagers do not expect adults to be sinless. But they are sensitive to dishonesty, lying, hypocrisy, and what they see as double standards or inconsistency. When you are trying to figure out who you are, it doesn't help to have adults demonstrating that they aren't sure who they are.

Adolescent psychologist David Elkind suggests that many parents of teenagers today are undergoing their own ideological crises. They may be sorting through their own past and present, unwilling to render value judgments as severely as their parents did. So, they hesitate. But teenagers do not interpret parental hesitation as mixed feelings. They interpret this ambivalence as complacency.[2]

We can think of several areas in which Christians are questioning the advisability of what they learned as children—things such as the jewelry issue, what to do about television and movies, dancing, drinking, and doctrine. And when we say to teenagers, "I don't know; I am rethinking that value. Give me space to sort that through," teenagers often interpret us to be saying, "I don't care. It doesn't really matter." And that provokes them.

TEENAGERS NEED HONESTY

Here teenagers need real honesty. They need to see the whole process through which their parents clarify their own value system. They need to have a value system modeled, not simply asserted. But because parents are often involved in their own rebellion against former or present role models, teenagers are provoked to anger.

> [4] Do not provoke your children to anger, but bring them up in
> the discipline and instruction of the Lord. (Ephesians 6:4)

Paul's words suggest an unswerving commitment of parenthood that involves understanding, care, loving concern, and the place of reasonable,

---

2. Elkind, *All Grown Up and No Place to Go*, Chap. 1.

responsible limits. This counsel includes more than just parents. Teenagers today, need the combined efforts of home, school, and church to provide the protection necessary for a minimum of stress and a maximum of security.

CHAPTER EIGHT

The Shockability Factor

> "The acquiring of culture is the developing of an avid hunger for knowledge and beauty."
>
> —Jessie Lee Bennett

PHILIPPIANS 4:4–9

> [4] Rejoice in the Lord always; again I will say, Rejoice. [5] Let all men know your forbearance. The Lord is at hand. [6] Have no anxiety about anything, but in everything by prayer and supplication with thanksgiving let your requests be made known to God. [7] And the peace of God, which passes all understanding, will keep your hearts and your minds in Christ Jesus.
> [8] Finally, brethren, whatever is true, whatever is honorable, whatever is just, whatever is pure, whatever is lovely, whatever is gracious, if there is any excellence, if there is anything worthy of praise, think about these things. [9] What you have learned and received and heard and seen in me, do; and the God of peace will be with you.

DESIGNED TO SHOCK

Scene 1: The young lady was a plainly dressed elementary school teacher by day. But during her college years she had acquired an insatiable sexual appetite and so she pursued a double life. Like Dr. Jekyll and Mr. Hyde, as the sun went down, she became transformed. But rather than becoming a monster she became a sexual drifter—discos, bars, the street—anywhere she could find a semblance of relief for her burning passion.

Night after night she searched only to find her need growing greater. She was on a collision course with destiny and her search came to an end in what began as a routine sexual encounter. Her lover, paranoid over his impotency, became her assailant, slashing a dagger into her starving body in his own attempt to compensate and establish some identity for himself. As a viewer of this slice of life you may watch the movie credits as they roll across her bloody bed.

Scene 2: The family anticipated the move to the new town for some time and they were thrilled that the day had finally come. The movers filled the new house with the family belongings and a new routine of life began. But it was not to prove so normal a routine after all, for the house was the habitation of demons who somehow claimed possession of it.

Whenever a family member introduced religion as a topic of discussion, the devils went berserk. They entered people, things, anything connected with the house. Whole rooms became like tornadoed wrecks. Just when you thought it was safe to move to the suburbs you are given the message that supernatural evil lurks in the bushes and closets eagerly anticipating your arrival.

Scene 3: He was not the Messiah but if one knew the story of Christ it would not take much imagination to conclude that there was more than a coincidental likeness to the Christian savior. You have touchpoints all along: the wisemen, the unmistakable allusions to the gospel story, the crowds. A chorus of the crucified, kicking their legs from the cross like Radio City Hall dancers, sang, "Forget your sin—give the audience a grin! Enjoy it—it's your last chance anyhow. So always look on the bright side of death. Just before you draw your terminal breath . . . And always look on the bright side of life (whistle) . . ."[1] The obvious message is different as one laughs one's way through it: you only go around once, so live it with gusto!

---

1. Idle, "Life of Brian."

SHOCK CAPACITY

How much of this does it take to shock you? Whatever happened to shock? Undoubtedly the above scenes from three popular, contemporary movies are certainly not the most shocking we could cite but they illustrate some of our generation's apparently indefatigable appetite for sex, violence, and cynicism. Nevertheless, when I ask whatever happened to shock I mean have you lost your capacity to be shocked? What is your "shockability factor?"

Shock is that expression of outrage that occurs when one's own sense of propriety or decency has been offended. The "shockability factor" is directly related to one's conscience identity, which is in turn the result of the internalizing of one's value system. As an individual allows his conscience to be violated through the vicarious viewing of ideology, attitudes and actions that are deviant to his Christian values, he will find a corresponding dulling in his shockability factor.

Moviemakers insist that what they give the public is (1) what the public wants, and (2) what the public is. In other words, movies (and television) are an accurate reflection of modern society as is: if not in deed, at least in thinking.

If we assume that claim to be accurate should it not produce a sense of shock? How would we rate our society: G, PG, PG-13, R, Mature? Is society so obsessed, in either act of thought, with schoolteachers who live a double life, streets filled with rapists, homes possessed with evil spirits, or common citizens who are at heart incurable sacrilegious cynics, that it is necessary to fill the popular screens with vividly dramatized delineations of such things?

KINDS OF SHOCK

Not all shock is of the same intensity nor is it caused by the same type of situation. A few years ago, a friend of mine died in a tragic airplane crash. The shock of this event rendered his family and friends immobile for some time. Divorce can create an initial shock wave that is hardly overcome for years as the disillusion caused by the breakup stubbornly refuses to dissipate. We might refer to this kind of shock as "a state of shock."

Occasionally this state of shock can come in the form of what has been termed "culture shock," where one's mind is paralyzed when confronted by new ways of life that are foreign. Here a person may respond,

"I know that's true, but I am too old to change." Or sometimes one's attitudes and behaviors may imply that everyone else needs to do the changing—"if only the world would fall in line with my perceptions." Consequently, we may start insulating ourselves from the need or the desire to make changes that keep us updated with a new culture.

Closely related to culture shock is what Alvin Toffler popularized as "future shock"—a sort of psychological *rigor mortis* brought on by the effect of too-quick change in our society.[2] An example of this could be seen in the wake of Vatican II. The quick, radical changes in the Roman Catholic worship and lifestyle left many Catholics in an emotional shock that saw great numbers of them searching for another expression of faith. Many felt betrayed and spiritually homeless. These examples are concerned chiefly with automatic or involuntary responses caused by death, crisis, change, etc.

Ivan Pavlov, a Nobel prize winning Russian physiologist active at the turn of the century and founder of behavior therapy (classical conditioning), ran his famous experiments on involuntary reactions demonstrated in animals. Attaching sensing devices to the salivary glands of dogs he discovered that when they associated the ringing of bells with food their saliva began to flow. It was not a question of the animals' choosing to make their mouths water—that was automatic.

VOLUNTARY SHOCKABILITY

Not all responses are involuntary. Human beings are creatures capable of morality, religion, and spiritual perception. There is an aspect of humankind that yearns for wholeness and feels a definite undoneness in a world where things do not seem whole. This moral or religious dimension entails a voluntary response.

In observing the subject matter and the manner of depicting "reality" cited above, it may appear that morality is no longer an option for postmodern humans. Is it legitimate to experience shock at what is being portrayed on America's movie screens? Is it legitimate to feel shock at what is happening to the marriage failure rate in America? Is it permissible to express shock at the ease with which one can obtain an abortion or at the injustice of the rich over the poor or of one race over another? Is it allowable to demonstrate shock over where the world is going in terms

---

2. Toffler, *Future Shock*.

of nuclear brinkmanship? Is it okay to express shock over political corruption? Indeed, should it not be expected that a Christian with a view of common uprightness and positive concern for society express voluntary shock at what should be perceived as twisted views of reality?

Today there seems to be an inordinate desire to avoid anything that would render one being judged to be prudish. Rather, it seems to be a mark of worldly status to pose oneself as quite insulated from shock—especially that caused by subjective moral considerations. One who shows shock about the display of moral evil in the world, particularly in the area of individual lifestyle, often tends to be perceived as reactionary, fanatical, unsophisticated, old-fashioned, or simply out of touch.

Leon Morris, an Australian theologian, has described it thus:

> As a generation we are shocked by nothing. We seem rather proud of this and regard it as a virtue. But is it? It implies a profoundly pessimistic view of mankind. People who can't be shocked confess by that fact that they expect nothing better.[3]

Surely young Christians expect something better than what they see in their society today. So much of what is depicted by the mass media as "normal" life is little less than gratuitous and indulgent immortality and violence.

THE POPULARITY OF SHOCK

The shockability factor on a societal level made a temporary cultural comeback in the 1960s. The look on the now famous face of the young girl who bent over her classmate gunned down at Kent State University was hardly one of passive observation. This look may have been involuntary, but probably it was more than that. Shock emanated from her face as suddenly the impersonal abstraction of violence (as often portrayed on the screen) became the personal experience of brutality.

There were a few who had the courage to stand and show their indignation and shock over racial discrimination and what it does to the human spirit. They emphasized the moral blight it had brought on America, and they laid in the streets, protesting, forcing the issue, and even dying, to underscore their belief that humans, as created by God had certain inalienable rights. They demanded reforms and often on moral principle born of righteous shock, they introduced major changes.

---

3. Morris.

Thousands of young people exploded in riots and protest over the immorality of the war in southeast Asia, because, among other reasons, it shocked them into action.

One could hope that such shock would have been for the betterment of America, and in some ways it has been. Yet the real heart-changes often go unrealized as we can see prejudice, lying, lust and hostility persisting.

HOPE FOR THOSE IN SHOCK

Is there a legitimate place for shock? Can one truly be shocked by evil today and respond to it in a realistic, rational, and creative way? I believe so. If you are a struggling Christian in a world that seems very hostile; if you have observed that not everything goes the way you believe God would have it go; if you ever have lingering questions as to where it will all end; if you are tempted to be shocked or to reside in a state of shock; you are in good company. Such illustrious spiritual giants as Moses, Daniel, Jeremiah, and Jesus expressed similar concerns.

Habakkuk, an obscure Biblical prophet, cried out to God.

> [3] Why dost thou make me see wrongs and look upon trouble? Destruction and violence are before me; strife and contention arise. [4] So the law is slacked and justice never goes forth. For the wicked surround the righteous, so justice goes forth perverted. (Habakkuk 1:3–4)

These are words born of an active, positive shockability factor. Perhaps they sound like your words at times. Where is God? Why doesn't he act?

For centuries it seems God did nothing. And then he sent Jesus Christ to judge sin, to show where God stood on the subject. And the sinners treated him just like they treat anyone else who poses a threat to their society. The world under Satan is a hostile place. And it is especially so to those who disagree with its goals and direction—to those who cast themselves in a position contrary to its intrinsic evil. Yet God has made clear what sin is and what the penalty of sin is. He has revealed where evil leads long before it gets there. In Christ God showed the nature of sin itself, and he showed his attitude toward it. Herein lays a positive approach to shock.

The following suggestions may help a Christian to maintain a spiritual equilibrium in the fact of all kinds of shock.

RECOGNIZE THAT SHOCK OVER EVIL IS A CHRISTIAN ATTITUDE. Such shock need not be debilitating or paralyzing. Furthermore, it should not be embarrassing to be sensitive to that which corrupts life. There are many things in an evil world that one should be shocked over. While not all times and places are necessarily appropriate for showing this shock, one should cultivate the attitude of shock itself.

RECOGNIZE THAT A STATE OF SHOCK CAN IMMOBILIZE YOU. This means that the shock you experience must drive you to action—either socially or personally. It is not enough simply to be carried along by shock. Moral sensibility is a capacity we have which seeks expression in order to develop. And such action needs to subject itself to the methods and models of scripture. The great people of all ages are revered by posterity because of their courageous willingness to allow shock to motivate them to positive, constructive correction of the mental, spiritual, or social status quo.

RECOGNIZE THAT IN THE PRESENT EVIL AGE THERE WILL CONTINUE TO BE THE HOSTILE ATTACKS OF EVIL. Wickedness and righteousness live together to the end. Since no valid complementariness exists between wickedness and righteousness, a distinction between the two must ever be made. Jesus suggested this when he prayed for his disciples.

> [13] But now I am coming to thee; and these things I speak in the world, that they may have my joy fulfilled in themselves. (John 17:13)

He knew that his disciples of all ages would face the same kind of ambivalence as he did, but he showed that we need not be overcome by debilitating shock expressed in hopeless discouragement and paralyzing depression.

RECOGNIZE THAT GOD HAS ALREADY STATED HIS OPINION ON SIN AT THE CROSS OF CHRIST. Those who refuse that judgment and reject God's salvific plan end up the objects of judgment. Shock should lead us to re-consider the judgment of God on evil and to make personal application of that divine opinion with regard to the eternal implications of our choice.

Those who are shocked by injustice in the world, by the free display of promiscuity in our society, by the maltreatment of human beings by other human beings in all areas of life are indeed demonstrating their desire to participate in God's opinion toward evil.

In short, to accept God's value judgment on evil and act accordingly has ever been considered by genuine piety to be a mature step in the Christian life. That suggests that "the shockability factor" is really the progressively maturing conscience that is finding itself attracted by the wishes of the eternal God.

CHAPTER NINE

Grace Under Fire

"To persevere in one's duty and be silent, is the best answer to calumny."

—George Washington

ROMANS 12:14–21

[14] Bless those who persecute you; bless and do not curse them. [15] Rejoice with those who rejoice, weep with those who weep. [16] Live in harmony with one another; do not be haughty, but associate with the lowly; never be conceited. [17] Repay no one evil for evil, but take thought for what is noble in the sight of all. [18] If possible, so far as it depends upon you, live peaceably with all.

[19] Beloved, never avenge yourselves, but leave it to the wrath of God; for it is written, "Vengeance is mine, I will repay, says the Lord." [20] No, "if your enemy is hungry, feed him; if he is thirsty, give him drink; for by so doing you will heap burning coals upon his head." [21] Do not be overcome by evil, but overcome evil with good.

THE IMPORTANCE OF ENDURANCE

It is not surprising that Christians have usually stressed the importance of endurance under personal trial and faithfulness to God in the face of persecution or difficulty and loss. The scriptures emphasize this faithfulness. "Do not curse" when you are persecuted, wrote Paul.[1] "Live in harmony," "Repay no evil for evil," "Live peaceably with all."[2] "Take thought for what is noble in the sight of all."[3] "Never avenge yourselves."[4] "Do not be overcome by evil."[5]

LET GOD BE FAITHFUL

All these admonitions are strong moral imperatives indicating what it means to be true and loyal to God when things get rough. But have you ever tried to carry them out under pressure? They make wonderful sermon material and great platitudes when things are going well, but how about when you are really suffering? When you stand for what you believe to be right is met by scorn and alienation, what is your response? When you are lied about and everything you say or do is twisted and distorted through the prism of gossip and speculation, how do you go on?

In times of difficulty, we demand a hearing. We hunger for meaningful justification for abuse. Our emphasis on "being faithful to God" sounds good before the pressures come and after they are resolved. But what is the value of such instruction in the eye of the storm?

TAKE CARE OF THE REVENGE

At the tough, rough times of our experience, when we are suffering severely, it is time to think about the second perspective in Paul's admonition—that which may not be emphasized enough: Let God be faithful and take care of the revenge.

> [19] Beloved, never avenge yourselves, but leave it to the wrath of God; for it is written, "Vengeance is mine, I will repay, says the Lord." (Romans 12:19)

Perhaps we should begin to emphasize the other side of the coin—not our faithfulness to God, but God's faithfulness to us.

1. Rom 12:4.
2. Rom 12:16–18.
3. Rom 12:17.
4. Rom 12:19.
5. Rom 12:21.

> [13] If we are faithless, he remains faithful—for he cannot deny himself. (2 Timothy 2:13)

No matter what the hardship suffered for the sake of the Christian ethic, the maintaining of your integrity or for the clear presentation of the gospel, God is faithful—he will see to it that suffering for the sake of right is justly avenged.

> [22] The judgment was given for the saints of the Most High, and the time came when the saints received the kingdom. (Daniel 7:22)

Plus, he will see to it that a powerful witness is the offspring of your suffering gracefully under fire.

Once you internalize by faith the notion that God is always faithful to his children you will have a sense of security. You will begin to see indications of his faithfulness in little ways and later in bigger ones. Once you grasp that God does not leave those who need him, you will demonstrate a grace under fire that others will sense, though you may not.

The behavior of the Christian in suffering carries a power in witness that little else can match. It does not come from psyching oneself up to remain true to God. Its source is far deeper—it comes from trusting that God means it when he promises to be faithful. Internalizing that principle has a staying effect that makes remaining faithful to God under fire a reality.

CHAPTER TEN

"Patient Endurance" in the End-Time

> "Patience is the companion of wisdom."
> —St. Augustine

REVELATION 14:6–16

⁶ Then I saw another angel flying in midheaven, with an eternal gospel to proclaim to those who dwell on earth, to every nation and tribe and tongue and people; ⁷ and he said with a loud voice, "Fear God and give him glory, for the hour of his judgment has come; and worship him who made heaven and earth, the sea and the fountains of water."

⁸ Another angel, a second, followed, saying, "Fallen, fallen is Babylon the great, she who made all nations drink the wine of her impure passion."

⁹ And another angel, a third, followed them, saying with a loud voice, "If any one worships the beast and its image, and receives a mark on his forehead or on his hand, ¹⁰ he also shall drink the wine of God's wrath, poured unmixed into the cup of his anger, and he shall be tormented with fire and sulphur in the presence of the holy angels and in the presence of the Lamb. ¹¹ And the smoke of their torment goes up for ever and ever; and

they have no rest, day or night, these worshipers of the beast and its image, and whoever receives the mark of its name."

¹² Here is a call for the endurance of the saints, those who keep the commandments of God and the faith of Jesus.

¹³ And I heard a voice from heaven saying, "Write this: Blessed are the dead who die in the Lord henceforth." "Blessed indeed," says the Spirit, "that they may rest from their labors, for their deeds follow them!"

¹⁴ Then I looked, and lo, a white cloud, and seated on the cloud one like a son of man, with a golden crown on his head, and a sharp sickle in his hand. ¹⁵ And another angel came out of the temple, calling with a loud voice to him who sat upon the cloud, "Put in your sickle, and reap, for the hour to reap has come, for the harvest of the earth is fully ripe." ¹⁶ So he who sat upon the cloud swung his sickle on the earth, and the earth was reaped.

ENDURING AS A GOOD SOLDIER

Paul encourages Timothy to endure hardships as a good soldier. It is not clear just what Timothy's hardships were or for what reasons he had to endure them. Paul had to endure imprisonment and physical abuse. Perhaps the same could be said for Timothy's hardships—common occurrences for the early missionaries.

What relation does this endurance have to "patient endurance?"

> ¹² Here is a call for the [patient] endurance of the saints, those who keep the commandments of God and the faith of Jesus. (Revelation 14:12)

No doubt the end-time saints will have to endure hardships like those suffered by Paul and Timothy. Yet could it be that these last-day believers will be called to a more specific type of endurance, that of relating to the intense destruction which comes as a result of God's wrath being demonstrated on earth? Are the saints in some way tested as they try to solve the paradox of God's love amidst sulfur, wine, fury, and pain? One can only wonder how much "wrath" one can observe while maintaining the notion that God is loving and wise and acts always in the best interest of humanity.

THE CUP OF HIS WRATH

As the final events consummate, it may seem that the God of the Old Testament has been revived for one last inexplicably vindicating moment. But just as Jesus' first coming helps to put into perspective the Israelite God, so the second coming of Jesus will help us to understand the "cup of his wrath."[1]

Some have suggested that God does not destroy. Others have pointed out that the Bible makes it clear he does. Regardless of how one interprets the texts, the saints still must deal with the circumstances. Somehow, if confidence in God is maintained in the midst of this holocaust until Jesus appears on the white cloud, then humans will understand much better the realities of justice in its purest form.

"Wrath" is God's attitude toward sin. "Grace" is God's attitude toward sinners. But for the grace of God, we would all suffer his wrath. It has ever been difficult for human beings to relate to God's wrath as an unimpassioned, non-emotive attitude. Some have viewed God as a benevolent grandfather who stands for little or nothing. Others have seen him as an arbitrary ogre bent on punishing those who are out of step with him. It seems difficult, even for thinking people, to grasp the concept that God's wrath is an attitude similar to that of the living and professional surgeon who must carefully extract a cancer from a debilitated body.

But to wed those notions of justice and mercy while seeing them displayed takes the experience of "patient endurance." Perhaps the apostle Peter had a taste of it when he fled the scene of the cross. Perhaps Judas represents the only realistic alternative to patient endurance.

Somewhat easily Christians have said, "God loves the sinner and hates the sin." But what shall we say when the sinner has become so identified with his sin that they are one and the same? Patient endurance then becomes indiscernible from trust.

The events of the end-time, when sin/sinners are extracted as malignant tumors from God's universal body, are so awesome that even those who keep the commandments of God and remain faithful to Jesus will surely have their trust tested to the uttermost. The tender, sensitive Christian will, for a fleeting moment which seems like an eternity, endure with patience the viewing of God's strange act.

---

1. Rev 14:10.

SECURING THE MORAL BALANCE

It is incredible, but there is a paradoxical relief expressed in the response of the righteous when the act is finally consummated.

> [1] After this I heard what seemed to be the loud voice of a great multitude in heaven, crying, "Hallelujah! Salvation and glory and power belong to our God, [2] for his judgments are true and just; He has judged the great harlot who corrupted the earth with her fornication, and he has avenged on her the blood of his servants." (Revelation 19:1–2)

The recognition that Christ's coming is the only answer to the situation is intimated in the words of the believers.

> [9] It will be said on that day, "Lo, this is our God; we have waited for him, that he might save us. This is the LORD; we have waited for him; let us be glad and rejoice in his salvation." (Isaiah 25:9)

Patient endurance will play its part to secure for eternity the moral balance of God's universe for the free moral agents who dwell therein.

CHAPTER ELEVEN

GOD'S PROMISE OF QUALITY TIME

> "Do not squander time, for that is the stuff life is made of."
> —BENJAMIN FRANKLIN

MARK 2:27-28

> [27] And he said to them, "The sabbath was made for man, not man for the sabbath; [28] so the Son of man is lord even of the sabbath."

THE ROUTINE OF LIFE

"I exist, and I am miserable." I've known people who could honestly say that. Geoffrey was such a person. He came home at night, watched TV, drank two six-packs of beer, went to bed, got up the next morning, had a couple cups of coffee, went to work, got off work, went to the bar, came home, watched TV, drank two six-packs of beer, went to bed, got up the next morning, had a couple cups of coffee, went to—so now you know his routine.

Geoffrey retired some time ago, and I have lost track of him, but I occasionally wonder what he does with his time during that additional eight hours a day that he used to work at his job. How do you think Geoffrey responded when I asked him excitedly if he would like to live *forever*?

QUALITY VERSUS QUANTITY

Which is better? The length (*quantity*) of your life? Or the richness (*quality*) of your life? My senior class was the smallest one my high school had graduated for years. "It's the *quality* that counts, not the *quantity*," we would say. But we suspected that biggest and best probably meant the same thing.

I have a hunch that most of us find quantity attractive. We hear about people winning the $50 million state lottery and secretly imagine ourselves in their place believing that they will be happier now. We drive through Beverly Hills or its equivalent and speculate that plush carpets, luxurious automobiles, swimming pools, and manicured lawns produce satisfaction.

The "good life" as interpreted on television is more than just fantasy for us—we believe it. Millions of viewers every night imagine what a quantity of money and things could do to improve their existence. Miserable or not they accept the notion that life could improve if they just accumulated a few more things.

However, quantity often proves to be of transient value. Marriages built on physical beauty alone fail when that beauty fades. When well-known, wealthy celebrities or businesspeople take their own lives we feel confused because quantity apparently did not prove satisfying for them. Those who live like quantity is their major concern in life, or quantity leads to quality, often testify that they feel empty, dissatisfied, and unfulfilled. Striving for possessions or fame stole time that could have been spent developing lives of service and loving relationships.

Older married couples who have accumulated a good share of this world's goods frequently witness that they have warm remembrances of the early days of their marriage when they had little. Uncomplicated life and simple things symbolized commitment, acceptance, and belonging—deeper values.

The Bible speaks of quantity and quality in terms of priorities.

> [19] Do not lay up for yourselves treasures on earth, where moth and rust consume and where thieves break in and steal, [20] but lay up for yourselves treasures in heaven, where neither moth

nor rust consumes and where thieves do not break in and steal. (Matthew 6:19–20)

Fleeting material things can corrode or be stolen. The quality of life has a chance to last.

GOD CARES ABOUT THE QUALITY OF LIFE

Jesus concerned himself with the quality of people's lives. He went about healing bodies and relationships.[1] He spent time with people to improve the quality of their lives.[2] He had both wealthy and destitute disciples, but they shared a common interest in the quality of the life he provided. In his presence they felt worth something, they experienced acceptance and companionship. Through this fresh experience they came to understand God, who had become distant, exacting, even judgmental for them. Their lives took on meaning. They received direction. Their existence became authentic.

Jesus viewed his mission to earth as rescuing people from meaninglessness. That mission involved healing all significant areas of their life.

> [10] The thief comes only to steal and kill and destroy; I came that they may have life, and have it abundantly. (John 10:10)

> [15] Whoever believes in him may have eternal life. (John 3:15)

When Jesus talked about eternal life he implied quality more than quantity. The richness of the present makes the thought of the future enticing.

A BIBLICAL EXAMPLE OF QUALITY

If God knows we need quality, but we think we need quantity, how do we ever come to appreciate his eternal life enough to accept it? To answer that question, God took the initiative and gave us something that symbolizes quality. He gave us the Sabbath, which at first glance appears as quantity because of our orientation to time. We think in terms of how much time we can spare, and what amount of time we have for our various duties and activities. But the Sabbath was not to be just so much time. It was to be quality time—a foretaste of heaven.

1. Matt 12:15.
2. John 4:7–42.

When people tell me, "every day is the Sabbath for me," I know they have misunderstood the basic notion of the Sabbath. The way God means for the Sabbath to be kept would preclude that every day could be the Sabbath. The person who says, "Every day is the Sabbath for me," misunderstands the meaning of quality time as well as the intention of God.

God never instructs us to make every day the Sabbath, any more than he expects us to give all our money to the church. Rather he means for the other six days to be quality time in other pursuits.

⁹ Six days you shall labor, and do all your work. (Exodus 20:9)

But the seventh day is to be quality time devoted in a different way to God and to social relationships that appropriately enhance that experience.

GOD'S WAY IN THE SABBATH

Therefore, since God dreamed the Sabbath, we need to hear him out on the subject—to let him interpret which day and how to keep it. First, he declared "the seventh day" of the week to be a "holy" day, that is, a day set apart for a purpose in a way that other time is not.[3] Only human tradition has ever suggested a change in either the day or the way of celebrating it. But human tradition lacks divine authorization. Obviously, God knew that change would damage the intrinsic meaning of the symbol itself.

Second, though the Sabbath was "made for man"[4] it was not to be a day of self-seeking.[5] Quality time can be enjoyable, but it goes significantly beyond selfish amusement. The day is for "doing good."[6] Quality is like an onion—it has layers, each important, but each one closer to the center.

Likewise, God declared the Sabbath a day of physical rest, but much more. To be "made for man" meant that the day was not to be burdensome. Service and worship were to be delightful. Walking with God, when fully appreciated, is joy. A fascinating phenomenon occurs when a believer in Christ celebrates the Sabbath. Participating in the symbol moves one layer by layer to an ever-richer understanding of one's quality as a person—to the deeper implications of a life of faith.

---

3. Gen 2:1–3, Exod 10:8–11.
4. Mark 2:27.
5. Isa 58:13.
6. Matt 12:12.

Third, in the living symbol of the Sabbath God points us to our roots and to his position as our Creator.

> [1] In the beginning God created the heavens and the earth. (Genesis 1:1)

> [26] Then God said, "Let us make man in our image, after our likeness; and let them have dominion over the fish of the sea, and over the birds of the air, and over the cattle, and over all the earth, and over every creeping thing that creeps upon the earth." [27] So God created man in his own image, in the image of God he created him; male and female he created them. (Genesis 1:26–27)

> [2] And on the seventh day God finished his work which he had done, and he rested on the seventh day from all his work which he had done. [3] So God blessed the seventh day and hallowed it, because on it God rested from all his work which he had done in creation. (Genesis 2:2–3)

To symbolize that he had completed his creative work, he "sanctified" (lit. "set apart") the day for us to remember him.

> [11] For in six days the LORD made heaven and earth, the sea, and all that is in them, and rested the seventh day; therefore the LORD blessed the sabbath day and hallowed it. (Exodus 10:11)

Sabbath is the Hebrew word that is translated in English as "rest." When we are invited to rest in memory of God's rest at our creation we are reminded that we did not evolve from simple, non-moral, non-responsible, unintelligent forms—we were created in the image of God.[7] The implication is awesome: created originally in the image of God, we are responsible, intelligent, and valuable persons. Accepting God's view of us will produce a self-concept that affects positively everything we do.

Fourth, when the Hebrews were delivered from their many years of enslavement to the Egyptian pharaohs, God used the Sabbath to commemorate their deliverance.

> [15] You shall remember that you were a servant in the land of Egypt, and the LORD your God brought you out thence with a mighty hand and an outstretched arm; therefore the LORD your God commanded you to keep the sabbath day. (Deuteronomy 5:15)

---

7. Gen 1:27.

The Sabbath now became not only a symbol of *creation* but a reminder of *freedom*.

Being created "in the image of God" suggests freedom. But this new insight of the Sabbath illustrated freedom more vividly. So meaningful was the picture that virtually all non-Jews came to think of the Sabbath as strictly Jewish tradition, connected almost exclusively with the Exodus from Egypt. This conclusion overlooks the clear witness of scripture. The Sabbath clearly transcends the Jews. All of us were created, not just Hebrews. All of us are free moral agents, not just Hebrews. All of us need and can receive God's salvation, not just the Hebrews.

TIME IS A MODERN CONCERN

The modern mind recognizes the crucial importance of the gift of time. "You never have time for me"—are words that often escape from the mouths of the frustrated teenagers seeking identity. I talked to a young man whose father was a world-famous church man. He was proud of his father and he told of his father's great feats for God. "But he never had time for me," he said with noticeable dejection in his voice.

We need to think about quality time as a gift. We have no problem with things as gifts. When I come home from a business trip I bring a shirt, a book, a piggy bank, or some other souvenir to my kids. Our house is full of trip junk. The rich show their wealth with lavish gifts—cash, cars, castles. But we should recognize that these things can be substitutes for giving ourselves. It is often harder for us to give people time than it is to give people things. Viewed from that standpoint, the Sabbath becomes one of God's most precious gifts. The Sabbath, if kept according to the commandment, will ensure time. You will ensure the quality of that time.

Marriage researchers consistently find that marriage and family successes and failure in America stem largely from time-related factors. Marriage experts Stinnet, Walters and Kaye list the six factors that research has shown to make strong families: appreciation, spending time together, commitment, good communication patterns, high degree of religious orientation, and the ability to deal with crises in a positive manner.[8] All these factors emphasize the priority of giving quality time over giving material things.

---

8. *Relationships in Marriage and the Family,* 8–12.

Despite all this, we are surprisingly miserly with our time. Family specialists estimate that the average American father spends less than six minutes of quality time a week with his children. When a man asks, "Dad will you play racquetball with me," a father often finds it easier to hand the boy a $20 bill and reply, "I don't have time right now, but here—go get yourself some new racquetballs." And the boy falls for it, at least initially, because things have some immediate attractiveness.

You can handle things. You can play with things. But because things don't play back, or handle back, they grow boring, old, and common. As time goes on their attractiveness fades. The tee-shirts become paint rags. The piggy banks are smashed with hammers for their contents. The racquetballs wear out and get replaced. In quality time, on the other hand, parents pass on crucial intangibles: the formation of personal identity, the development of personal worth, a spiritual dimension that gives life direction. These intangibles give children security, meaning, and direction in life. They are the stuff that produces leaders.

Unfortunately, even with the best of intentions, parents often realize the significance of quality time too late. A specialist on the home recently confessed that his children grew up and left home without much input from him. While his children were small he was getting educated. When his children became pre-adolescents, he was catching up on his work. As his children entered their teens he was establishing himself in his field.

Now he is educated, caught up, and established, and finally he has time for them. But they are grown up and gone. He feels a strange jealousy that while he was taking care of all those important career tasks, his wife was home with the children—learning their peculiarities, crying, and laughing with them in sad and happy moments. He would like to reclaim some of that relationship-building time for himself.

Time does not guarantee quality, but it does provide the opportunity for quality. Time, like money, can be squandered or invested. But if one does not set apart time, no investment will be made. Those who study social trends share an ever-growing concern that the erosion of the American family, largely caused by changing values related to the use of time, has already set the future of our society in serious jeopardy.

WHAT MAKES SABBATH A BLESSING?

The most significant words of Jesus regarding the Sabbath are perhaps those found in Mark 2:27–28. He directs them to people who have made the Sabbath a burden.

> ²⁷ And he said to them, "The sabbath was made for man, not man for the sabbath; ²⁸ so the Son of man is lord even of the sabbath." (Mark 2:27–28)

As Jesus and his disciples walked through a grain field one Sabbath, his disciples, apparently lost in conversation with him, picked some of the ripe heads of grain, rubbed them together in their hands and tossed the kernels in their mouths. Immediately their actions were questioned.

> ² But some of the Pharisees said, "Why are you doing what is not lawful to do on the sabbath?" (Luke 6:2)

According to Jewish tradition these disciples had just broken four Sabbath laws: reaping, winnowing, threshing, and sowing. These were not laws that came from divine sources, but rather the result of years of rabbinic analyzing and honing. Legalistic calculations had turned the Sabbath into a complicated obstacle course of "do's" and "don'ts." Jesus took issue because these traditions were interfering with the quality time the Sabbath was supposed to protect. He did not attack the Sabbath—it was the gift of God, it had spiritual significance, it provided quality time. The Sabbath was to be preserved. Rather, he attacked the tradition. The Sabbath was never meant to enslave.

To illustrate his point that we are to find the spirit in the laws of God, Jesus gave three challenges. First: the great King David, universally revered throughout Israel, when he was hungry, went into the holy place of Hebrew sanctuary (where only the priests could go) and took bread from the table of showbread (which only the priests could eat) and ate it, and fed his men with it. Technically he broke the law. Why did nobody condemn him for what he did?

Second, on every Sabbath the priests were hard at work in the temple. They lifted things and moved things about in a way that clearly put them in conflict with rabbinic Sabbath tradition. If anyone else did those things on the Sabbath they would be condemned immediately by a series of Sabbath regulations. Yet no one said a thing about the priests working on Sabbath. Why did nobody condemn them for what they did?

Third, you say it is unlawful to heal a man on the Sabbath, but if a sheep fell in a pit you would do all in your power to pull it out even on the Sabbath. Are you suggesting that a sheep is more valuable than a man who is sick?

> [1] At that time Jesus went through the grainfields on the sabbath; his disciples were hungry, and they began to pluck heads of grain and to eat. [2] But when the Pharisees saw it, they said to him, "Look, your disciples are doing what is not lawful to do on the sabbath."
> [3] He said to them, "Have you not read what David did, when he was hungry, and those who were with him: [4] how he entered the house of God and ate the bread of the Presence, which it was not lawful for him to eat nor for those who were with him, but only for the priests? [5] Or have you not read in the law how on the sabbath the priests in the temple profane the sabbath, and are guiltless? [6] I tell you, something greater than the temple is here. [7] And if you had known what this means, 'I desire mercy, and not sacrifice,' you would not have condemned the guiltless. [8] For the Son of man is lord of the sabbath."
> [9] And he went on from there, and entered their synagogue. [10] And behold, there was a man with a withered hand. And they asked him, "Is it lawful to heal on the sabbath?" so that they might accuse him. [11] He said to them, "What man of you, if he has one sheep and it falls into a pit on the sabbath, will not lay hold of it and lift it out? [12] Of how much more value is a man than a sheep! So it is lawful to do good on the sabbath." [13] Then he said to the man, "Stretch out your hand." And the man stretched it out, and it was restored, whole like the other. [14] But the Pharisees went out and took counsel against him, how to destroy him. (Matthew 12:1–14)

> [23] One sabbath he was going through the grainfields; and as they made their way his disciples began to pluck heads of grain. [24] And the Pharisees said to him, "Look, why are they doing what is not lawful on the sabbath?"
> [25] And he said to them, "Have you never read what David did, when he was in need and was hungry, he and those who were with him: [26] how he entered the house of God, when Abiathar was high priest, and ate the bread of the Presence, which it is not lawful for any but the priests to eat, and also gave it to those who were with him?"

[27] And he said to them, "The sabbath was made for man, not man for the sabbath." (Mark 2:23-27)

[1] On a sabbath, while he was going through the grainfields, his disciples plucked and ate some heads of grain, rubbing them in their hands. [2] But some of the Pharisees said, "Why are you doing what is not lawful to do on the sabbath?" [3] And Jesus answered, "Have you not read what David did when he was hungry, he and those who were with him: [4] how he entered the house of God, and took and ate the bread of the Presence, which it is not lawful for any but the priests to eat, and also gave it to those with him?" [5] And he said to them, "The Son of man is lord of the sabbath."

[6] On another sabbath, when he entered the synagogue and taught, a man was there whose right hand was withered. [7] And the scribes and the Pharisees watched him, to see whether he would heal on the sabbath, so that they might find an accusation against him. [8] But he knew their thoughts, and he said to the man who had the withered hand, "Come and stand here." And he rose and stood there.

[9] And Jesus said to them, "I ask you, is it lawful on the sabbath to do good or to do harm, to save life or to destroy it?" [10] And he looked around on them all, and said to him, "Stretch out your hand." And he did so, and his hand was restored. [11] But they were filled with fury and discussed with one another what they might do to Jesus. (Luke 6:1-11)

Jesus involved himself in this conflict in two ways: he exercised his authority over the rabbis to interpret divine law.

[28] So the Son of man is lord even of the sabbath. (Mark 2:28)

Jesus was essentially saying, "You pick and choose who you will condemn. You formulate your laws to fit your prejudices and preconceptions. You condemn my disciples, but you don't condemn your priests. I will give you the true meaning of the Sabbath since I gave the Sabbath in the first place." Those were hard sayings for the people.

Not only did he claim to have authority to give God's view on this issue, he then proceeded to present the divine interpretation of the Sabbath.

[27] And he said to them, "The sabbath was made for man, not man for the sabbath." (Mark 2:27)

And Jesus' actions were not lost on the Pharisees—they understood exactly what he was doing and were infuriated by it.

> ⁶ The Pharisees went out, and immediately held counsel with the Herodians against him, how to destroy him. (Mark 3:6)

According to Jesus the divine priority regarding the Sabbath could be summed up in this way: God did not invent the Sabbath and then create men and women to keep it. He did just the opposite. Mankind took priority. The Sabbath was a gift of quality time. If the spirit is beaten out of the Sabbath the day becomes an enslaving thing when it was designed to guarantee quality time freed up from the rest of the week.

There is much good to say about the modern and ancient Jewish approach to the Sabbath. The personification of the Sabbath as "queen" of the week has positive value in helping children to conceptualize God's presence. The Jewish emphasis on the Sabbath as a day of happiness, consecration, divine peace, morality, and joy is consistent with scripture.

One of the finest works on the subject ever published is *The Sabbath* by the late Jewish professor, Abraham Joshua Heschel.[9] But for a Christian the Sabbath goes beyond the historical events of Judaism that gave it meaning. Creation and the Exodus both provide the Sabbath with something to say to us in everyday life: we are created, and we are not to be enslaved. But the atoning work of Jesus Christ provides even more meaning in the Sabbath.

Shortly after the Sabbath was given in Eden humans fell into sin through a refusal to trust God.[10] They became enslaved in sin[11] and found it impossible to free themselves of this slavery.[12] Jesus not only instructed us in the way to live—he lived perfectly according to God's will.[13]

As the "second Adam" he succeeded where the first Adam failed and proved that the race, as God created it, could live in harmony with God's law.[14] He vindicated God and offers his righteousness a substitute for ours.

> ²¹ For our sake he made him to be sin who knew no sin, so that in him we might become the righteousness of God. (2 Corinthians 5:12)

---

9. Heschel, *The Sabbath*.
10. Gen 2:16–17; 3:1–24.
11. Rom 5:12–21.
12. Rom 7:7–12.
13. Heb 4:15.
14. Rom 5:19.

This is the transaction of salvation. The work of providing righteousness is complete in Christ at the cross.[15] Salvation is sure for all believers and we can rest in his completed work.[16]

Originally, God rested from his creative work and the Sabbath was given to symbolize that. Then God freed Israel from bondage—saved them from their enslavement—and the Sabbath became a symbol of that freeing bond between God and his people. But today the Sabbath means more. God frees us from sin at the cross, and the Sabbath symbolizes even that.[17] When Christians celebrate the Sabbath, they rejoice in the completed work of Christ's salvation on their behalf. Their obedience of the commandment adds nothing to that completed work. But it demonstrates a loyalty to God as one enters the enriching life of the symbol. For the Christian, celebrating the Sabbath typifies "entering into God's rest."[18] Just as God rested on the seventh day at the completion of creation, so Jesus rested in the tomb on the seventh day at the completion of redemption.[19] The Sabbath is a very rich Christian symbol.

A PRACTICAL EPILOGUE

The Sabbath is a living symbol that guarantees one full day of spiritual, social, physical, and mental rest each week. While many of us are workaholics who manufacture personal guilt if we are not working every waking moment, God gives us permission to rest on the Sabbath day and says, "Remember the Sabbath day to keep it separate"—separate from selfish pursuits, conversations, pleasures, and work.[20] It is lawful to do good on that day.[21] The time is guaranteed for quality potential and what God has joined together (you and the Sabbath) let no one tear apart.

As we remember the Sabbath God reminds us of some things. GOD REMINDS US OF OUR ROOTS. You were imagined in the mind of God. Such noble roots are flattering but also profoundly serious. For as such we were

---

15. John 19:30.
16. Rom 5:8.
17. Heb 4:3–10.
18. Heb 4:10.
19. Matt 27:62—28:1; Mark 15:42—16:3; Luke 23:55—24:3; John 19:41—20:2.
20. Isa 58:13.
21. Matt 12:12.

created dependent on him, which means we will be restless until we find rest in loyalty to him.

We are moral beings set in charge of this earth and therefore are accountable for what happens to this planet ecologically—animals, plants, atmosphere, soil. Our moral responsibility also extends to each other. We are caretakers of ourselves and are answerable to God for what we do to our being physically as well as spiritually. During the Sabbath rest we have time to think about these roots and allow that thought to bear experiential fruit in doing good things for others.

GOD REMINDS US WHO WE ARE. Our roots are intricately connected to who we are. Once you realize you are royalty then you begin to think like royalty. The royal child's life is disciplined and directed. One day he thinks for himself, but the guidance he has had seriously limits the extent of his deviation from the norm. Believers in Christ live under strict restraints and those restraints that give direction and meaning to moral being in a world that seems out of control.

Living according to those principles gives quality to life. Through the power of Christ living in the life those things are measurable, possible, and correspondingly rewarding. Not for the praise one gets but for the satisfaction of living according to one's reason for being created. During the quality Sabbath time the believer has a chance to think about who he is and to allow those thoughts to become enfleshed in his being.

GOD REMINDS US OF WHERE WE ARE GOING. There is a sense in which the Sabbath is symbolic of heaven. This is not to suggest that heaven is a place of inactivity and sleep, but rather to remind that quality time creates a kind of equality. For example, those who attend worship services on Sabbath will find pews filled with mechanics, nurses, teachers, farmers, doctors, business people, engineers. They worship God together as mutually dependent moral beings in God's presence. They worship God periodically freed from the artificial social distinctions in which they live during the week. Sabbath was to free us, for at least one day each week, from society and its social judgments as well as its pressure cooker pace.

Celebrating on Sabbath was to keep ever before the believer the understanding that this life is not all there is—a fact that has slipped out of the minds and hands of many human beings and causes great insecurity as a result. People give up when they are no longer clear on where they came from, who they are, or where they are going.

I often challenge my university classes that if they study for my classes on the Sabbath (and many of my classes are in some area of religion) they have failed to realize their freedom from me and are thereby cheating themselves. By studying on Sabbath, they have allowed me to intrude their life when God guaranteed they could be free from such intrusion. Students have God's permission not to do their assignment on Sabbath. Enjoying that freedom opens a great range of possibilities for personal Bible study that they cannot have when I am dictating their assignments. The same principle applies in the realm of work and play as well.

What is true of freedom from teachers and bosses is also true of social expectations. To make Sabbath a day of common business keeps humans in bondage—to the worries of balancing the budget, to the intensities of life that God promised to set you apart from. So much so that quality time may be lost, and we accidentally set into the routine that produces the old realization: "I exist, and I am miserable."

Years ago, a national advertiser popularized a slogan that is apropos regarding the Sabbath—a promise of quality time: "Try it, you'll like it!" The Sabbath was made for you!

CHAPTER TWELVE

THE SMOKE OF THEIR TORMENT

> "Coolness and absence of heat and haste indicate fine qualities."
>
> —RALPH WALDO EMERSON

REVELATION 14:8–16

> [8] Another angel, a second, followed, saying, "Fallen, fallen is Babylon the great, she who made all nations drink the wine of her impure passion."
> [9] And another angel, a third, followed them, saying with a loud voice, "If any one worships the beast and its image, and receives a mark on his forehead or on his hand, [10] he also shall drink the wine of God's wrath, poured unmixed into the cup of his anger, and he shall be tormented with fire and sulphur in the presence of the holy angels and in the presence of the Lamb. [11] And the smoke of their torment goes up for ever and ever; and they have no rest, day or night, these worshipers of the beast and its image, and whoever receives the mark of its name."
> [12] Here is a call for the endurance of the saints, those who keep the commandments of God and the faith of Jesus.
> [13] And I heard a voice from heaven saying, "Write this: Blessed are the dead who die in the Lord henceforth." "Blessed

indeed," says the Spirit, "that they may rest from their labors, for their deeds follow them!"

[14] Then I looked, and lo, a white cloud, and seated on the cloud one like a son of man, with a golden crown on his head, and a sharp sickle in his hand. [15] And another angel came out of the temple, calling with a loud voice to him who sat upon the cloud, "Put in your sickle, and reap, for the hour to reap has come, for the harvest of the earth is fully ripe." [16] So he who sat upon the cloud swung his sickle on the earth, and the earth was reaped.

SHARING THE FATE OF THE BEAST

The great warning of the last day message in Revelation is that all who identify with "the beast" will share its fate, and all who identify with "the Lamb" will receive his reward. But what do we make of the violent horror of the beasts' punishment? How should we understand the unmixed wine of God's wrath? And particularly the "smoke of their torment" which ascends "for ever and ever." For many Christians, the question of hell's eternal duration poses no problem. The white heat of God's anger represents the natural response to rebellion and manifests itself in eternal punish*ing*.

John Walvoord, a well-known evangelical scholar, has no difficulty with this passage. He maintains that God's justice is as certain as his love and that love spurned is love nullified. With no love there is only justice. The eternal duration of justice finds emphasis in such expressions as "day or night," "the ages of ages," and the use of the Greek present tense which stresses linear, continuous action. The great truth here, according to Walvoord, deals with the danger of trifling with false loyalties that dishonor God and contradict his word.[1]

While no Christian who takes the Bible seriously would disagree with Walvoord's insistence that justice is an important principle in Revelation, there are those who have seriously challenged the notion of a hell that burns sinners without end. Such a concept, they say, presupposes that man has immortality, a gift granted only to the righteous.[2] Those who hold this view are called "conditionalists," i.e., immortality is granted only on condition of faith in Jesus.[3]

---

1. Walvoord, *Revelation of Jesus Christ*, 219.
2. 1 Cor 15:53.
3. Walvoord, Chap. 3.

THE NATURE OF CONDITIONALISM

A conditionalist from the nineteenth century, George Storrs, argued that scripture teaches that "the wages of sin is death," *not* pain. Not only would keeping man alive in hell require a miracle of God, it would change the eternal results of sin from punish*ment* to punish*ing*. While pain, he argued, was a consequence of sin and naturally involved, only death could be the ultimate result.[4]

Not wishing to surrender the traditional evangelical position, English scholar John Wenham has nevertheless confessed that the subject is not fully settled, and Christians should seriously consider the views of conditionalism on this issue.[5]

Major problems of both exegesis and divine ethics are involved for the "orthodox" viewpoint that the smoke ascending forever somehow involves the eternal inflicting of pain on those who are lost. Discussion of these is far beyond the space of this chapter. However, Jacques Ellul has done justice to the language and context of Revelation in this summation:

> As the duration of this separation and these torments, they are declared to be "for eons of eons," and it is not a question of a duration limited by a passage or time but by the proclamation: "I make *all* things new," and "there will be no more curse" (chapter 22); then God by grace puts an end to this impossible situation.[6]

---

4. Storrs, *Six Sermons on the Inquiry.* 2d ed., 20–44.
5. Wenham, *Goodness of God*, 41.
6. Ellul, *Apocalypse*, 176–77.

CHAPTER THIRTEEN

Unconditional Love

> "Be such a man, and live such a life, that if every man were such as you, and every life a life such as yours, this earth would be God's paradise."
>
> —Phillips Brooks

HOSEA 6:1–3

> ¹ "Come, let us return to the Lord;
>   for he has torn, that he may heal us;
>   he has stricken, and he will bind us up.
> ² After two days he will revive us;
> on the third day he will raise us up,
>   that we may live before him.
> ³ Let us know, let us press on to know the Lord;
>   his going forth is sure as the dawn;
>   he will come to us as the showers,
>   as the spring rains that water the earth."

VARYING RESPONSES

A colleague recently went through a divorce. He shared some of his pain with me; what hurt him most was a note from his mother-in-law, someone he loved very much. It went like this:

"You surely must be miserable today thinking of what you have done to your wife, your family, your friends, your students, and your church members. You have disappointed so many. We will all go on, but what about you? We feel betrayed and rightly so. We pray for you every day."

He testified to the pain that the note inflicted. I wondered what he expected, yet I saw his point. At times when we need nourishment from other Christians, we often get stepped on. "She treats me as if I am totally responsible for this breakup," he said. "Doesn't she understand that it takes two to tangle?" Where was the Holy Spirit in their marriage? Where was the Holy Spirit in her treatment of him?

WE FEEL BETRAYED

At another time and another place, another friend and his wife divorced. He had not lived an exemplary life and had caused great pain in his relationship. His problems went far beyond his home and his wife. Society judged him guilty of crimes, and he ended up in jail. No one came to see him except his father-in-law. Instead of condemning him for the treatment of his daughter or blaming him for the embarrassment he had caused the family, his father-in-law saw him as a pilgrim in this world, struggling to find answers to life's questions.

This father-in-law had come to grips with life because he had experienced the work of the Holy Spirit in a special way. He himself had been hurting and made mistakes. Swallowing his own offense at the young man's craziness, this father reached out to bring a spot of encouragement to his son-in-law.

My colleague is doing fine despite the note. My friend in jail got out and continued his crimes. But what of the mother-in-law and the father-in-law? What kind of joy came to these two witnesses for Christ? Reaching out is not always going to bring the closure we would like. Unconditional love does not try to manipulate, control or create guilt. It simply allows the Spirit to do his softening work.

THE WORK OF THE HOLY SPIRIT AS "RAIN"

I remember hearing and reading a lot about the "latter rain." Much of it seemed very esoteric. The preaching and the theorizing were lost on me and, if anything, tempted me with arrogance at knowing something others didn't know. But if we mean by the "latter rain" that there are people whom God touches in such a way that they swallow their own hurts and reach out when we are hurting to bring us comfort, then I will appreciate this teaching as something every one of us needs.

CHAPTER FOURTEEN

What Does "the Latter Rain" Mean Today?

> "There is a divinity that shapes our ends—but we can help by listening for its voice."
>
> —Kathleen Norris

JOEL 2:23–32

> [23] "Be glad, O sons of Zion,
> And rejoice in the Lord, your God;
> for he has given the early rain for your vindication,
> he has poured down for you abundant rain,
> the early and the latter rain, as before.
> [24] "The threshing floors shall be full of grain,
> the vats shall overflow with wine and oil.
> [25] I will restore to you the years
> which the swarming locust has eaten,
> the hopper, the destroyer, and the cutter,
> my great army, which I sent among you.
> [26] "You shall eat in plenty and be satisfied,
> and praise the name of the Lord your God,
> who has dealt wondrously with you.
> And my people shall never again be put to shame.

> ²⁷ You shall know that I am in the midst of Israel,
>> and that I, the LORD, am your God and there is none else.
> And my people shall never again
>> be put to shame.
> ²⁸ "And it shall come to pass afterward,
>> that I will pour out my spirit on all flesh;
> your sons and your daughters shall prophesy,
>> your old men shall dream dreams,
> and your young men shall see visions.
> ²⁹ Even upon the menservants and maidservants
>> in those days, I will pour out my spirit.
> ³⁰ "And I will give portents in the heavens and on the earth,
>> blood and fire and columns of smoke.
> ³¹ The sun shall be turned to darkness, and the moon to blood,
>> before the great and terrible day of the LORD comes.
> ³² And it shall come to pass that all who call upon
>> the name of the LORD shall be delivered;
> for in Mount Zion and in Jerusalem there shall be those who escape,
>> as the Lord has said,
> and among the survivors shall be those whom the LORD calls."

THE DOCTRINE OF THE LATTER RAIN

One of those pieces of Christian tradition that can be confusing to young people is the doctrine of the latter rain. We shouldn't call it a doctrine, since it is just an analogy to the work of the Holy Spirit, but it is a thought that is vintage eschatology. We need to look at the work of the Holy Spirit in the latter days of human history. And there are some insights that may be helpful as we face our daily opportunities.

PROMISES OF ATTAINMENT

We will find it constructive to see the work of the Spirit as a work of enabling. God cares about people, their dreams, and their hopes. He gives them power through the Spirit to attain those hopes. Much of this power is built into us, and with a little encouragement from each other we can do it. Our life can have structure, focus and direction. Those things give us clarity.

Scripture often encourages believers.

> [18] Then the LORD became jealous for his land, and had pity on his people. [19] The LORD answered and said to his people, "Behold, I am sending to you grain, wine, and oil, and you will be satisfied; and I will no more make you a reproach among the nations." (Joel 2:18–19)

Much of the descriptive language seems foreign to us, especially if we are from the cities, because the analogies are made to the growing season and agriculture. But with a little application we can understand these promises in our own setting. Overarching these promises of attainment is the notion that life is not a project so much as a process. We are growing; thus, we need nourishment. We are in process of attaining. We understand progressively. Our understanding of life today will invariably change tomorrow as we gain new insights from the experiences of each day.

How we look at life at twenty will be different from how we look at life at fifty. Christians have not always allowed for this. We baptize people after they have gone through a set of Bible studies, sometimes leaving the impression that there is nothing important left to learn about God. We accept people based on their behavior and then reject them when they don't live up to their profession, forgetting that change may indicate a further maturity in truth.

The outpouring of the Spirit on receptive ground (hearts) means that some change and depth of growth is inevitable and that a plant that is not watered, or that does not grow inevitably dies.

PICTURES FROM THE FARM

Pictures of rains, pastures, fruit, trees, barren lands, parched fields, storm clouds, abundant showers, and the like fill the pages of scripture. They are significant illustrations of the life with or without God, and they form wonderful pictures on the walls of our soul. So intimate is this language in our Christian religion that we can scarcely describe our perception of God's activity without them.

The fruit of the Spirit is evidence of the power of the gospel. Our souls are watered with the sweet rains of the Holy Spirit. Storms in life drive us back to our starting point with the Lord. At times we go to church and feel our parched souls filled with the water of life. These are all expressions we can call "pictures from the farm." And though most of us don't live on a farm, few of us misunderstand this picturesque way of describing God's work. Most of us went to summer camp or had to keep up our yards. We understand to some degree, the pain of thirst and heat. We can relate to the need for food and drink.

When we study the early and latter rain analogy, we should not be dogmatic or arrogant about who is going to receive the Spirit and who is not. We should rather be concerned that the Spirit can find a friendly atmosphere in our hearts and that we are open to the chances of understanding and tolerance he proposed to bring to us. As the seeds are gently awakened by the autumn rain (to use the biblical illustration), so the plants are attractively sprouting with the spring rain. The church could use a crop of tolerant and accepting plants like never in its history.

PREROGATIVES OF THE SPIRIT

From the earliest days some Christian leaders and writers had trouble with the Spirit. For one thing, some of them were not trinitarians. They believed that Christ was a created (or "begotten") being and that the Spirit was a pervading, impersonal influence of God.

Although the creedal position has been shored up, many church members still act as if there is no need for the Spirit. They scurry around as if they must "finish the work," as if the Holy Spirit does not exist, does not care or is not able. How is the Spirit alive in our experience?

Judging, discriminating, deciding who is real and who is phony is really the work of the Spirit. Giving gifts to individuals is the work of the Spirit. Our task is simply to recognize those gifts in people and honor them. There are prerogatives of the Spirit: watering, nourishing, teaching, giving the gifts, producing the fruit. That doesn't leave us with nothing to do, it just assures us that there are some things for which we are not responsible.

Releasing us from the compulsion to take the place and do the work of the Holy Spirit will bring us more security in our Christianity and set us free to witness to the power of the Spirit in our lives.

CHAPTER FIFTEEN

Saul the Monarch Tested

> "Study without reflection is a waste of time;
> reflection without study is dangerous."
>
> —Confucius

1 SAMUEL 13:11-12

> [11] Samuel said, "What have you done?" And Saul said, "When I saw that the people were scattering from me, and that you did not come within the days appointed, and that the Philistines had mustered at Michmash, [12] I said, 'Now the Philistines will come down upon me at Gilgal, and I have not entreated the favor of the LORD'; so I forced myself, and offered the burnt offering."

Israelites Had No King

When the Israelites were organized, they did not have a king like the surrounding nations. This made them different in a very striking way. Where the Amalekites and the Philistines had a visible leader to rally around, Israel did not. This is not to say Israel had no leaders. They had prophets who spoke for God delivering the "word of the Lord," and they had judges who made decisions and ruled territories on the basis of divine moral instruction. These leaders carried out the work of the theocracy—a government where God was king.

As time went on, Israel saw what they considered were advantages in having a tangible, visible king like other nations. And their insistence finally led to divine approval provided God made the choice. The story of Samuel the prophet and Saul's appointment as Israel's first king is well-known. But now the question arose, how would a king function differently than a prophet or a judge? And how would he relate to the priests?

The monarchy differed from the judge/prophet rule in that it rested on military prowess and dynastic rule. Secular life and religious life, being the same in the theocracy, began to diverge in the monarchy. The relationship between Israel and God may not have changed a great deal on a day-to-day basis, but it changed fundamentally and philosophically a great deal with the inception of the monarchy. Never again would it be as close.

SAUL'S FIRST MISTAKE

We cannot be clear on how long Saul had been king when the attack at Geba occurred.

> [11] When I saw that the people were scattering from me, and that you did not come within the days appointed so . . . [12] I forced myself, and offered the burnt offering. (1 Samuel 13:11–12)

The Hebrew text omits the time reference[1] so the English versions differ (NIV—Saul had reigned for 42 years; NEB—22 years; NASB—32 years; RSV— . . . and 2 years; KJV—2 years; Amplified—2 years; Douay—2 years). The extensive variance shows the speculative nature of the translators' work.

However, the time factor is not of significance to us here. Kings, prophets, and priests each had important functions even in the monarchy. But Saul either decided that these distinctions were no longer important, or that as king he need not follow the rules. Even though he was a Benjamite, he decided to try his hand at the priesthood, offering up burnt offering and fellowship offerings.[2]

---

1. 1 Sam 13:1.
2. 1 Sam 13:9.

Instead of waiting for a word from the Lord through his prophet, Saul decided to get his own word from the Lord directly. This proved to be a serious mistake. The end had begun.

> [13] And Samuel said to Saul, "You have done foolishly; you have not kept the commandment of the Lord your God, which he commanded you; for now the Lord would have established your kingdom over Israel for ever. [14] But now your kingdom shall not continue; the Lord has sought out a man after his own heart; and the Lord has appointed him to be prince over his people, because you have not kept what the Lord commanded you." (1 Samuel 13:13-14)

We should not think that making a mistake decides our destiny. Saul's problem resided not in making the mistake but in his handling of the mistake. Rather than confessing his disobedience and repenting of it, Saul justified himself, shifting the blame to Samuel[3] and by implication to God who had appointed Samuel. So, the issue was trust. In not obeying God's instructions through his spokesmen of old, Saul demonstrated that he really didn't trust God.

What do we do when God seems to be giving us the "silent treatment?" Does shifting the blame for your problems (to circumstances, parents, friends, authority figures, etc.) enhance your reputation as a strong, intelligent person? What do we think of people who always make excuses for their problems?

SAUL'S FOOLISH COMMAND

It was no mean challenge to fight the Philistines with rakes when they had all the swords. At this time, the Philistines held the monopoly on iron.[4]

> [24] And the men of Israel were distressed that day; for Saul laid an oath on the people, saying, "Cursed be the man who eats food until it is evening and I am avenged on my enemies." So none of the people tasted food. (1 Samuel 14:24)

Despite that, Jonathan let God fight for his army and he routed the Philistines soundly. The combination of Jonathan's creative approach to warfare (a result of his daring trust in God) and God's earthquake intervention,

---

3. 1 Sam 13:12.
4. 1 Sam 13:19-23.

led the Philistines into total disorientation. In their confusion they turned their one advantage, namely their swords, on each other and did the work Jonathan could not do alone.[5]

Meanwhile back at headquarters, Saul, acting from fear, issued the self-defeating command that no one in his army would eat food until he (Saul) was avenged.[6] But Jonathan, who had been at war, unknowingly broke the command and even when he was informed of it declared that if the men were hungry they would do a better job as soldiers if they were fed. We can see the profile developing: Maybe Saul was not so wise. In fact, some (even in his own family) thought he made dumb rules.

When Saul prayed for guidance and perceived no answer from God, he impetuously concluded that the silence was the result of some soldier's disobedience. So, he began the search for who was to blame (again!). But when the lot fell on his own household, i.e., his own son Jonathan (by now the national hero), he decided he could not carry out his own order.

Saul looked like a bumbler. He shifted blame, he was indecisive, he overstepped authority, he made stupid declarations, he tried unsuccessfully to cover his tracks. Such capriciousness was dangerous for the nation. But the drama was not over yet. Should Saul have carried out the declaration that the guilty party be executed whether his son was guilty or someone else? What did Saul's declaration reveal about his character? Is "casting lots" a good way to know God's will for my life? In a certain circumstance?

PIETY OR REBELLION

Even after the death-knell of his kingdom had been sounded, Saul won impressive victories and continued to function as king. But it was inevitable that his character flaws would eventually lead to his undoing.

> [3] Now go and smite Amalek, and utterly destroy all that they have; do not spare them, but kill both man and woman, infant and suckling, ox and sheep, camel and ass. (1 Samuel 15:3)

The Amalekite incident magnified Saul's character and vindicated God's evaluation.

---

5. 1 Sam 14:21.
6. 1 Sam 14:24.

> [sup]13[/sup] And Samuel said to Saul, "You have done foolishly; you have not kept the commandment of the LORD your God, which he commanded you; for now the LORD would have established your kingdom over Israel for ever. [sup]14[/sup] But now your kingdom shall not continue; the LORD has sought out a man after his own heart; and the LORD has appointed him to be prince over his people, because you have not kept what the LORD commanded you." (1 Samuel 13:13–14)

Ordered to annihilate the Amalekites and completely dispose of their goods, Saul displayed selective and creative obedience, picking and choosing what seemed to fit his fancy. He brought the Amalekite king back alive. He brought back the best of the flocks to offer as sacrifice to the Lord. At first he denied that he disobeyed, then he began giving reasons why his ideas were better than God's.

Saul represented all who insist they can improve on God's revelation. "I do keep the Sabbath; I just keep it on Sunday." "I don't fornicate; I love the girl I am sleeping with that I'm not married to." "I didn't steal this. I just borrowed it for a while." "I'm just watching this sex and violence; I'm not meditating on it." "I'm not committing adultery, my marriage just didn't work, it would be a sin to live with my husband when I don't love him anymore."

Samuel's answer to Saul's self-deception became the battle cry of the prophets.

> [sup]22[/sup] And Samuel said, "Has the LORD as great delight in burnt offerings and sacrifices, as in obeying the voice of the LORD? Behold, to obey is better than sacrifice." (1 Samuel 15:22)

Refusing to live in harmony with God's judgments and instructions, Saul acts out a sham, tacking on religion where it seems expedient, saying what should be said when it appears advantageous. Knowing that his position could be jeopardized, Saul cosmetically treats his character flaws, and then ironically ends up jeopardizing his position. He is a type of Pilate who washed his hands of Jesus' death in order to save his own skin, only to be driven out of office later because of his incompetence in solving problems. History extravagantly demonstrates that it is better to die for a cause than to live a sham.

A picture doesn't become religious art because it has a Bible verse as a caption. And so, a life does not become a committed life because it adheres to the culture of a religious tradition. Saul represents to us the shallowness of the uncommitted life that irrationally seeks to hang on to God but to do it in one's own way. Such attempts result in foolish decisions—both personally and corporately. The result is weak leadership, intrigue, and finally personal, national, organizational disaster.

By contrast, David, Saul's successor, made many of the same mistakes as Saul, yet his repentant attitude, his contrite pliability, and his humble obedience won him the distinction:

> [14] But now your kingdom shall not continue; the LORD has sought out *a man after his own heart;* and the LORD has appointed him to be prince over his people, because you have not kept what the LORD commanded you. (1 Samuel 13:14. Emphasis supplied)

If obedience is better than sacrifice, does that mean that obedience is more than following a set of rules? How do you know when you are obeying? Why was God so upset about having appointed Saul king? Had he made a mistake? Does God make mistakes? Here is a microcosm of living in anticipation of the end time.

CHAPTER SIXTEEN

The Hall of Shame

> "No public man can be a little crooked. There is no such thing as a no-man's-land between honesty and dishonesty."
>
> —Herbert Hoover

ROMANS 12:1-8

¹ I appeal to you therefore, brethren, by the mercies of God, to present your bodies as a living sacrifice, holy and acceptable to God, which is your spiritual worship. ² Do not be conformed to this world but be transformed by the renewal of your mind, that you may prove what is the will of God, what is good and acceptable and perfect.

³ For by the grace given to me I bid every one among you not to think of himself more highly than he ought to think, but to think with sober judgment, each according to the measure of faith which God has assigned him. ⁴ For as in one body we have many members, and all the members do not have the same function, ⁵ so we, though many, are one body in Christ, and individually members one of another. ⁶ Having gifts that differ according to the grace given to us, let us use them: if prophecy, in proportion to our faith; ⁷ if service, in our serving; he who teaches, in his teaching; ⁸ he who exhorts, in his exhortation;

he who contributes, in liberality; he who gives aid, with zeal; he who does acts of mercy, with cheerfulness.

INDUCTION IN THE HALL OF SHAME

King Saul was an enigma. He had so much going for him, yet he ended up in the scripture Hall of Shame. There were several people with him. Cain was the first to be inducted. Perhaps the next real notables were Esau and then Pharaoh. We could list a precious few kings of Judah and Israel who really qualify as "very bad guys." Perhaps Ahab achieved this status. In the New Testament only Judas truly achieved such infamy, though Paul was on his way until he turned around. Other members of the Hall of Shame would certainly include Pilate, Herod the Great, Herod Antipas, and Caiaphas.

There is also a scripture *Hall of Fame*. The list there is longer because the Bible is salvation history and is trying to show how to aim at a good destination. These people have become household words: Abel, Seth, Noah, Abraham, Isaac, Jacob, Moses, Samson, David, Solomon, Hezekiah, Daniel, Nebuchadnezzar, Mary Magdalene, Dorcas, John, Paul. The list goes on.

I can remember in church school learning the Israelite kings on the basis of the good guys and the bad guys, and seriously wondering: what turned them bad?

HALL OF SHAME INDUCTEES

The Hall of Shame inductees shared one trait—they let circumstances mold them into a shape which left them useless to God, society, or themselves. A profile of each of their lives would make a fearful biographical work. Starting with great potential they allowed themselves to believe that their natural abilities were somehow a credit to them. Inheriting intelligence is out of our control. How intelligence is used is very much within our control. The position is often termed "went to their heads." They became the *prima donnas* of scripture and allowed themselves to indulge the illegitimacy of thinking they were "special."

A particularly evil person is a person with spectacular potential for good. C. S. Lewis, in his book *A Case for Christianity,* addresses the question of how a good God could make a bad devil, by reasoning that in creating a person with magnificent potential for good, God also opened the possibility of frightful evil.

A cow with little potential for mischief also has little hope of offering anything but meat, milk, or calves. But a dog with its superior intelligence (as compared to a cow) has a greater capacity for troublemaking. We take dogs into our homes to live and show affection. We teach them tricks, we house-break them. Can you imagine having a Holstein cow residing in your living room? Some people adopt dogs and find their reciprocal affection quite delightful. But you don't hear of people doing that in the same way with a Guernsey.

So, it is not impossible that very capable people will turn out to be very evil, but it is still curious and enigmatic. Here is Saul:

> 1 There was a man of Benjamin whose name was Kish, the son of Abdiel, son of Zero, son of Becorath, son of Aphiah, a Benjaminite, a man of wealth; ² and he had a son whose name was Saul, a handsome young man. There was not a man among the people of Israel more handsome than he; from his shoulders upward he was taller than any of the people. (1 Samuel 9:1–2)

Saul was initially thoughtful of others' feelings, humble, handsome, spiritual, and hand-picked by God to lead his people. And in the over three hundred scriptural references to him, we watch him literally deteriorate before our eyes.

WHAT CHANGES FOR A PERSON OF THE HALL OF FAME?

Saul habitually modified God's instructions. He constantly sought to improve on God's ideas. Rationalization, selfish adjustment, shifting the blame, self-justification, impetuous self-seeking, all coalesce in Saul's experience and become easier to indulge. Until finally jealousy, envy, pride, clamoring to exert authority for its own sake, become not temptation but lifestyle for Saul.

Realizing that he is getting consistent silence from God he blames his soldiers. Jealous that David is more popular he seeks to kill David. When you are king you have options you don't have as a peasant subject in a kingdom. Saul succumbs consistently to the temptation to exert those prerogatives for his own gain. He lets the circumstances decide his character.

People do not start out life in the Hall of Shame. They work at it. Cain allowed circumstances to make him bitter. Pharaoh allowed the plagues to turn him into a tower of obstinacy. Judas let greed turn him into a traitor. Pilate became a world-class example of the futility of self-serving in political office.

Paul offers this advice for the potential Sauls of today.

> [2] Don't let the world around you squeeze you into its mold, but let God remold your minds from within, so that you may prove in practice that the plan of God for you is good, meets all his demands and moves toward the goal of fine maturity. (Romans 12:2, Phillips)

CHAPTER SEVENTEEN

WITH EMOTIONS MIXED

> "The true test of a great man—that, at least, which must secure his place among the highest order of great men—is, his having been in advance of his age."
>
> —HENRY BROUGHAM

DANIEL 12:3

> ³ And those who are wise shall shine like the brightness of the firmament; and those who turn many to righteousness, like the stars for ever and ever.

ASTONISHMENT AND ADMIRATION

My first impression of Dr. Frank Knittel[1] was one of astonishment and admiration. As a first-year Seminarian at Andrews University who had learned the basic strum on the five-string banjo, I had been invited by a friend to join a group of guitars in accompanying a community sing in the student union building. It was there that I saw the new vice-president for student affairs in action.

---

1. Dr. Frank Knittel was President of Southern Adventist University from 1968–1983.

Dr. Knittel was addressing the students at this social event. There was no whispering or goofing around among the students—only rapt attention. I had heard deans before speaking at, straightening out, intimidating, praising, etc. But this dean was communicating. And he looked like no other dean I had ever seen—crewcut, informally dressed, fidgety and straight-forward with his machine-gun rhetoric. His talk was periodically interrupted by spontaneous applause, responsive chuckling, and warm pensiveness. The reverence of his student body was obvious.

A short time later my wife, a junior English major at the time, enrolled in a class in the *History of the English Language* (one of the more potentially dull courses available, I guessed). But the teacher, Dr. Knittel, brought little dullness to the subject and each day my wife testified to some new energetic antic or exciting piece of knowledge by way of her professor.

WHO WAS THIS MAN?

Who is this Frank Knittel and how had Southern College and the Collegedale Church deserved the blessing of his presence for sixteen years? He was born in Bakersfield, California, in 1927, of Seventh-day Adventist parents. His father was a church schoolteacher and for a time an academy principal. Dr. Knittel grew up in the church and was educated by the church. His formal schooling started unintentionally at three years of age when his mother took a job and left him with the first-grade teacher while she taught the upper grades. By the end of the school year, he had finished the first grade.

The course of his elementary schooling seemed patterned after that first freakish year. He advanced so rapidly that by the seventh grade he was only ten years old, and his parents decided to keep him home to let his chronological age catch up. When the truant officers found him, he was returned to the eighth grade and graduated two weeks later.

At eleven he entered high school and finished that in three years. This swift movement became known by many in the school district. But this time his family had moved from California to New Mexico, and on to Texas, and students were anxious to meet this intellectual "exhibit" when he entered Southwestern Junior College in Keene, Texas. By the age of sixteen he had graduated from junior college.

Dr. Knittel's first administrative/teaching appointment was at Plaquemine, Louisiana, where he taught twenty-one students spread over eight grades. The assignment included running the school, teaching all the elementary grades and high school level World History, English, Algebra, and New Testament History. Since that first assignment Frank Knittel's professional life involved administration, teaching, and lecturing competently on a wide variety of subjects of interest and help to the academic community. These tasks were carried out with a deep sensitivity to the needs of the students and the best interests of the church's institutions.

PROFESSIONAL ADVANCEMENTS

Some administrators seem to be simply scientists carrying on their work for the good of humanity as though humanity did not include people. But humanity was individualized for an administrator like Frank Knittel. His door was always open to his junior administrators, his teachers, and his students.

Through the years he gained a reputation for patience with professionals who were having a rough go of it. Gathering them closely to him he gave them chance after chance to succeed in their work. Rather than merely a scientific administrator, Dr. Knittel functioned as an artist who was sensitive to the brittleness of the stuff with which he had to work and the goals of the task he was to accomplish. With a rare combination of wisdom and knowledge, energy, and decisiveness, he brought out the best in others and built the institutions of the church into respectable pursuits.

Leaving his first teacher/administrator job, Knittel returned to college to finish three majors—English, History, and Religion—and graduated from Union College at the age of eighteen. He next attended University of Minnesota where he taught as a graduate assistant for a year and two summers. And in 1947 he became dean of boys at Enterprise Academy in Kansas. One evening at a dinner party could yield story after fascinating story from his stay at Enterprise which lasted a scant three years. But the thread running through all the accounts was clearly discernible—people meant a great deal to Dr. Frank Knittel.

COMPLICATIONS ON THE WAY

The Korean War interrupted further educational pursuits for a time. For two and a half years Frank served his country as a First Lieutenant in the

U. S. Army and remained in the active reserves before retiring as a Major in 1967.

In 1953, he became dean of boys at Campion Academy where he taught Geometry. Two years later he enrolled in a master's and Doctoral program in Medieval Studies at University of Colorado and graduated in 1959. He wrote his doctoral dissertation in six weeks. During his time at U. C., he taught for the university and worked as assistant dean of men.

By this time Frank had met Helen Smith, a secretary at the Colorado Conference office in Denver. After marriage in 1956, Helen also pursued academic goals and finished her BA in Business and her MA in English from Andrews University. She had previously attended Southern Missionary College, Union College, and the University of Colorado.

In 1959 a call to Andrews University returned the Knittels to denominational employment. Frank taught English full-time for four years—such subjects as Middle English, History of the English Language, Chaucer, and honors English. "They were the most glorious years of my life," he recalls, "simply working with students and watching them grow." However, because of his innate administrative ability, coupled with his uncanny ability to motivate young people, he was invited to become vice-president for student affairs.

Here I saw him function for the first time. I only remember observing him. I did not know him. My perception of him was that his rapport with students was electric. He could quell potential mass movements with an expertise rare to his office. He could reason with and motivate students with unusual competence. He could lead a student individual or students in a group to a spiritual commitment with an understanding envied by the finest of gospel ministers. He could handle the stickiest of problems with a decisiveness and perception that was incredible. By his own admission he had always been "unique," but that uniqueness was transferred to others in the form of thorough-going leadership and ability.

When Dr. Knittel was invited to Southern Missionary College to serve as academic dean in 1967, the students at Andrews University staged a demonstration to dissuade him from leaving. They organized on campus with placards and speeches and marched in mass the three-quarters of a mile to the Knittel home where they proceeded to appeal to him. But to no avail. The Knittels decided to come to Collegedale.

MOVING SOUTH

Andrews University carries some good memories for the Knittels. It was there that their two children, Jeff, and Sherry, were born. Many close personal relationships begun there continue to this day. But it also conjures up such recollections as snowbanks and snow shovels, long hard winters, and geographical flatness. All these are Michigan facts of life that Californians, and southerners have difficulty adjusting to.

Since 1967 the Knittels gave untiringly to the Collegedale community. Helen taught for the college in both the English and the Business Departments. She served as secretary in the division of religion and managed the Georgia-Cumberland Adventist Book Center in Collegedale. All of this has been in addition to the frightening demands thrust upon her by her husband's position—entertaining, traveling, and public exposure.

Frank served the church for two and one-half decades and was known through the North American Division as one of the ablest administrators and teachers this church has ever produced. In 1981 he was honored by Andrews University as the recipient of the Charles Weniger award for outstanding leadership—the highest administrative award offered by the Adventist Church.

The recent committee for accrediting Southern College showered praise on him for the outstanding job he did as president of the college for twelve years, and especially through the exceedingly difficult three years of unprecedented and largely unwarranted criticism of the college and its staff.

ACCOMPLISHMENTS OF FRANK KNITTEL

During Dr. Knittel's twelve years as president the enrollment of Southern College grew from 1440 to a high of over 2000. In addition to the rise in enrollment the growth budget expanded from $4,000,000 to $16,000,000.

William Iles, an executive officer with Florida Hospital, and member of the SC Board of Trustees recently revealed to the faculty and Board that 70% of all the students who have ever graduated from Southern College (since 1892) did so with Frank Knittel on the platform to shake their hands. And 61% of all who graduated did so during Frank's tenure as president.

It is not stretching the truth at all to suggest that no other one person was more responsible than Frank Knittel for the fine academic reputation

Southern College now enjoys around the circuit of church higher education. Tired from the beleaguerment of his last three years and from the general fatigue that all administrators suffer, Dr. Knittel left his position at the summer of 1983 at his own request. He began a fifteen-month sabbatical with no intention of returning. And while the Knittels' plans for the future were not final at the time of our honoring him, the Collegedale Church wished them the kind of blessing they had brought to us.

Our college teaching staff would miss his honest openness, his keen scholarship, his decisive leadership, and the open-handed comradeship we had enjoyed. Our church would miss the undying optimism, the incisive articulation of issues, the challenges to do our best. Our students would miss the bond they had felt, and they would wonder how long it would be until someone treated them with such understanding. Our Sabbath School class would miss the exciting discussions and the probing questions that only Frank Knittel could introduce. And we all pledged that the work of educating and motivating young people for the faithful service of God would move with energy and devotion in the spirit which Frank and Helen Knittel had modeled for us. We prayed for God's richest blessings to be on our friends wherever God might lead them.

For years I have heard Frank Knittel give tributes to those retiring or leaving our faculty. Both his favorite words and his favorite text which follow aptly apply to him and to Helen. "Nobody is indispensable, but there are some people who are irreplaceable." (Frank Knittel).

> [3] And those who are wise shall shine like the brightness of the firmament; and those who turn many to righteousness, like the stars for ever and ever. (Daniel 12:3)

CHAPTER EIGHTEEN

East of Eden

> "To live without loving is not really to live."
>
> —Moliere

GENESIS 4:1–8

> [1] Now Adam knew Eve his wife, and she conceived and bore Cain, saying, "I have gotten a man with the help of the Lord." [2] And again, she bore his brother Abel. Now Abel was a keeper of sheep, and Cain a tiller of the ground.
> [3] In the course of time Cain brought to the Lord an offering of the fruit of the ground, [4] and Abel brought of the firstlings of his flock and of their fat portions. And the Lord had regard for Abel and his offering, [5] but for Cain and his offering he had no regard. So Cain was truly angry, and his countenance fell. [6] The Lord said to Cain, "Why are you angry, and why has your countenance fallen? [7] If you do well, will you not be accepted? And if you do not do well, sin is couching at the door; its desire is for you, but you must master it."
> [8] Cain said to Abel his brother, "Let us go out to the field." And when they were in the field, Cain rose up against his brother Abel, and killed him.

AN ANTHROPOCENTRIC CONCERN

In holy writ the earliest illustration of man's inhumanity to his fellowman is seen in the story of Cain and Abel. The first children to be born into the world, these brothers brought great hope to their parents. But events took a dastardly turn when, in a fit of rage born of deep jealousy and nurtured hatred, the first-born Cain turned his hand against his brother and murdered him.

In his well-known novel, *East of Eden,* written in 1952, John Steinbeck (1902–1968) alludes frequently to the ancient tale of Genesis. But this is hardly an exposition of the biblical story. Were a Christian to have written such a novel he may have elaborated on the meaning of sacrifice, or on the importance of obeying God, or even on the difference between God's way of salvation and man's perverted suggestions as to how God could improve.

But Steinbeck's concern is anthropocentric and lays in that aspect of the story, which suggests man's plight—the emotional and sentimental situation. He explains,

> As I went into the story [of *East of Eden*] more deeply I began to realize that without this story [of Cain and Abel]—or rather a sense of it—psychiatrists would have nothing to do. In other words this one story is the basis of all human neurosis—and if you take the fall along with, you have the total of the psychic troubles that can happen to a human.[1]

Thus, it is in this matrix of hatred and love, envy and cruel discrimination, strength and weakness, beauty, and ugliness that Steinbeck gestates his philosophical message.

THE FILM ADAPTATION OF THE BOOK

The 1955 film version of "East of Eden," starring James Dean, and directed by Elia Kazan, covers only the last ninety pages of Steinbeck's novel. It provides the viewer with a slice of life from the family of Adam Trask and his two sons Caleb and Aron. The story line goes like this: Caleb, the black sheep of the family, finds it virtually impossible to win his father's favor. In an involved identity search brought on by the relationship with Adam, Caleb discovers that he and his twin brother were born by a prostitute.

---

1. Steinbeck, *Journal of a Novel,* 104.

When Adam loses his money in a bad business deal Caleb gives him the money for his birthday, but the gift is spurned. "Give me a good life—that could be something I'd value," says his father. Caleb, in a rage, hauls his brother to Monterey where he discloses the secret of their origin. Unable to cope with the reality of his roots, Aron (who has been studying for the ministry) joins the army, goes to war, and is killed in action. Adam suffers a stroke. But through this complex maze Caleb finally receives the forgiving acceptance of his father, marries Aron's sweetheart, and begins again.

THE SLICE OF LIFE

This slice in the life of the Trask family is large enough for Steinbeck to reveal his naturalism.

> I believe that there is one story in the world, and only one, that has frightened and inspired us, so that we live in a Pearl White serial of continuing thought and wonder. Humans are caught—in their lives, in their thoughts, in their hungers and ambitions, in their avarice and cruelty, and in their kindness and generosity too—in a net of good and evil. I think this is the only story we have and that it occurs on all levels of feeling and intelligence. Virtue and vice were warp and woof of our first consciousness, and they will be the fabric of our last, and this despite any changes we may impose on field and river and mountain, on economy and manners. There is no other story. A man, after he has brushed off the dust and chips of his life will have left only the hard, clean questions: Was it good or was it evil? Have I done well—or ill?[2]

Steinbeck shows, through the story, the ill-frustration of favoritism, the importance of identity, and the great human need for acceptance and understanding. The story line is complex and constitutes naturalistic philosophy at its finest.

The viewer's understanding of the film will be enhanced if he has some grasp of naturalism. Briefly, this philosophy is atheistic (does not assume the existence of a personal God who involves himself in human affairs) and deterministic (basically all things are beyond the control of humanity being fixed in nature). Writing from this perspective the literary naturalists of the twentieth century sought to be objective and detached.

---

2. Steinbeck, *East of Eden*, Chap. 34.

They attempted to provide a description of the way things are rather than suggestions about why they are like that or how they could be changed. Value judgments and normative ethics are in logical secondary position for naturalism. However, like all atheistic philosophies, naturalism has always suffered in its inconsistencies and this can be seen in *East of Eden.*

Steinbeck's emphasis on emotion and sentimentality is so convincing and involves his reader so effectively that the message comes across: man's plight is truly awful. Such a value judgment immediately provides a subjectivism that pure naturalism had sought to avoid.

CHAPTER NINETEEN

THE INFLUENCE OF A TEACHER[1]

> "It is a great mistake to think of being great without goodness; and I pronounce it as certain that there was never yet a truly great man that was not at the same time truly virtuous."
>
> —BENJAMIN FRANKLIN

1 CORINTHIANS 12:28

[28] And God has appointed in the church first apostles, second prophets, third teachers, then workers of miracles, then healers, helpers, administrators, speakers in various kinds of tongues.

THE PLANTING OF MENTAL TIME BOMBS

What is the value of a true teacher? James Garfield once said, "Give me a lot hut, with a simple bench, Mark Hopkins on one end and I on the other, and you may have all the buildings, apparatus, and libraries without him."[2] Probably all of us could identify a teacher or two who held a

---

1. Zackrison, "Edward Heppenstall." Paper, Andrews Society of Religious Studies, Anaheim, California.

2. Riles, in Pullias, *A Teacher is Many Things*, ix.

comparable place in our personal and professional lives. We can all point to teachers and moments of truth that have stuck with us.

One day in class Dr. Robert Johnston likened a good teacher to a person who plants land mines and time bombs. Thoughts placed in our minds may lie dormant for years, even decades, he said, but when their fuse is spent—when their time has come—when their relevancy is personally realized—those thoughts explode into our intellectual bloodstreams, and they are incarnated in us.

That observation was a moment of truth for me. It made me more aware of how life works. It made life a search for what was happening in my mind. It fed into my educational strategy for it told me something about the subtleties of my task as a teacher. Most of the information Dr. Johnston gave in class is confined to my notebooks, but that moment of insight continues to grow in my thinking.

THE VALUE OF A TRUE TEACHER

In a philosophy class Dr. Fritz Guy related an experience that became another moment of truth for me. When he was attending University of Chicago a concerned church member asked him, "Aren't you worried that what you are learning at that school is affecting your thinking?" Dr. Guy answered, "I certainly hope so. I'm devoting four years of my life and committing an awful lot of expense and personal inconvenience to it."

At first his answer struck me as clever, but as the fuse burned I began to see that Dr. Guy was not trying to be clever. At a time that I needed it I received a perspective on the importance of cultivating breadth in the thinking enterprise. Here is the value of great teachers in our lives: Men and women who have gone before and committed themselves to relating what they saw and how they saw it. Such commitment provides us with hints of meaning.

Another example will suffice to illustrate my point. One morning as college sophomores we sat around a table in Dr. Walter Specht's office at La Sierra College. Our *Introduction to Theology* class had met to discuss the nature of Christ. I had done my homework. I had read *Bible Readings for the Home Circle*. I had collected those prophetic statements that supported my view. I had avoided *Questions on Doctrine*. I had done everything right.

Fatefully, my professor, Dr. Wilber Alexander called on me. For once I was ready. I demonstrated my fidelity to my confessional tradition by presenting "the denominational view"—Christ was born exactly as we are—of a woman with our fallen human nature. He is our example and to be such it was logically necessary that he be exactly like us. As a result, we can overcome as he overcame—such is the nature of the "good news."

I quoted those texts from Romans and Hebrews that supported my views and, before the jury of seven students and the judge Alexander, who in the end held all the votes in his grade book, I rested my case. The cross-examination process began and with the skill of Perry Mason, Dr. A demolished me.

That was another moment of truth. That was also the last day I remember any student in that class ever asserting his theological stance without first prefacing his remarks, "I suppose you're going to tear this apart, but here goes anyway . . ." I learned that Dr. A had been trained by Dr. Heppenstall.

In that moment there was born in me a fascination for theology in general, and the gospel in particular; not for its demolition value but for its help in making sense of life. Now I realize that from that moment of truth, that day in class, the seeds were sown that would grow over the years into my doctoral dissertation project.

Great teaching provides great moments of truth. Great teachers recognize how to maximize the significance of those moments. Due in part to their deep commitment to truth, their natural abilities, their spiritual gifts, and their developed observational skills, these teachers enrich our lives and bring us not only to the conclusion that our tuition money was well spent, but that our lives are worth living and sharing. We can all point to teachers who have had an intensive influence in our lives, but most of us can point to one or two who had a pervasive influence.

I am honored by the invitation to share thoughts on the influence of Dr. Edward Heppenstall as a teacher, for he holds a unique position in my experience and some of yours as well.

A COLLAGE OF CARING

In a Festschrift presented to Dr. Heppenstall at one of his retirements (we call it "the retirement of 1970"), Dr. Norval F. Pease wrote this accurate and suitable description:

> Dr. Heppenstall could never be described as a calm, phlegmatic personality. He has always been like a racehorse—prancing, chewing at the bit, eager for action. He is always ready to match wits with anyone who wishes to discuss a significant idea. In debate on theological issues he is a formidable opponent. But there is another side to Dr. Heppenstall's personality that must not be overlooked. He has demonstrated a tremendous ability to inspire enthusiasm and confidence. Students have been attracted by his brilliance and inspired by his dedication. Many have looked to him as a counselor.[3]

It is doubtful that Dr. Heppenstall ever conceived of education as taking place solely in a classroom. His interest in people and his commitment to personal work, whether in the form of colporteuring, Bible studies or counseling, precluded that. His formal teaching career began at the age of twenty-two when, upon graduation, he was immediately invited to join the staff of his alma mater, Stanborough College in England. For a short time, he taught logic, Greek, and English, while serving as dean of men.[4] But he left England to obtain further education in America. There he completed a BA at Emmanuel Missionary College (now Andrews University), a master's degree at University of Michigan, and later a Ph.D. at University of Southern California in Los Angeles.

His charming Norwegian wife Margit, whom he met in Michigan and refers to as the "Queen of Norway," never tires of telling the story about his arrival at Emmanuel Missionary College as the strutting proper English gentleman with his stuffy clothes and white spats. He later became the father of the Adventist junior camp, when after spending some time doing pastoral and evangelistic work in Michigan, he negotiated the purchase of Gull Lake as Missionary Volunteer secretary for the Michigan Conference.[5]

One of the first stories I remember him telling in his home was about the far-sightedness of the brethren for allowing him to buy that camp. The next story I remember him telling in his home was about the short-sightedness of the brethren for selling it. His perception of the wisdom of that move seems rivaled only by his perception of the wisdom of moving the Seminary from Washington to the "Arctic Circle."

---

3. Pease, "Edward Heppenstall," in Carner and Stanhiser, *The Stature of Christ*, 7–8.

4. Murdoch, "Edward Heppenstall," in Carner and Stanhiser. 2.

5. Murdoch, "Edward Heppenstall," 2.

My earliest memories of Dr. Heppenstall are from the mid-1940s. I was young. He seemed old. He was pastor of the La Sierra College Church where we had moved from Glendale. We sat in the front row of the balcony in Hole Memorial Auditorium, and I remember him preaching. He was a dynamo. I don't remember what he said, I just remember thinking he was fun to watch. My five-year-old mind told me that we visited the Heppenstalls a lot because my grandma needed someone to speak Norwegian with and his mother-in-law fit the bill. Malcolm and Astrid and I became friends as our grandmothers talked Norwegian. I think Dr. Heppenstall was working on his doctorate at USC at the time, but I didn't know that then. I can only remember thinking it was fun that a man *so old* should like us kids so much!

A COLLAGE OF COMPETENCE

We know that the influence of a teacher goes far beyond his classroom in the form of students who pass through it. In Dr. Heppenstall's case, he took his influence beyond the classroom. A student testified: "Dr. Heppenstall was the most balanced teacher I ever had. He gave solid content, but he always showed us its relevancy to the pastorate. He always reminded us we were going to be pastors as he lectured to us on theology. He knew what we would face, he told us what to expect. He encouraged us to stay committed. He knew our audience. To this day my pervasive model for ministry is Dr. Heppenstall."

In talking to Dr. Heppenstall's students of all ages I found that he represents for many of them the finest demonstration of the spiritual gift of pastor/teacher[6] that they have seen. Jesus explained the principle in this spiritual gift:

> [40] A student when he has fully learned will be like his teacher.
> (Luke 6:40)

Christian educators argue that the task of the Christian teacher goes beyond teaching the student to knowing what the teacher knows to inspiring the student to become who the teacher is. Intellectual integrity, personal honesty, theological veracity, personal concern, Christian nurture, and evangelistic fervor coalesced in Dr. Heppenstall's classes to

---

6. Eph 4:11.

leave us feeling he did not just teach us, he also pastored us. As such he left us with a real, warm, human model.

One Friday night at Pioneer Memorial Church, Dr. Heppenstall spoke for vespers about the atonement. The sermon was a literary work of art. The king's English was flawless, the descriptive phraseology made the sermon live, the basic idea was transparent and exciting. I immediately headed for the podium to thank him for the talk. Thinking to compliment him I commented that I hoped someday to become as eloquent—that I wished I could put words together like that. He responded, "I'm sorry the words got in the way." His response was no feigned humility. He meant it. This was an honest recognition that he had overstepped himself and inadvertently moved attention away from his subject.

Dr. Lawrence Richards writes that teaching is most effectual when it is "experienced reality."[7] That is, we learn best in informal situations. That which is learned best is that which is learned together. Teachers often must create these situations because our job descriptions include more primarily classroom work and committee work. Part of what made Dr. Heppenstall the pastor/teacher was his calculated approach to students outside the classroom. Students knew he was available at any time. He was a familiar sight in the dormitories at night religiously spending one night a week there but on call anytime.

Wherever I go I run into doctors, lawyers, administrators, nurses, teachers in all disciplines who talk about Dr. Heppenstall—a man who cared about everyone on campus during their college experience. From my earliest serious conversations with Dr. Heppenstall I received consistent counsel about working with young people from a solid base. "I tried the buttons and bows route to young people," he told me; "that might be fine for some men but not for me—and it will never work for you either. You must be a college teacher!"

Paraphrasing my memory of a conversation we once had on the golf course and later replayed through the lips of his wife: "Ed, you want to stay with the young people—they're fun, they keep you young, they're pliable, you can teach them. You have to be a college teacher, Ed." So, one day I got a call from the president of a midwestern Adventist college saying the Board had voted to extend me a call. I immediately called Dr. Heppenstall.

"Ed," he said, "you don't want to live in the Midwest. You must teach college, Ed, but let me just say this—you must go where it's pleasant to

---

7. Richards, *Theology of Christian Education*, 76–77.

live—where your colleagues are supportive, where the community is progressive, and the administration is dynamic. Hold out for Southern Missionary College!" And I did. And it changed my life!

I have painted the picture of an educator in whose presence we feel accepted. Education is not simply being able to prove a theological point, as much as I enjoy that. To be an educator is not simply to have the degrees even though I believe in that. Those are "intensive" qualifications. But there are also pervasive requirements to being an educator. I knew students who were not particularly turned on by Dr. Heppenstall's theology. I can't say I understood that, but I knew it. But those same students often confided—"he inspired me."

A PROFESSOR WITH A SENSE OF HUMOR

I asked Dr. Wilber Alexander for his favorite story about Dr. Heppenstall, but since he is speaking next I really didn't expect him to give it. He did, however, throw me a crumb which he said I could share. One day at La Sierra College, Dr. Heppenstall walked into class and saw a student chewing gum. "You know you will never get an A in my class if you chew gum," he warned. The student disposed of his gum. Next class period one of the girls in the class brought gum for everyone, so that when he entered the room Dr. Heppenstall was greeted by a classroom of what looked like cows from the dairy. His response was predictable—a march around the classroom with a trash can to guarantee that someone would get a higher-than-average grade.

That was an intensive aspect of his influence as a Christian educator. That's what a teacher has to do when faced with such a confrontation. What is important here is the freedom the students felt to do what they did and the acceptance that they knew would be forthcoming in spite of their "sin." Their action speaks loudly about the pervasive aspect of his influence as a Christian educator. Here was a case of "sinning boldly" in the face of knowing the unmitigated grace that would follow.

I know how he looked at them with a bit of a twist in his mouth and twinkle in his eye. I know because I have been looked at that way. During my second year at Seminary, I took "Law and Covenants" from him. John Duge and I were pastoring the Bangor Michigan Adventist Church. I'm not sure how or when the idea came to us, but after listening to Dr. Heppenstall talk about California, and how much he was looking forward to retirement, and how glad he would be to get out of the ice and snow, we decided to prolong his stay.

Somewhere we found a letter someone had received from the General Conference, and we cut the letterhead off of it. Next we clipped Elder Figuhr's signature from his column in the *Review*. Then in the privacy of Garland Apartments we composed a letter, which we believed would be almost believable but have just enough tip-offs that he would catch it was a hoax. I have the letter here and all of you who have had classes from Dr. Heppenstall will recognize the terminology we included:

January 5, 1965

Dr. Richard Hammill, President
Andrews University
Berrien Springs, Michigan

Dear Dr. Hammill:

We have received an urgent request from the North Pacific Union Conference for an extension school in Icy Cape, Alaska. In this picturesque little town 560 miles north of the Arctic Circle, we have a little company of believers. The request is for three eight-week sessions of six Seminary credit hours each. This will make it possible for all the workers in the great white Alaskan harvest field to attend.

The Executive Committee of the General Conference has voted to ask the Seminary to establish such a school and to send Dr. Edward Heppenstall for the 24-week period beginning September 1, 1965 and ending February 25, 1966. We regret that it will be impossible for Dr. Heppenstall to return upon conclusion of this session as travel is impossible until the spring thaw. The Conference President in Alaska assures us that he will be able to get out by the middle of June 1966.

The Committee saw fit to vote Dr. Heppenstall a small parka allowance of $5.00 per month. His regular mileage allowance will adequately cover dog food expenses. The local congregation has promised him the use of a sled and dog team.

The Conference President has called to the attention of the Committee that there may be some dietary inconvenience. If you don't eat meat in the winter, you won't be around in the spring. The Committee was hesitant to approach Dr. Heppenstall on this matter. Please advise. Please counsel Dr. Heppenstall that whale blubber is unclean.

We are anxious that you pass this invitation on to Dr. Heppenstall and await in anticipation his affirmative reply.

My wife joins me in warmest Christian greetings for the New Year, and with best wishes, I am

Most cordially yours,

R. R. Figuhr
President

RRF:deb

We xeroxed the letter so it would look more authentic coming from the president's office as a copy. And we waited. Since my wife was Dr. Heppenstall's secretary we had someone to monitor the office. The mail came. Dr. Heppenstall came into his office and began to go through it. The door was open, and my wife heard him opening his letters. Then there was silence, and she knew he had gotten to it.

There were no sounds as he read it. Then he came out of his office, passed her desk and went into Dr. Edward Vick's office with whom he shared the office suite. He read the letter to Dr. Vick and she recalls hearing him say something like, "Do you think it's for real?" Then laughter. Then he left. She assumes he went to see Dr. Hammill. He never discussed it with her even though he apparently had it all figured out.

For the next two weeks Dr. Heppenstall's lectures were filled with innuendoes about Alaska and whale blubber and the advantages of riding on dog sleds. Nobody caught the innuendoes in class except John and me. When he figured it out (and how I will probably never know) but every time he would begin talking about how much he wanted to go to California, but Alaska might interfere, he would look at me with that twinkling eye.

John Duge and I have evaluated our own actions. We are both veteran teachers now. That we would admire a professor so much as to take the time to do something like that is self-revealing for us. Most teachers you just do assignments for, but pervasive teachers you also have fun with—they are unthreatened, secure, and challenging.

EVALUATION: THE MAKING OF A TEACHER OF INFLUENCE

In my opinion, Dr. Edward Heppenstall is one of the easiest teachers to evaluate for greatness. Gilbert Highet suggests that there are six essential qualities to being a good teacher.

> A good teacher knows his subject.
> A good teacher likes his subject.
> A good teacher likes his students.
> A good teacher knows his students.
> A good teacher has wide and lively intellectual interests.
> A good teacher has a sense of humor.[8]

I think the case has been made. Thousands of ministers and former students could join me in exclaiming that the influence of Dr. Heppenstall as a teacher is incalculable. The clear and consistent witness of over sixty years of ministry has been a constant inspiration to us. His incisive thinking expressed in sermon, worship talk, Seminary and college lecture, discussion group in the mountains or by the sea or simply in a dormitory room has made us come to grips with the issues of life.

His undying adoration for Margit expressed in over 52 years of marriage stands us in awe—not out of sheer quantity of time but in the fact that he has matured not a bit and continues to act like a teenager in love for the first time. His theological awareness and clear thinking have challenged us to value truth. His scriptural certainty has provided us with a surety that gives us direction in a world of ambivalence and ambiguity. His pastoral concern has made us realize that devotion to people may at times prove more important than theological rightness. His treatment of people has inspired us to realize that in this world people are all that really count. His worship of God has helped us believe there is a God. His counsel has shown us his humanness. His pathos has brought us courage to care. His acceptance has made us feel our worth.

I close my case with my favorite illustration, stolen from out of Dr. Heppenstall's sermons. Picture yourself at Yosemite National Park. You are watching two climbers through your binoculars as they climb ever so slowly, ever carefully up El Capitan, that great boulder of granite that rises 3,000 feet from the valley floor. As you watch you notice that the two men are roped together—for safety—for speed. But as you watch you see the

---

8. Highet, *Art of Teaching.* (1950). 8–65.

man on the bottom slip and begin to fall—and he slides along the rock until he comes to the edge of a great crevasse in the rock and over the side he goes. But he is tied to the man above—so you know he will be safe.

As you watch helplessly to your horror the rope breaks and the man falls to his death on the jagged rocks below. Light-headed you go with the search party to take up the remains. And when you arrive at the spot you examine the body, and then the rope, to see what kind of imperfection led to the terrible and fearful death. And then you discover that the rope *has been cut!*

What a thing for the man at the top to live with—that in the hour when his friend needed him most he cut the rope and let him fall. But the man at the top, perhaps he was a young man, and the man at the bottom was an old man with his life mainly spent. Maybe the man at the top, he was a married man with a family awaiting his return, and the man at the bottom, he was a single man with no one to go home to. Perhaps the man at the top, he was a rich man with many employees needing his business acumen, and the man at the bottom, he was an apprentice. The man at the top may be needed by society to lead a great movement to freedom, and the man at the bottom may just be a common soul who has little or no influence. Yet this man will go back into society living with the dubious distinction that in the hour of greatest need he cut the rope on his friend.

In this church we are bound together with tender cords of love.

Great teachers help us to know how to preserve and strengthen those cords. Great teachers do not cut ropes. Great teachers show us how to edify and build up the church. We thank Dr. Heppenstall, for his influence as a teacher, for his love of Christ, and for a model of faithfulness that enfleshed the effects of the gospel.

CHAPTER TWENTY

A *Jesus-Model* of Communication

> "The language of love is spoken with a look, a touch, a sign, a kiss and sometimes a word."
>
> —Frank Tyger

MATTHEW 13:24–30

> ²⁴ Another parable he put before them, saying, "The kingdom of heaven may be compared to a man who sowed good seed in his field; ²⁵ but while men were sleeping, his enemy came and sowed weeds among the wheat, and went away. ²⁶ So when the plants came up and bore grain, then the weeds appeared also. ²⁷ And the servants of the householder came and said to him, 'Sir, did you not sow good seed in your field? How then has it weeds?' ²⁸ He said to them, 'An enemy has done this.' The servants said to him, 'Then do you want us to go and gather them?' ²⁹ But he said, 'No; lest in gathering the weeds you root up the wheat along with them. ³⁰ Let both grow together until the harvest; and at harvest time I will tell the reapers, Gather the weeds first and bind them in bundles to be burned, but gather the wheat into my barn.'"

THOSE WHO CAN, TEACH

A familiar saying among teachers goes, "Those who can, teach; those who can't, go into some less significant line of work." Our society, one that pays its major league baseball players on average salary of 3.4 million dollars a season and its teachers thirty-two to fifty-five thousand dollars a year, does not reflect the enthusiasm suggested in this saying, but an important fact of life remains—all of us are teachers. Professional teachers are paid a salary for their activity; the rest of our society enjoys teaching for nothing. Most people probably don't even think of themselves as teachers.

We can look at ways to success in teaching. Far from trying to outline a job description for the teaching profession we emphasize here that the life of Christ forms a model for effective teaching, or sharing, or even better, communicating. Everybody communicates in some way. We are especially concerned here with communicating the gospel, nevertheless the elements employed in a Jesus-model of communication will affect every level of our meaningful interpersonal relationships.

CONVERSATION

Jesus' personal interchange with Nicodemus at night is typical of his conversational approach.[1] Think about the meaning of conversation. Let's say you had been dating for three years and then you decided to break up. How would you tell the other person? Talk face to face? Call by phone? Write a letter? Send an email?

Most people answer "talk face to face" because they naturally sense that a personal conversation would show respect for the person who devoted three-years to this relationship. This ensures a degree of accuracy in communicating intentions. They think that in a meaningful conversation they would stand the best chance of being understood. And they are right.

In an age of mass media and social programing, we may minimize the importance of conversation. Sharing our experience personally may seem rather trivial next to Oprah Winfrey or Sean Hannity who can communicate their ideas to audiences of millions every day on TV and radio (would Jesus have a talk show if he were here today?). But notice that the talk shows are popular because of their conversations. As viewers enter those conversations they are taught and their outlooks on life are formed.

---

1. John 3:1–21.

TRANSFORMATION

Jesus' conversations were directional, and they always stimulated a desire for change.[2] Always a controversial figure, Jesus never left people in the same state of mind, being or action as he found them. He healed, and lives were redirected. He modeled, and people were enlivened. He brought controversy and people began to think about the possibility of or need to change.

> [7] "Do not marvel that I said to you, 'You must be born anew.'" (John 3:7)

Transformation followed in his wake wherever Jesus went.

In Jesus' declaration we should see more than a simple theological doctrine of original sin and conversation. Effectively communicating always includes disequilibrium—"stirring up your pure minds," as one of my professors used to say. Jesus' ministry continually gave evidence that the Christian mission includes the breakup of shallow worn-out thinking, acting, and talking. The old clichés cannot meet the modern dilemmas.

ILLUSTRATION

The parable of the weeds forms well-known pictures in our minds.[3] The metaphor of the shepherd brings heavenly insight to our earthly life.[4] Picture Jesus' dilemma of dealing with sinful minds bent on self-indulgence. Communicating unknown but sensed realities and striking friendly chords of relevance were Jesus' greatest teaching challenge. Theologians call Jesus' words about God "anthropomorphisms" or "analogical language." But these are simply technical terms for "illustration."

St. Thomas Aquinas wrote: "All words used metaphorically of God apply primarily to creatures and secondarily to God,"[5] that is to say, every evidence of God finds its expression in common human terms; otherwise, we could not understand anything about God.

Because of this reality Jesus told stories. Look at your favorite people—the best communicators in your life—they all tell stories. Our witness—our pilgrimage—sparkles when it comes in the form of stories.

---

2. John 3:3.
3. Matt 13:24–30.
4. John 10:1–18.
5. St. Thomas, *Summa Theologiae*, 3:1a:12–13.

Christ spoke with authority because when he had finished his stories people knew truth. His stories communicated the complexity and simplicity of truth—that's the genius of a good story. Truth without complexity is simplistic. Truth without simplicity is unduly abstract. Christ's verbal and experiential communications of truth were illustration. Often the most effective communication comes in story form.

REVELATION

There can be little doubt that Jesus claimed to bring people into contact with "revelation"—the self-disclosure of God.

> ³ No one has ascended into heaven but he who descended from heaven, the Son of man. (John 3:13)

Divine perspectives on the meaning of life have not always been well-received by humankind. Almost immediately upon hearing appeal to God many find a natural tendency to respond—"Who do you think you are—holier than thou?" And Jesus continually suffered that criticism even though he communicated effectively.

Paradoxically, the hostile response of the world to the gospel contributes to its effective communication. Revelation brings a sword. And out of this disequilibrium God's voice directs us. Not all who receive reproof come to hate God. The Bible chronicles the lives of great men and women who responded positively to revelation. Revelation is what gives authority to our witness. Somewhere in our communicating we must be confident of a "Thus said the Lord." We need assurance of God's approval on our direction in life.

INCARNATION

Incarnation means simply "in flesh." To incarnate truth means to live it. Jesus became human to incarnate truth. When Christians speak of "the word" they do not just refer to Scripture. They mean also, the Incarnation—God in human form.

Philip inquired of Jesus,

> ⁸ "Lord, show us the Father, and we shall be satisfied." (John 14:8)

> ¹⁰ "Do you not believe that I am in the Father and the Father in me? The words that I say to you I do not speak on my own authority; but the Father who dwells in me does his works. ¹¹ Believe me that I am in the Father and the Father in me; or else believe me for the sake of the works themselves. ¹² Truly, truly, I say to you, he who believes in me will also do the works that I do; and greater works than these will he do, because I go to the Father." (John 14:10–12)

Every Christian can "show us the Father" as the truth is incarnated—as the principles of truth are consistently internalized and lived out.

HE TAUGHT WITH AUTHORITY

Sharing genuine faith experience exudes authority because these principles of effective communication work to make life meaningful.

> ²⁸ And when Jesus finished these sayings, the crowds were astonished at his teaching, ²⁹ for he taught them as one who had authority, and not as their scribes. (Matthew 7:28–29)

Nicodemus at Night[1]
A Readers Theatre Script

NICODEMUS: Rabbi—

JESUS: Yes?

NICODEMUS: I know you are a teacher who has come from God.

JESUS: Why do you say that?

NICODEMUS: No one else could perform miracles like you do.

NARRATOR 1: And so one night—

NARRATOR 2: a conversation began between Jesus and Nicodemus—

NARRATOR 1: a conversation between Jesus—

NARRATOR 2: a Nazarene carpenter,

NARRATOR 1: and Nicodemus—

NARRATOR 2: a man of the Pharisees—a member of the Jewish ruling court.

NARRATOR 1: Jesus taught Nicodemus great truths.

---

1. Campbell and Zackrison, "Nicodemus at Night," *Readers Theatre for Christian Worship*, 166–71.

JESUS:	No one can see the kingdom of God without being *born* again.
NARRATOR 2:	Nicodemus asked Jesus curious questions.
NICODEMUS:	How can I be born when I am old?
NARRATOR 1:	Jesus responded by teaching even greater truths.
JESUS:	No man can *enter* the kingdom of God without being born again.
NARRATOR 2:	Nicodemus acted confused.
NICODEMUS:	Surely I cannot enter into my mother's womb to be *born* again!
NARRATOR 1:	Nicodemus knew that bodies can create other bodies,
NARRATOR 2:	but the great truth he needed to learn was—
JESUS:	that the Spirit gives birth to spirit. You must be born again.
NICODEMUS:	Be born again?
JESUS:	Yes! You should not be surprised at this.
NARRATOR 1:	Then Jesus likened being born again
NARRATOR 2:	to the will of the wind.
JESUS:	The wind blows where it wills—
NICODEMUS:	I can hear it when it blows.
JESUS:	But you can't see it. You can't tell where it comes from or where it is going.
NICODEMUS:	What do you mean?
JESUS:	Being born of the Spirit is like that.
NICODEMUS:	Like what?
JESUS:	You are Israel's teacher?
NICODEMUS:	Yes.
JESUS:	And do you not understand these things?
NICODEMUS:	But—

JESUS:	I spoke of what we all knew, and I testified to what we all had seen.
NICODEMUS:	But—
JESUS:	And still you and your people do not accept my testimony.
NICODEMUS:	I have heard you speak of earthly things.
JESUS:	But you don't believe them. How will you believe heavenly things?
NICODEMUS:	What are "heavenly things"?
NARRATOR 1:	Then Jesus told Nicodemus that the things of the Spirit
NARRATOR 2:	are spiritual things.
NARRATOR 1:	That life consists of more than getting jobs and buying things—
NARRATOR 2:	That life consists of caring and concern for *people*—
NARRATOR 1:	That being truly alive means thinking about eternity.
NARRATOR 2:	And eternity requires the Son of Man, lifted up, living, dying,
NARRATOR 1:	winning and living again.
NARRATOR 2:	Finally, Jesus gave Nicodemus the conclusion of the whole matter:
JESUS:	*Believe in me and you will not perish but have eternal life.*
NARRATOR 1:	And so it was on that night in Jerusalem
NARRATOR 2:	at midnight, Nicodemus saw the Light.

CHAPTER TWENTY-ONE

Improving Your Church's Responsive Readings[1]

> "We may divide thinkers into those who think for themselves and those who think through others."
>
> —Arthur Schopenhauer

PSALM 5:7

But I through the abundance of thy steadfast love will enter thy house, I will worship toward thy holy temple in the fear of thee.

CAN RESPONSIVE READINGS BE IMPROVED?

Have you ever felt that the responsive reading in your worship service was not very responsive? Or that the scripture reading was just a form with little attention paid to it? In this chapter, we will suggest some revisions that could transform your responsive readings into an exciting part of your service.

---

1. Campbell and Zackrison, "Improving Your Church's Responsive Readings," *Worship Leader*, 19–25, 35.

We will propose some ways that you can use the dynamics involved in public reading to enhance more spontaneity in worship. We will first discuss the responsive reading of scripture, and then present an approach in which the reading of scripture is more a monologue or presentation.

WHY CHANGE IS NEEDED

The public reading of scripture has always been an important part of Christian worship. In fact, little revision of form has occurred in Christian liturgy since the first century. But in our fast-paced society and particularly in the more non-liturgical traditions, there is a real pressure on church leaders to fashion a worship service that is fresher and more appealing. Worshipers want more inviting forms, and visitors seem hard to attract with worship forms that escape their understanding.

We submit that an area that lends itself to rather easy change in the worship service is the public reading of scripture, which often appears to be lifeless routine. We suggest a responsive reading that is *truly responsive* and different in form from presentational reading.

The scriptures were not originally written for group or responsive reading in the way we do such readings today. While there may have been some responsive readings of scripture in public, this usually was based on memorization. In fact, many of the books of the Bible, especially of the New Testament, were letters written to individuals or groups. Letters do not necessarily lend themselves to public reading, and certainly were not written to be read responsively. Some letters were written to entire congregations and were meant to be read aloud by a central reader, but most of the Bible was probably not intended that way.

Part of our challenge lies in the fact that while the Bible was set and clarified in the context of its day, many of us no longer have an adequate understanding to relate to the world of the Bible in the way it was meant to be. Most of us are not captivated when someone reads a long letter from Paul in the same way that the original recipients might have been.

If we were the Corinthians, or if we understood more adequately the contextual setting of the Corinthians, we might not tire so quickly. But few contemporary worshipers will relate to original scripture in the same way as those to whom it was written. Hence we are confronted with deciding what in the Bible is cultural for its day and what is transcultural for our day. In reading the Bible, whether as a monologue or a responsive reading we must take our congregation and our culture into account.

In today's worship services, the sermon usually gets top billing. But the sermon never simply involves the reading of a scripture passage. Skilled preachers apply and relate scripture to the worshipers' needs and lives. Such preachers carefully craft their sermons to illustrate contemporary meanings drawn from the original preaching passage. Can a carefully structured reading of scripture enhance worship and set the stage for the sermon or homily? We think so.

SOME PRINCIPLES FOR EFFECTIVE READINGS

Christians have sensed for years that simply lifting a responsive reading from the back of a hymnal or a prayer book can be lethal to any worship service that has conceptual elements or intent. We may even be able to understand and enjoy the experience of biblical characters. But by most people's standards, traditional responsive readings are just not effective elements of worship.

Most of us were not taught (or maybe we rejected) the notion that choral *reading* is an art form in its own right and requires some practice to sound effective. We know that congregational singing is effective worship—but only with well-known and practiced hymns. Singing new hymns or new music is usually an embarrassingly painful experience. As with congregational singing, choral reading also takes practice.

Thus, short of scheduling regular reading rehearsals for the congregation, how can readings be structured to provide us with a worship experience? We suggest a few simple rules that we have found helpful in improving this situation and encouraging effective responsive reading.

THE CONGREGATIONAL RESPONSE SHOULD BE LIMITED TO SHORT SENTENCES OR PHRASES—perhaps no more than five words, preferably one or two. More than five words encourage the congregation to drag sentences and lose their expression. For most of us, responsive reading raises more memories of trying to stay together with the congregation than of a truly meaningful worship experience. The concept of short responses is illustrated in this passage.

A Hymn to the Fool[2]

Reader 1:	Fools say in their hearts,
Congregation:	There is no God.
Reader 1:	They are corrupt—
Reader 2:	Their ways are vile.
Congregation:	There is no God.
Reader 1:	A fool does no good—
Reader 2:	A fool is vile.
Reader 1:	Fools say in their hearts,
Congregation:	There is no God.

There is a cadence to this short response that the congregation can find inviting. Furthermore, there is a built-in rehearsal quality to the reading because of the repetition.

THE READING SHOULD BE DIRECTIVE AND PURPOSEFUL. Responsive reading tends to be rote already. A non-directional reading only exacerbates that tendency. In reading responsively, you are not trying simply to get people to read. The desire is for this to be something of a learning experience, one in which people can participate intelligently. In either choosing or writing a responsive reading, you should consider how the reading adds to the overall purpose of the worship service itself. This will encourage intelligent attention directed at meaningful worship.

Notice an example of direction and purpose:

A Hymn to the Fool[3]

Reader 1:	People of understanding delight in wisdom.
Reader 2:	Fools show their annoyance at once.
Congregation:	Don't tell me what to do!
Reader 1:	Reasonable people heed correction.
Reader 2:	Fools spurn their parents' discipline—
Congregation:	I want what I want when I want it.
Reader 1:	Wise people accept commands.
Reader 2:	Fools give full vent to their anger—

---

2. Campbell and Zackrison, *Interactive Readings*, 2.
3. Campbell and Zackrison, *Interactive Readings*, 2.

CONGREGATION:	You're crazy!	
READER 1:	A fool is hotheaded and reckless—	
READER 2:	From the mouth of the fool gushes folly.	
READER 1:	Wise people keep themselves under control—	
READER 2:	Fools fold their hands and ruin themselves.	
CONGREGATION:	Don't bother me!	

In this particular reading, the congregation is cast as the "fool" so that they could experience the attitudes and the words that the "fool" would utter. People may hear themselves when they examine the scripture in this way. They may experience a crucial self-revelation and find themselves impressed with the attractiveness of turning from being a fool.

THE READING NEEDS TO BE INTERACTIVE IF IT IS TO BE EXCITING AND FOSTER THE ATTENTION OF WORSHIPERS. We look for a chance to turn the reading into a dialogue between the reader and the congregation. We may cast the congregation in different roles as characters in the passages. For example, we look for an opportunity to cast people as God; or sinners; or Pharisees; or biblical heroes such as Paul, David, or John; etc., much as we did in the earlier example.

Here is a passage in which we cast the congregation as a Pharisee, and they had to respond with pharisaical righteousness:

Forgiveness for Certain *Persons*[4]

READER 1:	Now, do you—	
READER 2:	Now, do you see this *certain* woman?	
CONGREGATION:	I can see and smell!	
READER 1:	I came into your house.	
READER 2:	Did you give me any water for my feet?	
CONGREGATION:	I see a *certain* woman!	
READER 1:	But this woman	
READER 2:	provided water from her tears.	
READER 1:	Did you provide me with a towel?	
CONGREGATION:	I see a *certain* woman!	

---

4. Campbell and Zackrison, *Interactive Readings*, 2.

Reader 2:	This woman used her hair as a towel.
Reader 1:	Did you provide me with a towel?
Reader 2:	Did you give me a gift?
Congregation:	No, but she is a—
Reader 1:	She has used perfume on my feet.
Reader 2:	Her many sins are forgiven
Reader 1:	so she loves much.

We also look for opportunities to set up an antiphonal relationship in which leader and congregation answer each other with duplicate phrases or with parallel ideas. In this reading we divided the congregation into four parts and turned them loose to respond to each other.

Promise for the New Year[5]

Reader 1:	A nation has invaded my land—
Reader 2:	A nation powerful and without number—
Reader 3:	A nation with the teeth of a lion—
Reader 1:	A nation with the fangs of a lioness.
All readers:	Joy has withered away.
Congregation 3:	Mourn!
Congregation 1:	Wail!
Congregation 2:	Spend the night in sackcloth!
Congregation 4:	Declare a holy fast!
Congregation 3:	Call a sacred assembly!
Congregation 1:	Summon all who live in the land!
All readers:	Cry out to the Lord!

The passage you are working with has a lot to do with what approach you take. We would approach the choosing or writing of a responsive reading much like a scriptwriter looking for more creative interaction.

The narration in general must be short. The narration can easily get bogged down when read by a poor, unpracticed reader. Sometimes it may be more effective to break up the narration between readers.

---

5. Campbell and Zackrison, *Interactive Readings*, 34.

Look first at this typical example from a church service, and then we will suggest a more exciting possibility.

A Time for Everything

LEADER:	God has shown you what is good,
	What does the Lord require of you?
	To act justly and to love mercy
	And to walk humbly with our God.
CONGREGATION:	There is a time for everything.
	And a season for every activity under heaven.
	A time to be born and a time to die.
	A time to weep and a time to laugh.
LEADER:	A time to mourn and a time to dance.
	A time to embrace and a time to refrain.
	What good is it for anyone to gain the whole world,
	yet forfeit one's life?
CONGREGATION:	Seek first the kingdom of God and His righteousness.

Notice that both the leader and the congregation were expected to read long lines. When this occurs, readers often lose their focus on the message of the text and become anxious about reading together. This reading deals with the meaning of time. However, its experiential focus does not lend itself to expressive reading, and more than likely it will deteriorate into a dull, monotonic exercise when it is not broken up. By simply rewriting the response, using the rules above, a worship leader can involve the congregation in a sharpened focus:

A Time for Everything

READER:	There is a time for everything.
MEN:	A time to be born—
READER:	And finally,
WOMEN:	a time to die.
READER:	There is a season for every activity under heaven.

Congregation:	Weeping and laughing?
Reader:	Everything has its time.
Women:	Mourning?
Men:	Dancing?
Reader:	Everything has its time.
Women:	Embracing!
Men:	Refraining.
Reader:	Even though there is a time for every activity, what good is it for anyone if one takes time and gains the whole world, yet forfeits one's life?
Congregation:	Then time is wasted!
Reader:	What has God shown you is a good use of time?
Congregation:	To act justly.
Reader:	And—
Congregation:	To love mercy.
Reader:	What does God require of you?
Congregation:	To walk humbly with Him.
Reader:	Seek first the kingdom of heaven. Take time for His righteousness.

The focus of this reading suggests that in the midst of modern living there is an overriding responsibility to put God first. Ordinarily, the congregational responses are short. Punctuation marks give the congregation cues on how to read the sentence.

The words have been rearranged to bring closure to the reading. While the phrases have been rearranged and in some cases words changed from the exact biblical text, the spirit and the meaning of the text remain intact. It should go without saying that those who write responsive readings have a responsibility to be as true to the meaning of the text as they can be.

In the next example taken from a familiar parable of Jesus, the congregation is cast as who responds and interacts with the king and the poor servant. Two readers provide the setting and conclusion for the reading. The lines are short and should be read with feeling and meaning. Staging for the reading can be done with two readers in front standing on either side of the king and the poor servant. Readers chosen directly from the congregation or from the worship staff read only parts of sentences. With a little practice, they can learn to present these sentence parts smoothly and with a precision that resembles that of only one reader.

The Unmerciful Servant[6]

READER 1:	The kingdom of heaven is like a king
READER 2:	who wanted to settle his accounts with his servants.
READER 1:	A man who owed him several million dollars
READER 2:	was brought to him.
KING:	I need my several million dollars—pay up!
CONGREGATION:	I *can't* pay.
KING:	Pay up!
CONGREGATION:	I *can't* pay.
KING:	Pay up!
CONGREGATION:	I *can't* pay!
KING:	Sell his wife.
CONGREGATION:	*Please* don't.
KING:	Sell him!
CONGREGATION:	Please *don't!*
KING:	Sell his children, sell his lands.
CONGREGATION:	*Please don't.*
READER 1:	The servant fell on his knees
READER 2:	and cried:
CONGREGATION:	Be patient, I will pay.
READER 1:	And the king took pity on him.
KING:	Cancel his debt, he is free!
CONGREGATION:	I am free, I am free!

---

6. Campbell and Zackrison, *Interactive Readings*, 7–8.

READER 1:	But when the servant went out	
READER 2:	he found one of his fellow servants	
READER 1:	who owed him just a few dollars.	
CONGREGATION:	Pay up!	
POOR SERVANT:	*I can't pay.*	
CONGREGATION:	Pay up!!	
POOR SERVANT:	*I can't pay.*	
CONGREGATION:	Sell his wife!	
POOR SERVANT:	*Please don't.*	
CONGREGATION:	Sell him!	
POOR SERVANT:	*Please don't.*	
CONGREGATION:	Sell his children! Sell his lands!	
POOR SERVANT:	*Please don't!!*	

READER 1:	The servant's servant fell on his knees,
READER 2:	and cried:
POOR SERVANT:	Be *patient!* I will pay.
CONGREGATION:	SELL! SELL!! SELL!!!
KING:	I forgave you millions—can't you forgive a few dollars?

READER 1:	And so it was in this parable
READER 2:	that Jesus gave meaning
READER 1:	to what forgiveness
READER 2:	really means.

This reading can be used in conjunction with a sermon on the meaning of forgiveness. The same approach can be taken with any subject the pastor or minister plans to speak on.

A worship leader may need to do some rehearsing with a congregation that is not accustomed to responding creatively. It will help to give an overview of the reading, and to discuss the role they will play in it.

Here are some additional pointers we've given congregations on reading scripture that have proven to be effective. Tell the congregation to:

Read a response as if each one in the congregation was the biblical character involved.

Read a response as if each one in the congregation was the only person reading. Reading in perfect unison in not necessary or advisable.

Read a response with feeling and emotion.

Read a response so that others can hear the words (speak up!).

When the congregation is initially introduced to these types of readings, they will need to practice responding to a few lines. That is usually enough to make the reading more effective.

CASTING THE CONGREGATION

In a reading of the parables of the pearl and the treasure, titled "The Pearl" [next example], the congregation is cast as the sought-after pearl and treasure. Readers and congregation should respond as if they are becoming enlightened with the gospel and their great value to God. The two readers assume Jesus' storytelling role, and the congregation in the role of the disciples responds to the truths as perhaps the disciples would have responded 2,000 years ago.

The Pearl[7]

READER 1:	Jesus told a story about the kingdom of heaven
READER 2:	so that all could understand its importance.
DISCIPLES:	The kingdom of heaven, where is it?
READER 1:	The kingdom of heaven
READER 2:	is within you
READER 1:	and around you.
DISCIPLES:	But when is it?
READER 1:	The kingdom of heaven
READER 2:	is right now,
READER 1:	today,

---

7. Campbell and Zackrison, *Interactive Readings*, 63–65, for a variation of this reading.

READER 2:	tomorrow,
READER 1:	forever!
DISCIPLES:	But what is the kingdom like?
READER 1:	The kingdom of heaven
READER 2:	is like a merchant looking for fine pearls.
DISCIPLES:	That's it!
READER 1:	The kingdom of heaven
READER 2:	is also like a man finding a treasure hidden in a field.
DISCIPLES:	I do not understand.
READER 2:	This is the reason that Jesus told this story about pearls and treasures.
READER 1:	The kingdom of heaven
READER 2:	is about a man selling
READER 1:	all he has to buy a treasure.
READER 2:	Or—
READER 1:	You can think of the kingdom
READER 2:	like a man selling
READER 1:	all he has to buy a pearl.
DISCIPLES:	So pearls and treasures?
READER 1:	You see, you are the treasure.
DISCIPLES:	I am the treasure?
READER 1:	You are the sought-after treasure in the story.
DISCIPLES:	I am the treasure!
READER 2:	Furthermore, you are the pearl.
DISCIPLES:	I am the pearl?
READER 2:	You are the pearl of great price.
DISCIPLES:	I am the pearl!
READER 2:	You are the pearl.

Disciples:	Then the kingdom of heaven is about me?	
Reader 1:	And don't forget the man who purchased the treasure	
Reader 2:	and the merchant who bought the pearl of great price.	
Disciples:	I am the treasure; I am the pearl!	
Reader 1:	The kingdom of heaven	
Reader 2:	is about you	
Reader 1:	within and without,	
Reader 2:	today and tomorrow	
Reader 1:	and about the Christ,	
Reader 2:	the merchant man,	
Reader 1:	who gives all he has	
Reader 2:	to buy pearls and treasures.	

We have field-tested many readings and found encouraging results. "The Pearl" was used by one worship leader three times in conjunction with one sermon—before, during and at the end. In this case, the minister used the responsive reading to reinforce and teach the concept she was trying to get across in her sermon.

If you keep the creative spirit alive, you could present a group responsive reading weekly. That is not our goal, however. We are only advocating the presentation of the scriptures in a meaningful and listenable manner.

THE READERS THEATRE

Another way to present scripture that we have found to be effective is what is called Readers Theatre. This type of reading is presentational in nature [that is, the congregation does not participate], but the reading is written and presented in such a way that the congregation identifies with one or more of the characters in the story.

The story of David and Bathsheba can take on new and significant modern meaning when it is presented in the following way by four readers. In this type of presentation, the readers typically speak directly to the congregation and do not look at each other.

David and Bathsheba

READER 1: In the spring
READER 2: when the kings were off to war,
READER 3: when the whole Israelite army was off to war,
READER 4: David was in Jerusalem.

READER 1: One evening
READER 2: in that spring,
READER 1: while the men were off to war,
READER 3: David got up from his bed
READER 4: and walked about on the roof of the palace.

READER 2: While the men were off to war,
READER 3: he saw Bathsheba bathing.
READER 2: She was very beautiful
READER 4: and . . .
READER 1: she was very married!
READER 3: In fact . . .
READER 2: she was married to Uriah,
READER 4: who in that very spring
READER 2: and on that very evening,
READER 3: was off to war.
READER 1: But . . .

READER 4: King David, who was not off to war,
READER 2: sent for her,
READER 3: and slept with her.
READER 2: Later she sent a message to David,
READER 4: I am pregnant!
READER 3: Uriah, who was off to war,
READER 1: was called home and told,

READER 3:	Go to your house!
READER 2:	But he didn't go.
READER 3:	Go to your house,
READER 4:	lie with your wife.
READER 1:	But he didn't go to his house, and he didn't lie with his wife.
READER 3:	How can I go home?
READER 4:	How can I lie with my wife?
READER 1:	when the ark,
READER 2:	the men of Israel and Judah
READER 4:	are off to war.
READER 1:	All the men
READER 2:	of Israel and Judah are off to war.
READER 4:	Well, all except David.
READER 3:	I cannot go home
READER 4:	until all Israel and Judah come home!
READER 3:	Then David sent a message to Joab, the general, who was with Uriah.
READER 2:	David ordered Uriah to be put in the front of the battle
READER 1:	to be killed.
READER 3:	And so it was in that very spring
READER 2:	when all of Israel and Judah were at war
READER 3:	and while David walked the palace rooftop in the evening
READER 1:	that Uriah was killed in the war.
READER 3:	Bathsheba mourned for her husband
READER 1:	in the evening in that spring
READER 2:	while the men were off to war.
READER 4:	Then David brought her to his house
READER 3:	and she became his wife.

IMPROVING YOUR CHURCH'S RESPONSIVE READINGS

READER 2: But the thing David did
READER 1: displeased the Lord. The child died!
READER 3: But their next child, Solomon, the Lord loved.

READER 2: Here is a record of the genealogy of Jesus Christ.
READER 1: Abraham
READER 4: was the father of Isaac.
READER 2: Isaac
READER 1: was the father of Jacob.
READER 3: And on and on until—
READER 2: Jesse
READER 4: was the father of David.
READER 1: David
READER 2: was the father of Solomon,
READER 3: whose mother had been Uriah's wife.

READER 2: And finally
READER 4: to Joseph and Mary
READER 1: was born Jesus,
READER 2: who is the Christ
READER 3: who saved Abraham and Isaac and Jesse and Solomon and David from their sins.
READER 4: And especially David!

READER 2: It all started
READER 1: in the spring,
READER 3: one evening
READER 4: in Jerusalem,
READER 2: when the men
READER 1: were off to war!

For the "David and Bathsheba" reading, the four readers should rehearse sufficiently so that the sentences are read smoothly even though there are four different voices composing the sentences.

A FINAL EXAMPLE

We share selections from a much longer presentation that approaches scripture from a more traditional Readers Theatre form using the guidelines we have been discussing. This is from a Readers Theatre script. The entire presentation involves thirteen presenters and runs ten minutes in length.

Choice and the First Parents[8]

NARRATOR 1:	This is the story of the beginnings
NARRATOR 2:	of this earth,
NARRATOR 1:	of man,
NARRATOR 2:	of woman,
NARRATOR 1:	of choices,
NARRATOR 2:	of sin—
NARRATOR 1:	all from the book of Genesis....
NARRATOR 2:	In the beginning, God created the heavens and the earth.
INTERPRETER 1:	Genesis one, verse one.
NARRATOR 1:	On day one, God said,
GOD:	Let there be light, day and night,
READER 4:	And it was good.
NARRATOR 1:	On day two, God said,
GOD:	Let there be a heaven, a firmament!
NARRATOR 1:	And there was a heaven, a firmament,
READER 2:	And it was good.
NARRATOR 2:	On day three, God said ... [the creation story is continued]....

---

8. Campbell and Zackrison, *Readers Theatre for Christian Worship*, 1–11.

NARRATOR 1:	And Eve could help Adam
NARRATOR 2:	make good choices.
READER 2:	They could help each other!
READER 3:	But they didn't.
READER 4:	The first bad choice!
SATAN:	Eve, come over here and have some fruit!
EVE:	No, God said not to eat the fruit on that tree.
ALL READERS:	Good choice, Eve!
SATAN:	Come on, Eve! Eat and be like God. You don't die. Look at me. I ate it—do I look dead?
READER 2:	He is lying to you, Eve—choose not to eat.
NARRATOR 1:	But Eve took the fruit, and she ate it.
ALL READERS:	Oh no!
READER 1:	The second bad choice!
NARRATOR 1:	Eve felt no worse after eating it.
NARRATOR 2:	She wanted to share the fruit with Adam.
EVE:	Adam, eat this!

The example may seem too choppy to be enjoyable. But if readers will practice making the parts of the sentences flow together smoothly—as though only one person were reading them—the result will be exciting for both the presenters and the congregation. Such a presentation will maintain the dignity of the service and form a didactic element as well. We emphasize "adequate" and "sufficient" rehearsal. This means continuing to go over a presentation together until it is almost second nature to readers and characters.

We have found that the group responsive reading and the presentational Readers Theatre approaches to scripture reading, when they are done seriously and carefully, will augment and enhance the sermon as well as the overall worship service. We have suggested that the reading of scripture be done in a variety of ways, and that as much attention and practice be given to the reading of scripture as to a choral anthem or the sermon.

Making scripture meaningful in the lives of church members is ever in the mind of the worship leader. In a time of falling attendance especially, church leaders need to do all they can to make worship a place to learn of God while communing with him in exciting and significant ways.

CHAPTER TWENTY-TWO

A Week of Violence

> "Let us not pray to be sheltered from dangers
> but to be fearless when facing them."
>
> —RABINDRANATH TAGORE

TITUS 2:1-5

¹ But as for you, teach what befits sound doctrine. ² Bid the older men be temperate, serious, sensible, sound in faith, in love, and in steadfastness. ³ Bid the older women likewise to be reverent in behavior, not to be slanderers or slaves to drink; they are to teach what is good, ⁴ and so train the young women to love their husbands and children, ⁵ to be sensible, chaste, domestic, kind, and submissive to their husbands, that the word of God may not be discredited.

PAX AMERICA

We have just experienced a week of violence that has vaulted many of us back into those emotions and reminiscences of the 1960s. I shall never forget that Friday afternoon in 1963. School was over for the week. I was rushing to St. Joseph, Michigan to get a haircut, listening to the news on the car radio. The commentator was speculating whether Richard M. Nixon would try to run again in the upcoming presidential election campaign of 1964.

I parked my car, went into the barber shop, got my haircut, and returned to my car. In that few minutes of interlude it had happened. In the streets of Dallas, Texas, the president of the United States of America had been gunned down. And the world stopped for four days.

America has never been the same since. It was the end of the reign of peace. I grew up during the period I call the *Pax America*—a period of American peace. I was too young to remember the big wars, I vaguely remember the Korean war, but for me the 1950s were peaceful; that was my time of growing up. Grade school, high school, college—class of 1963. But the 1950s ended on November 22, 1963, when the bullet from the gun of Lee Harvey Oswald penetrated the head of the young president who typified a new America—as a "New Frontier."

THE STREETS OF RIOTING

From that moment on it was periodic rioting in the streets, racial unrest, assassinations of political persons—Martin Luther King, Jr., Malcolm X, Bobby Kennedy. And those were just the big names. Viet Nam had its own brand of treachery of which none of us will ever know the full extent. There was Watts and Kent State, and who can remember what else?

Another week it all came back. Another president gunned down; three people seriously injured because they got in the way. Two more children found dead in Atlanta. News bulletins expected momentarily—how we all hate it—and how we all look forward to it; not with love really—but with, what would you call it? Curiosity? We turn on the TV and it goes for hours keeping us posted on every raw detail. How many times did I see President Reagan shot that Monday—and again on Tuesday?

Go with me mentally to some of the country sides around mid-America to one of the hog ranches along the back roads. It is a sunny day, one of those marvelous spring days the region is famous for. The pigs are out of the pen—out in their fields. In one end of the field is a swampy, muddy, sloppy hole. The rest of the field is green, teeming with flowers and newly budding trees. Where are the hogs?

You don't even have to go out there to know—they are in the mud. Are they enjoying the forest and the flowers? No—they are where they love to be most—in the mud and slop. Look into their eyes—if pigs ever express enjoyment it is with their eyes when they are ear deep in slop. And they look as though they are saying—"We would never do anything else if we had it our way."

THE 1960S, THE VIOLENCE AND THE PIGS

There is a connection between my recollections of the 1960s, the violence we experienced that week, and the pigs in the slop. It is a paradoxical kind of connection, but these are related.

It appears that, as the pigs love their slop and much on an otherwise sunny and lovely day, so we love to wallow in violence. Yet when violence occurs we are upset and shocked by it. Now please try to understand me. Normal people do not really like to see others get hurt, or so they say. Particularly are we incensed when treachery is, or harm is done to someone we respect or like. No one loves to have a loved one hurt.

One of our students at the college lost his wife minutes after she had delivered a healthy baby boy. One minute she was nursing the baby, talking about the marvelous future he was going to have, sharing her fond hopes and dreams with her husband. Minutes later a blood clot took her life—just like that it was over. Several of us visited the family and the bereaved husband. Believe me, there was no happiness there over what had happened. Only deep hurt and loneliness. When I suggest that we love violence and death I do not mean we love to see healthy young mothers die.

But it is a strange paradox that the man who allegedly tried to kill President Reagan, complained that the bodyguards had hurt his arm when they wrestled him to the ground to retrieve the gun. Later he objected that his wrists were sore because of the handcuffs—couldn't they treat him a little nicer? Ironic? Yes. Sick? Yes. Normal, in its own negative way? Yes.

Now the news is full of stories about the accused would-be killer. He had a fantasy life with a young actress he had seen in a movie. He pictured himself as her lover and he imitated macho characters in the film. He staged his assault on the blueprint suggested to him in the movie. In his twisted mind he concluded that such an act of violence would make his fantasy come into real life—he would kill the president and by that act attract the attention of the pretty actress. Fantasy and reality would be fused. She would step off the screen and into his arms.

COPYING THE SCENE

I watched with intense concentration as network news synthesized the movie suspect had apparently copied with the actual scene at the side entrance to the Washington Hotel where President Reagan exited. The similarities were not contrived. The human mind is a delicate conglomerate of tissue. We say a mind that does something so extreme as this man attempted Monday is "sick," "disoriented," "confused," "twisted," and so on. I agree. What about the minds that put together the picture he got his idea from? What about a general, so-called "normal" public who continually pleads for ultra-violence via magazines, movies, and books.

We hate violence, we say, but we continue to wallow in it vicariously. Is it reasonable to believe that by beholding it we will not be changed by it?

Several years ago, I kept up to date on a dramatic murder trial in Southern California when a young lady was charged with murdering her husband. There was a love triangle involved but it was the mode of murder that intrigued the public. The lady had drugged her husband, put him on the passenger's side of their family car, and driven him out into one of the then plentiful orange groves of the San Bernardino valley. She had stopped the car, poured gasoline over the car and him, lit a match, and watched the car and husband enshrouded in flames.

In court she had pleaded innocent, that the car had caught fire, that her husband was sick and that she had not been able to get him free from the little car. It was all accidental she said. As the trial began to ferret out the inconsistencies in her story she finally came to admit that she had indeed premeditated the murder, that she was guilty of the crime and she subsequently went to the penitentiary.

Under cross examination she admitted that she had gotten the idea for the murder from a movie she had recently viewed at a local theater and thought that it would work. We will hear a lot of talk, in the aftermath of Monday's shooting incident about new laws for gun control. Some have suggested that the only answer to this problem is to make the penalties swift and severe so that people will be discouraged from committing such grizzly crimes. What kind of talk are we hearing about cutting out the viewing of violence? Of limiting vicarious treachery?

THE ATTITUDE OF HATE

It is true, of course, that behavioral scientists do not agree on how the viewing of violence affects a person. There is evidence on both sides of the question. Some say vicarious violence cuts down on real violence—if a person watches it he works through his emotions that may under other circumstances produce an anti-social action.

On the other side, professional studies line up evidence that ideas are born and carried out by viewing violence on the screen or reading about it in racy journals and books. Rape plans, bank robberies, vice, general dishonesty, and the like, are practiced freely in the homes of millions every day. For many TV has become a school of crime. Hence the paradox. We hate people who practice violence—and therein may lie one of the most serious problems this nation must come to grips with. The problem of hate.

Hate is an attitude. Are we born with it? Or is it something we acquire? Is it a learned response? And if we hate long enough and hard enough, will it manifest itself in hateful behavior? Undoubtedly it will. We say, that is true in the social misfit or the abnormal—true, but what put him into that category if hate did not. Somewhere at the heart of most anti-social activity you will find the elements of hatred. Hatred toward someone and some notion—some philosophy, some institution, some political party, or some authority figure.

I seriously question whether we do ourselves a favor by dwelling on hateful things—whether it is hatred toward minorities, toward authority figures, toward certain ideologies or toward groups. And our only alternative is the opposite of hate.

PARENTAL LOVE

Unfortunately, "love" has become one of those words that means anything one wants it to mean. So, to get the true meaning one ought to go to the Bible. There the term is best understood in the setting of "parental love." What kind of "love" would solve all the ills of this nation? Parental love. Of course, if you have parents for whom you have no respect, the concept tends to lose its meaning for you. But look at the qualities of "parental love."

A model parent (God, if you like), keeps everything in perspective—but his overall goal for his child is what will be best for that child. Thus, parental love is non-indulgent and yet merciful. It is patient. It is thoughtful, respectful, kind and understanding. It is rational, and it thinks of the best interest of the child.

Imagine a nation in which each person took it upon himself to manifest parental love for each other. Brotherly love is fine, but the Bible seldom uses "brotherly love" as the kind of love that will solve the problems we are facing. It is parental love it sets forth as the answer. Do you know where you are most apt to learn parental love? From your parents.

And so, we have a complex problem. Homes breaking up, parents who abandon and beat their children, television moguls who become the surrogate parents, children growing up in a violent environment, a society that, as the North Georgian children growing up in a violent environment, a society that, as the North Georgian pig loves its slop, wallows in that environment until out come the fruits of a sick society. I'm not picking on North Georgia—name your state. Sin is not geographical—it is universal.

No law will drive you back to God. But rest assured society will not change. A society that turns its back on God will become like that which it has turned its face toward. Yet you can come into that circle of friendship with God. The Christian response to violence is an intensely personal one in the end. We start by getting out of the mud and spending our time in the fields and forests of the sun of parental love. In God's presence you are loved and when you are loved you can love. Then you begin to think of other people instead of just yourself.

Wouldn't it be marvelous if the secret service could be dismissed because everybody in America thought so much of the other person's welfare that they were no longer needed? It won't happen. But you and I can respond this way.

THE CHRISTIAN ANSWER TO VIOLENCE

The Christian answer to violence is the gospel. God so loves us that in response we find it attractive and realistic to love others with a parental, caring love. We may pass our laws—and we should. We may speak out against such dastardly deeds as we saw demonstrated on our screens that week—and that too is necessary. But at the root of our chagrin, we must guard against demonstrating the very thing we are condemning: hatred merely in a more acceptable form.

"By beholding we become changed"—that law is true for hatred and violence, but it is also true for love and respect.

CHAPTER TWENTY-THREE

Togetherness in Community

"The world must learn to work together, or finally it will not work at all."
—Dwight D. Eisenhower

PSALM 133:1-3

¹ Behold, how good and pleasant it is
    when brothers dwell in unity!
² It is like the precious oil upon the head,
    running down upon the beard,
upon the beard of Aaron,
    running down on the collar of his robes!
³ It is like the dew of Hermon,
    which falls on the mountains of Zion!
For there the Lord has commanded the blessing,
    life for evermore.

INTRODUCING COMMUNITY

What does "community" mean to you? How important is it to feel the joys of living together in mutual trust, harmony and understanding? The psalmist wrote,

¹ Behold, how good and pleasant it is when brothers dwell in unity! (Psalm 133:1)

Do you know that feeling? Do you know what it is like to be trusted? Have you felt the delight of being able to be yourself with someone and not have it held against you because you did not totally conform to their tyrannical attitudes or methods? If so, you have felt community. Some people find it almost impossible to live in a community. They must always be the center of attention. They must always be lashing out at the community in some way that the whole community is alerted to their presence.

A REGULATED LIFE

A college student came to visit me. After a short visit I told him it was time for the family meal and that we would have to continue our talk some other time. He seemed reluctant to leave, but I assured him we could talk again later. Finally, he said, "Do you eat together for meals?" Yes. "How do you stand such a regulated life?" I never thought of it as regulated—we are a family. A family is a community of mutual trust, and we like to be together.

It was a thought that seemed foreign to him. Apparently he had not grown up in a home like that. Family togetherness seemed strange to him. It came as no surprise to me that later he became a chief antagonist in the community where he lived. From that short interchange of thoughts, together with others I had later, it became apparent that here was a child who had experienced little community.

As time went on the boy bounced from one kind of philosophical orientation to another. He went from atheism one year to super-piety the next. The vehicles of his wrath were different, but the theme was always the same—the community was always wrong. Like the clarinetist who thinks the entire orchestra is out of tune but him he invaded the symphonic sounds of the community and distorted the harmony that resided there. He made charges on the duly appointed leadership and he distributed distortions about those who had sought their level best to help him live in harmony. And finally, the community had had enough. They ostracized him.

This story can be repeated many times in the lives of people. The "jilted lover" syndrome is remarkably and alarmingly prevalent. Such people always have a cause, and they always present it as a legitimate cause. But they are sadly perceived by their neighbors and even some of their friends as "born losers."

Part of the problem with the born loser or the jilted lover is that he has not learned community. Of course, the most meaningful place to learn this is at home—in the family. But today's families are too often rather pitiful places and unfortunately they become kindergartens of alienation and pain.

Yet they remain the beginning place of learning harmony. It is in the home that a child learns to interrelate and interact. Parents who set the stage with fair discipline and concerned interest in the future of their child provide great benefit to the larger society. But those who refuse to set limits and are afraid to regulate their home may be training the tyrants of tomorrow. They could be preparing to foist on society more judgmental, often bitter, new antagonists.

WHERE COMMUNITY IS LEARNED

But it is not only in the home that community is learned. Fortunately, there are other homes that serve as surrogate training centers. Some children can be saved by drawing from the life of other homes. Here the church and the school play a part as well. But these agencies of training are more inclined to discipline-for-survival than are many homes. So, when a child has entered the larger society represented by the school or the church, he is expected to conform on a level that is related, but somewhat different, than the home.

My student left my home that day and drove over to another home in the neighborhood where a girl lived. The girl was his friend at a distance. He had tried to reach her and show affection, but she did not care for him. She called him a pest and treated him as such. So, he parked in front of her home and stared at her house. After an hour or so he left. He repeated this behavior several times and it did not go unnoticed. Finally, the girl's parents ordered him out of the area and to stay away. They had swatted the fly. And so, he lost again, this time as a jilted lover.

Why didn't he just go home and enjoy the community there? Where is one to go for community when there seems to be no community? Again, the words of the psalmist:

> [1] Behold, how good and pleasant it is when brothers dwell in unity! (Psalm 133:1)

What if there is no perceived community? He tried the church. But he was spurned there. First, the church members saw him as odd. Within minutes after he began to ask his questions about the church's teachings he experienced large doses of hostility from that group. In his classes he experienced the same pain. His very presence seemed to bring out the worst in people. He could not relate on the same level, or in the same way as the majority around him. It seemed obvious to those who cared about him that the pressure would someday become unbearable.

I watched with concern as he went through the steps of filling the needs caused by his social impoverishment. I could not put my finger on the exact cause of pain. But it soon became apparent that I too would be a victim of his wrath. When his family seemed to side with him the stage was set for his last great fling: clear anti-community behavior. It was *he against the world* now. When community spurns and becomes inaccessible—even in a legitimate attempt to save itself, those who are spurned, often by nature sensitive and deprived people, react in anti-social ways. He became bitter. It was predictable. The joy of community is only felt in harmony. Community involves common interest.

THE COMMUNITY OF THE CHURCH

Take for example the community of the church. I have heard people say, "I won't ever go back to that church—it was cold—nobody talked to me but the receptionist—and she was assigned the task." One person even said once, "I went to that church for the express reason of seeing how warm it was. Guess what? Just as I suspected—no one even knew I was there."

Some people act like church was made for them—that when they walk through the door everyone is to jump and bow as they take their royal walk down the red carpet to their throne near the front. But while people are surely central to the church's existence and ministry, it is not people that constitute the church's only hub of meaning.

The church is a result not a cause and what makes it a community are the justified saints. The church is not a service club, it is the body of Christ's disciples. Its purpose and central reason for existence is found in Jesus Christ, and out of that meaning service naturally proceeds. What the church has in common is a mutual love and trust in Jesus as the Savior of mankind. Thus, the church is community. And how delightful it is when the church lives together in unity. What a powerful witness to the world when the brethren dwell together in harmony!

What happens when this center of community—of this gospel—is misplaced or overlooked or misunderstood? The same thing that happened among the disciples of the savior: disputes. It is inevitable. When the hub is misapplied the wheel does not turn correctly.

The Bible records an incident that gives us understanding here:

> [46] And an argument arose among them as to which of them was the greatest. (Luke 9:46)

One way we handle our hurts, especially when they involve the community, is by lashing out at those who are perceived to have done the hurting. Whenever there is disruption in the community it is first rooted in a removal or misplacing of what we had in common in the first place.

WHO IS THE GREATEST?

The disputes are over "Who is the greatest?" And thus enter the critics in the community. There are three kinds of critics.

First, there are *the uncritical lovers*. In every attempt at community you have them. Anything the leaders of the community want to do they are ready to support it. If the leaders came up with the idea it must be a good idea. You never have to worry about a serious objection for these people.

They love the leaders. But such a position can make them vulnerable to tyranny. Nevertheless, they are not so concerned about that. If the leaders decide to tyrannize they will answer to God. They accept it. It is a comfortable position to take—that of being an uncritical lover, unless, of course, someone takes advantage of them. The uncritical lover can become the jilted lover.

Second, there are *the unloving critics*. These are people who find themselves incapable of fulfilling their emotional needs without living in constant or sporadic criticism of others in the community. They are consistent only in their critical ways. They will lie and slander to fulfill their need to be the greatest. They seem uninterested in facts or truth. They live to produce the latest smear.

Like attendants at a Halloween party, they wear different masks. One says he's doing the work of John the Baptist. Another claims to be cleansing the temple like Jesus did. Still another is Elijah reincarnated to clean up the horrible situation that exists in Israel. As such they feed off the community. They wear cloaks of piety with a silent stiletto in its folds aimed at every duly appointed leader they perceive. They come across as overbearing and unloving, loud, and forceful against established authority, but they always pose as great protectors of some tradition the community supposedly must hold.

It seldom seems to occur to them that those traditions were developed to be in some way meaningful to the unifying life of the community and that community involves people. To the unloving critic people mean ultimately little more than a vote in favor. The unloving critic is not altruistic. No wonder that the Bible assigns unloving criticism to its source in Satan.

> [10] And I heard a loud voice in heaven, saying "Now the salvation and the power and the kingdom of our God and the authority of his Christ have come, *for the accuser of our brethren has been thrown down,* who accuses them day and night before our God." (Revelation 12:10. Emphasis supplied)

"You will know them by their fruits"[1]—you will know their spirit by their product. They will even quote the Bible.

> [10] If you keep my commandments, you will abide in my love, just as I have kept my Father's commandments and abide in his love. (John 15:10)

But one of Christ's two great commandments escapes them:

> [39] You shall love your neighbor as yourself. (Matthew 22:39)

John wrote,

> [9] No one born of God commits sin; for God's nature abides in him, and he cannot sin because he is born of God. (1 John 3:9)

The unloving critic reserves the right to define who he is to love—anyone else is led by Satan in his eyes. But love is not earned in the Christian way of life. True Christian love is that attitude of dignity we have toward others because they are children bought by God. But this is a foreign concept to the unloving critic—no one in the end misses his venom, not even other unloving critics.

If we could pull back the masks and take away the cloaks we would see that the end to be gained by the unloving critic is the same. The theme

---

1. Matt 7:15–20.

of his life, whether he articulates or realizes it, is found in the revealing words of Jesus:

> [46] And an argument arose among them as to which of them was the greatest. (Luke 9:46)

"I will be the greatest," is an attitude that, with its subsequent methods, is tailor-made for one end-result: the destruction of the community. Ethics seem not to enter the picture. They will lie and slander to fulfill their need to be the greatest. They are always God's instruments to strengthen. But the brethren are only those who agree with the unloving critic for he is the spokesman of God and who would disagree with God? And it is little wonder that the community finally excludes them.

There is *the loving critic*. Here is someone who is not primarily centered in self but in the goals of the community. He follows the channels which the society has set up. Because of the genuine concern for the community, his presence is uplifting, unselfish, and edifying to the community. If a leader abuses his power, as human leaders are prone to do, he approaches him alone to talk it out in a manner that is conducive to understanding. He does not run campaigns of embarrassment, he does not try to get something on the leaders of community, he does not seek to pass on and embellish rumors about those who lead, and he does not gloat over others' mistakes. He is kind, thoughtful, altruistic, patient, and above all, he is truthful. He can be firm and disciplined, but he is such in love—a principled love. And in the end it is the loving critics that make a community work and prosper.

JOINING A GROUP

As I watched my student leave my home I suspected that he would join one of these three groups: he would become an uncritical lover, or an unloving critic, or a loving critic. But because of the impoverishment he had experienced, I suspected the worst. What so often happens happened. He teamed up with a few others who found a temporary goal in the destruction of the community and joined the ranks of the unloving critic under the guise of saving the church.

To some extent a community can thank itself for its unloving critics, because somewhere along the line it has been unloving—either in the homes it has allowed to develop in its midst, or because it gradually abandoned the methods of loving criticism itself. Jesus' secret for community is carefully laid out in Matthew 18, and it is sad to discover how many Christians seem totally illiterate in that counsel for Christian life together.

Community is the result of brethren who love the Lord dwelling together in unity. One day every community must decide how important it is to dwell together in unity, because any community that doesn't will cease to exist.

CHAPTER TWENTY-FOUR

The Middle Rain

> "Our growth depends not on how many experiences
> we devour, but on how many we digest."
> —Ralph W. Sockman

JOEL 2:23

> [23] "Be glad, O sons of Zion,
>   and rejoice in the Lord, your God;
> for he has given the early rain for your vindication,
>   he has poured down for you abundant rain,
>   the early and the latter rain, as before."

THE TENNESSEE RAIN

I knew little about rain until I moved to Tennessee many years ago. The college chaplain gave me a complimentary umbrella (something I had never owned in Southern California). That was a hint of what was coming. The college pastor told me that if I could walk across the campus under a large umbrella and make it to the other side without getting wet above my waist that was only a squall—not really a Tennessee rain. He was right.

I have learned to drive in the rain and to walk in the rain without having all my notes and books destroyed by water damage. I have even learned to enjoy being weaned from my set sprinklers in California when I care for my lawn and garden. Perhaps no one knows the importance of rain more than the farmer who depends on it for his livelihood. In these modern times rain is guaranteed through sophisticated irrigation techniques. But this was not so in the ancient times. Then the farmers were at the mercy of nature.

Our concern here is not to understand the weather but to understand the word of God and how it employs the figurative language of the harvest in illustrating the work of the Holy Spirit. Our church is not unacquainted with the terms of Joel 2:23—the "early" and the "latter" rains. These are concepts we have understood to refer typologically to both the Christian era in general and to those last days. In fact, we tend to wait for the "latter rain" of the Holy Spirit, a concept we will examine here.

THE BACKGROUND OF THE RAINS

In the Bible these terms occur several times. Moses makes clear that the grain, the oil, and the wine of the land are dependent upon these showers.

> [14] He will give the rain for your land in its season, the early rain and the later rain, that you may gather in your grain and your wine and your oil. (Deuteronomy 11:14)

In the Psalms the pilgrim on his way to the tabernacle is blessed by the coolness and freshness of the early rain.

> [5] Blessed are the men whose strength is in thee, in whose heart are the highways to Zion. [6] As they go through the valley of Baca they make it a place of springs; the early rain also covers it with pools. [7] They go from strength to strength; the God of gods will be seen in Zion. (Psalm 84:5–7)

Old Testament prophets point out that it is God who brings the rain that we might have harvest. Jeremiah recorded that,

> [24] They do not say in their hearts, "Let us fear the LORD **our God, who gives the rain in its season, the autumn rain and the spring rain,** and keeps for us the weeks appointed for the harvest." (Jeremiah 5:24)

And Joel added,

> [23] Be glad, O sons of Zion, and rejoice in the Lord, your God; for he has given the early rain for your vindication, he has poured down for you abundant rain, the early and the latter rain, as before. (Joel 2:23)

TOKENS OF GOD'S BLESSING

All these texts share two things: (1) they present the rains of nature as tokens of God's blessing; and (2) they speak in the context of harvest. No wonder that this illustration has become so popular in understanding the final work of God in a sin-sick world.

Jeremiah uses the expressions "autumn rain" and "spring rain."[1] The early rain of Palestine was the autumn rain. The latter (or last) was the spring rain. The early rain started the rainy season and the latter rain ended it. The season began in the month of Tishri, which would be the rough equivalent of September and October. The harvests began in Iyar, our April and May, with the final rain.

The climate of Palestine is quite different from that of the wet parts of the United States. Actually, there are really only two seasons in that land: summer and winter. Summers are sunny, warm, virtually rainless, moderate, with regular winds, and run from May to November. Winters are mild to cool, with intermittent wet and stormy weather, and run from November to May. The brief transitional periods between summer and winter bring the former and latter rains—they are really the first and last installments of the winter rains.

THE EARLY AND LATTER RAINS

In intensity, depending on where you might be in Palestine, the early and latter rains are virtually indiscernible. For example, if you are north and west in Palestine you get more rain. If you move south and east you get less. If you were to winter in Jerusalem you would experience about three days of rain in October—the early rains. If you stayed until January you would need your umbrella about thirteen days out of the month. But if you can last out the winter until May you will only have two more days of rain that month—the *latter* rain.

---

1. Jer 5:24.

If, on the other hand, you went east to Jericho—only some ten to twelve miles toward the desert—in October you would have only one day of rain—the *early* rain. In January you would have about seven days of rain, and if you stayed until May you would be back to one day of rain—the *latter* rain.

Why this meteorological lesson? Because one does not understand the symbols of scripture without first understanding the literal terms.

> The early rain is also applied to a preparatory personal experience prerequisite to receiving the latter rain. As a result of the early rain experience of the individual, the heart is emptied of every defilement, and cleansed for the indwelling of the Spirit. The latter rain, in turn, qualifies the church for bearing witness in the "loud cry" and to stand firm during the last great time of trouble.[2]

THE DOUBLE APPLICATION OF JOEL

Some traditions see this prophecy of Joel as having a double application. First, it refers to the primary fulfillment at Pentecost as made by Peter.

> [17] And in the last days it shall be, God declares,
> that I will pour out my Spirit upon all flesh,
>   and your sons and your daughters shall prophesy,
> and your young men shall see visions,
> and your old men shall dream dreams;
> [18] Yea, and on my menservants and my maidservants in those days
> I will pour out my Spirit; and they shall prophesy.
> [19] And I will show wonders in the heaven above
> and signs on the earth beneath,
> blood, and fire, and vapor of smoke;
> [20] The sun shall be turned into darkness
> and the moon into blood,
> before the day of the Lord comes,
> the great and manifest day.
> [21] And it shall be that whoever calls on the name of the Lord shall be saved. (Acts 2:17–21)

There is the cosmic pouring out of the Spirit in the Christian era. Thus, can we legitimately expect the final or latter rain of the Spirit at the close of the age—the days in which we are living?

---

2. "Latter Rain," *SDA Encyclopedia*, 766.

THE GIVING OF THE HOLY SPIRIT

There is a second, and perhaps more personal lesson, that we can learn from this farm illustration. As mentioned above, in Jerusalem in October one gets three days of rain and in May gets two days of rain. So, if the illustration can be pushed this far, it is not really the *quantity* of rain that is so crucial. In other words, antitypically speaking, the lesson is not so concerned with *how much* of the Holy Spirit we get.

Even measures are figurative. The acceptance of the Spirit is measured more by the reception of the heart than by quantitative means. Thus, it is the quality of the rain, or the function of the rain, that is important. It is the timing. It is the purpose, and it is the operation of that rain on the crop. That is to say, it is the effectual operation of the Holy Spirit in our lives.

The rain in October served to soften the ground. Can you imagine how hard it tends to get after five months of no rain? A plough could hardly crack it. But the first rain readied it for the plough and had a penetrating effect. This is a brilliant illustration of the initial work of the Spirit, not only at Pentecost, but in the life of every would-be follower of Jesus Christ.

The Spirit penetrates the heart like rain on the parched earth, softening it so the plough can work, and the seed can germinate. Then the rain came, and the seed was nourished. And by the final rain puts on the last touch of full fruition—the final spurt for harvest.

And here comes the rub so far as our personal emphases are concerned. Have you ever thought of the "latter rain" as something we are all waiting for? Like someday the Spirit is going to seep through our church and the sick will be healed and the miracles of Christ will be reenacted, and we will all go out with great power and finish the work? And you have even wondered: I wonder when it will occur? Will I be alive? Will I be faithful?

A WORLD WITHOUT "RAIN"?

Perhaps one can even come to act like one believes that the parable of the ten virgins is not a parable at all but an allegory which predestines God's church to be devoid of the Spirit between the initial filling of the lamps and the final coming of the bridegroom. But such a view can leave the impression that there is little if any connection between the initial and the final falling of the rain. Yet the rain is falling all around during the rainy season.

Have you ever taken a hike and wished you had some water? No creek, no rain, no river, no canteen. Perhaps you drank two quarts before you left. No good. You need to drink all along the way. If you drink six quarts of water in one day and try to make it all the rest of the month without water those six quarts will not do it. If you know you have only six quarts of water to last you for the month you can make it by drinking a little each day.

Likewise, one rain does not do it. Seeds need continual watering. I planted a new section of lawn last August. The first two weeks went fine— we got enough rain for the seed to germinate and even got the sprouts above the ground. Then came the drought—three weeks without rain. My lawn would have died but I got out the sprinklers and kept the rain coming. It is no different in the antitype—this illustration tells a great deal about the Holy Spirit as well.

The early and latter rains were not the only rains Palestine got. If it had been there would have been no crops, no harvest, no agriculture industry. Three days in October and two days in May will not produce a harvest. In Jerusalem, between November and April there are fifty-three days of rain! The early and the latter rains are connected with a rainy season: the middle rains!

CHAPTER TWENTY-FIVE

WHEN ORTHODOXY COSTS TOO MUCH

> "Christianity is the good man's text; his life, the illustration."
> —JOSEPH P. THOMPSON

JOHN 13:34-35

> [34] A new commandment I give to you, that you love one another; even as I have loved you, that you also love one another. [35] By this all men will know that you are my disciples, if you have love for one another."

THE BASEBALL FORFEIT

A few years ago, as a young youth pastor, I played shortstop for a church softball team sponsored by my local church in a city church league. We played the Baptists, Presbyterians, Episcopalians, Church of God, and others.

One Thursday evening we played the Assembly of God and things did not go well. The umpire must have been a member of their church. There were many bad (we thought) calls. Our head elder was pitching, and he heckled the umpire so much that he finally got thrown out of the game. So, he did what any self-respecting head elder might do—he sat in the stands and heckled the umpire from there.

In utter desperation the umpire eventually stopped the game and ordered our head elder out of the park with the ultimatum that he had two minutes to exit the ballpark. By now it was a dual. He threatened, "If you aren't out of the park in two minutes your team will forfeit the game!"

So, our elder started walking slowly for the exit, dramatizing the situation by holding his watch up in the air to time his arrival at the gate with the stroke of the second hand. But he didn't make it. We forfeited the game. And by then we were all mad. We protested the game; we took the decision to the City Parks and Recreation Department Board. We asked for a city hearing over the results. We protested the incompetence of the umpire. But we lost all around.

That night as we walked off the field grousing about the unfortunate situation, licking our wounds with pitiful sarcasms, one of our elders shouted angrily, "Well, they may have won, but we keep the Sabbath!"

I have often thought of that evening and its subsequent events with horror—especially in the light of the above text. I wonder if those brethren in the Assembly of God were impressed by our witness to the Sabbath? What kind of experience would I have if while knocking on the doors in that city one day I should come upon a member of that opposing church softball team? I wonder if he would say to me, "Oh yes, you are with that church we played the other night—you are from that church that keeps the Sabbath!"

Obviously, it wouldn't occur that way. He would not remember our biblical "orthodoxy." He would only remember our behavior. This is Jesus' truth:

> [35] By this all men will know that you are my disciples, if you have love for one another. (John 15:35)

HUMAN PROCLIVITIES

We were not unique that night on the ballfield. All through church history Christians have had a hard time keeping the tension between orthodoxy and love for the brethren. In almost any era of the past you can drop in for a visit and find a religious war. In the early centuries Christians fought and killed each other if they disagreed on the nature of Christ. In the middle ages, monks fought over how many angels could stand on the head of a pin. In Reformation times John Calvin set up a city of refuge for those fleeing the persecuting fires of Rome only to burn those who were not orthodox according to his standard of truth. And what a marvelous witness Northern Ireland was to the non-Christian community in our world!

There are many ways to kill. Christ taught his disciples in the Sermon on the Mount that anger, and evil attitudes are as effective as physical killing. So, in modern times when we have become more civilized we have become more sophisticated in our methods of killing—we kill reputations through gossip and half-truths. We kill other people's spirit and drive through criticism and envy. Sometimes we attack verbally—other times we just utter sarcasms—"You may have won the game, but we are orthodox!"

Perhaps there is nothing more ironic than when two church elders, both claiming to love the Lord and follow him, both claiming to be getting more holy, engage in a fist fight over a disagreement on righteousness by faith. It may well be that if that fist fight continues to the gates of heaven that neither will be admitted—not because both are unorthodox but because neither would be safe to take into a kingdom where all is harmony and love.

CAN ORTHODOXY COST TOO MUCH?

"Orthodoxy" means straight thinking, right belief, and correct doctrine. We believe that the place to find correct doctrine is in scripture. Scripture is clear that we are to "test everything" and hold to that which is good.

> [20] Do not despise prophesying, [21] but test everything; hold fast what is good, [22] abstain from every form of evil. [23] May the God of peace himself sanctify you wholly; and may your spirit and soul and body be kept sound and blameless at the coming of our Lord Jesus Christ. (1 Thessalonians 5:20–23)

Scripture warns about the possibility of being misled.

> [15] Beware of false prophets, who come to you in sheep's clothing but inwardly are ravenous wolves. [16] You will know them by their fruits. Are grapes gathered from thorns, or figs from thistles? [17] So, every sound tree bears good fruit, but the bad tree bears evil fruit. [18] A sound tree cannot bear evil fruit, nor can a bad tree bear good fruit. [19] Every tree that does not bear good fruit is cut down and thrown into the fire. [20] Thus you will know them by their fruits. (Matthew 7:15–20)

> ²⁰ To the teaching and to the testimony! Surely for this word which they speak there is no dawn. (Isaiah 8:20)

God's word does not in any way minimize the importance of orthodoxy provided the objective tests are right. My question here is: Does something ever take priority over orthodoxy? Just recently it struck me that all the people who crucified Christ were orthodox. It dawned on me that one reason they put the spear through the side of Jesus was to make certain he was dead so that they could get him off the cross in time to keep the Sabbath.

With these questions in mind, we should look at Revelation 2:1–5. Our Lord was one of a handful of great religious leaders in history who left behind no collection of philosophical, ideological, or religious writings. The only record we have that he ever wrote anything was when he wrote in the sand—and then we are not told specifically what he wrote.

But in the last book of the Bible, we have a series of letters that he gave to John, his beloved disciple—at a time when John was in exile after having served as pastor of the church of Ephesus.

> ¹ To the angel of the church in Ephesus write: "The words of him who holds the seven stars in his right hand, who walks among the seven golden lampstands.
> ² "I know your works, your toil and your patient endurance, and how you cannot bear evil men but have tested those who call themselves apostles but are not, and found them to be false; ³ I know you are enduring patiently and bearing up for my name's sake, and you have not grown weary. ⁴ But I have this against you, that you have abandoned the love you had at first. ⁵ Remember then from what you have fallen, repent and do the works you did at first. If not, I will come to you and remove your lampstand from its place, unless you repent." (Revelation 2:1–5)

Ephesus was a productive church. The chances for preaching the gospel seemed endless—it was in the center of the Roman empire—the crossroads of Asia Minor. The challenges of paganism should have kept the people always seeking new methods of witnessing. The charter members were baptized by John the Baptist and later re-baptized by Paul.[1]

Paul had spent three years teaching in a school room donated by one of the citizens.[2] Such famous leaders as Aquila, Priscilla, Timothy,

---

1. Acts 19:1–7.
2. Acts 20:28–31.

and John worked in the church.³ Exciting miracles of healing and the casting out of demons occurred there.⁴

Ephesus was a hard-working church—a church busy in its service, patient in its suffering and orthodox in its belief. And the Lord commended it for all these things. It was a church that responded to God's blessing. Paul met with the elders of Ephesus and delivered a warning.

> ²⁹ I know that after my departure fierce wolves will come in among you, not sparing the flock. (Acts 20:29)

Paul didn't use the term "kooks," but he meant that—he used the term "fierce wolves."⁵ He wrote more:

> ³² What do I gain if, humanly speaking, I fought with beasts at Ephesus? If the dead are not raised, "Let us eat and drink, for tomorrow we die." (1 Corinthians 15:32)

Be alert, Paul warned these elders—test what they say and how they act by the word.

> ³² And now I commend you to God and to the word of his grace, which is able to build you up and to give you the inheritance among all those who are sanctified. (Acts 20:32)

Not to tradition, not to opinions, not to one man's notions of what he thinks he has always believed, not to some private interpretation of scripture—but by scripture as perceived by the church.

Apparently the Ephesian members followed Paul's counsel. They developed a knack for heresy detection and Christ commends them for it. By the gift of discernment, they recognized the wolves in sheep's clothing—Jesus had told them how—by their fruits, that is, by their behavior, by their principles, you will know them. Wolves leave a trail of prints that are discernible. It is possible to know their spirit by their actions. It is possible to know their goals by their spirit. Heresy must be recognized for what it is, or it will do its work of distortion—it should be corrected.

Orthodoxy, right thinking, is—it is crucial to think right. The apostle wrote,

> ²⁰ Do not despise prophesying, ²¹ but *test everything*; hold fast what is good, ²² abstain from every form of evil. ²³ May the God

---

3. Acts 18:24–28.
4. Acts 19, 20.
5. Acts 20:29.

of peace himself sanctify you wholly; and may your spirit and
soul and body be kept sound and blameless at the coming of our
Lord Jesus Christ. [24] He who calls you is faithful, and he will do
it. (1 Thessalonians 5:20–24. Emphasis supplied)

The church of Ephesus did it and Christ commended them for doing it.

You can read about the miracles and advance of the work in Ephesus in Acts 19–20. Sick were healed, devils were cast out, books were burned—the modern equivalent of four million dollars' worth of books in one bonfire—heretical books on magic and superstition. It was a truth-filled, truth-loving bunch in Ephesus.

Jerome preserved the story that John, when he became too old to walk, was carried into church and brought by the deacons to the front. He was too old to talk at length, but the members still wanted to hear what he had to say; and so, he would say each time, simply, "Little children, love one another." Some of the saints got weary of this continual repetition and asked him why he always said the same thing. "Because," he replied, "It is the Lord's commandment, and if this only is done, it is enough."[6]

WHAT WENT WRONG

But something went wrong.

> [4] But I have this against you, that you have abandoned the love you had at first. (Revelation 2:4)

There are two ways to understand this rebuke. (1) Enthusiasm, or (2) Love. We often apply it to enthusiasm—a person comes into the church, he is in love with the message—"he is on fire," we say, he is excited, and we all wait for him to get like the rest of us—because you know that a red-hot coal in a tub of ice water eventually goes out.

The more natural way to understand this text is that it was *love* that waned. The Old Testament is filled with pictures of God and his people having a love affair—Israel is the bride.

> [8] When I passed by you again and looked upon you, behold, you were at the age for love; and I spread my skirt over you, and covered your nakedness: yea, I plighted my troth to you and entered into a covenant with you, says the Lord God, and you became mine. (Ezekiel 16:8)

---

6. Stott, *Epistles of John*, 49. Citing St. Jerome's commentary on Gal 6.

God loves her and then she "plays the harlot"—she leaves that love.

> ² Go and proclaim in the hearing of Jerusalem, Thus says the LORD, I remember the devotion of your youth, *your love as a bride*, how you followed me in the wilderness, in a land not sown. (Jeremiah 2:2. Emphasis supplied)

The New Testament follows the same imagery—"I have betrothed you," the new Israel.

> ² I feel a divine jealousy for you, for I betrothed you to Christ to present you as a pure bride to her one husband. ³ But I am afraid that as the serpent deceived Eve by his cunning, *your thoughts will be led astray from a sincere and pure devotion to Christ*. (2 Corinthians 11:2–3. Emphasis supplied)

Too often this beautiful bride falls out of love—and makes a deliberate choice to walk no more with her lover God—so the book of Hosea tells of the wooing process on the part of God—the hope of restoring—the long-suffering and patience of a loving God.

Ephesus was over thirty years old when Jesus sent his letter to the church—love was waning—but work without love is drudgery. Jacob could work for seven years for Rachel and then another seven years and testify that it seemed like but a few days[7] because he loved her—there was excitement in that love—but when love is gone all becomes sour and cold. And people in this condition look for substitutes. Here is the picture of a church that has chosen deliberately to leave the love she had at first. The original language does not say she "lost" that love. It says she "left" it—she decided not to love because something more enticing had lured her away.

The love Jesus speaks of is a Godly love—a love that seeks the best for others. It is a seeking love, one that is limited only by the capacity of the hearts on which it is poured out. It is a love that cares about the credibility of the church, a love that places supreme value on other human beings. It is a love for God and a love for people—not just enthusiasm of faith—but love for others. It is the love by which Christians are identified. "If we love one another, God abides in us and his love is perfected in us."[8]

Apparently those early traits of real love, of no dissension, of a heart ready to be kindled through sensitivity to God's wooing and recognition of human need, of hands ready to help, began to be enamored with a

---

7. Gen 29:30.
8. 1 John 4:11.

new phase of orthodoxy—one that need not be but is a self-centered perversion. The pride that comes from being right—heresy-detection became heretic-hunting. And once that transition is made love dies. Some churches early rejected the idea of creeds because of the terrible history of creeds among other Christians. It became grounds for hunting heretics and thus diverted believers from the gospel mission.

A young ministerial student once visited his teacher and confided that he had become embroiled and caught up in the theological controversies of the day. His time was spent in arguing, in ferreting out heretics, in fighting to the bitter end over infinitesimal issues that he had begun to question whether he would want to be a minister if there were no controversy. He was perceptive and loved the Lord enough to fear this trend in his life. So, he came seeking counsel.

The counsel he received was this: God has called you to minister not to control. He has called you to serve not to accuse. God's work will succeed with or without you. You will neither defeat it, nor will you finish it—but you can be a witness to Christ's work for you and thereby be used by God in his cause on this earth.

If you choose to be that kind of minister you will discover great fulfillment for your own soul. Your desire to be right at the expense of fellowship, your selfish perusal to make other people know you are right regardless of what it does to them, will finally destroy your will to love if you do not gain control of it. It is important to be right—but you must constantly strive to avoid controversy—it is more important to love.

By God's grace that young man turned around, left his professor's office, gave up his fanatical, egocentric, compulsive obsessions to lord orthodoxy over love. Today he is a successful young pastor ministering to the needs of God's people.

This inordinate preoccupation with heretic hunting killed the love Ephesus had come to be characterized by. It was one thing to test and detect—it was altogether a different thing to hunt heretics. The church is made up of delicate trust relationships—many of which are very fragile, especially at first. Once those trust relationships begin to break through the tyranny of a few self-styled judges, it does not take long to destroy the fabric. And the natural result is that everyone becomes a threat—everyone becomes a potential heretic. The ultimate result is that *the candlestick is removed*—the witness dies.

Just as surely as our immature behavior on the ballfield placed in jeopardy our witness with the members of the opposing team, so the Ephesian church was in danger of darkness if she did not follow Christ's counsel.

THE COUNSEL OF CHRIST

Christ's counsel was characteristically clear and simple: (1) Remember, (2) Repent, and (3) Return. As the prodigal son was wooed back to his father by the love he remembered experiencing there, so Ephesus is enticed to remember what it used to be like before she became unloving.

Remember the fellowship you once had? Remember what it was like to have an open church free of suspicion and intrigue? Remember what it was like when you could ask questions and not be suspected of backsliding? Remember the love you enjoyed when you were accepted as yourself—a being created in the image of God—instead of one who was expected to submit to the inordinate molding of your human judge?

Remember what it was like when you could teach a class or preach a sermon without being accused of undermining the church? Remember when you could just bask in the glory of what God was doing without being suspected of destroying the youth of the church? Remember when you could share the gospel without being misquoted?

If you can remember that, Jesus says to Ephesus, and you like what you remember—then repent. Turn your back on your proclivities toward *unlove*. Quit passing on the ugly rumors when they come to you. Stop the insipid obsessive gossiping. Quit destroying the credibility of the brethren—refrain from attacking that which you do not understand as heresy or something worse. Read your Bible and share your concern and show that your repentance is from God.

Return! It's not too late—you can still be the loving community you once were. Make your restitutions and your confessions and straighten out your breaches of relationship. Re-focus your attention on your fellowship with God—re-study the message that attracted you and remember that I love you, Christ says. I don't love you any less for your waning love. But return to that pure love relationship that we once enjoyed.

THE STRONGEST ARGUMENT

Love is not a cover for heresy. It is not an umbrella for falsehood. It is not a cop-out for truth. Love is a component of truth—the experiential component. Love is evidence that our truth is really God's truth; truth is not just something we believe it is but something we are as well.

When orthodoxy is maintained at the expense of fellowship, the cost is too great—it is possible to be as straight as a pillar but as cold as the marble out of which the pillar is made. And when that occurs, the lampstand of witness, the fire of concern for people, *the love* dies.

The church cannot last without love. A traveler tells of visiting the village at modern Ephesus and looking for Christians, he found three. For a time after the letter came to the church there was a reversal and a return—but then the church fell back into its unloving ways. These three Christians whom the traveler found he described as "so ignorant that they scarcely had heard of the names of Paul and John. Like the city, the local church began in a desirable condition and ended in ruins."[9]

In 1623, as John Donne the famous English poet and clergyman lay ill and close to death, he picked up his pen and began to write his *Meditations:*

> No man is an island entire of itself; every man
>   is a piece of the continent, a part of the main;
> If a clod be washed away by the sea,
>   Europe is the less, . . .
> Any man's death diminishes me,
>   because I am involved in mankind.
> And therefore never send to know for whom
>   the bell tolls;
>   It tolls for thee.[10]

---

9. Bunch, *Seven Epistles of Christ*, 119.
10. Donne, *Devotions upon Emergent Occasions.*

CHAPTER TWENTY-SIX

Enhancing the Preaching of the Parousia

> "We judge ourselves by what we feel capable of doing, while others judge us by what we have already done."
>
> —Henry Wadsworth Longfellow

MATTHEW 24:29–35

²⁹ "Immediately after the tribulation of those days the sun will be darkened, and the moon will not give its light, and the stars will fall from heaven, and the powers of the heavens will be shaken; ³⁰ then will appear the sign of the Son of man in heaven, and then all the tribes of the earth will mourn, and they will see the Son of man coming on the clouds of heaven with power and great glory; ³¹ and he will send out his angels with a loud trumpet call, and they will gather his elect from the four winds, from one end of heaven to the other.

³² "From the fig tree learn its lesson: as soon as its branch becomes tender and puts forth its leaves, you know that summer is near. ³³ So also, when you see all these things, you know that he is near, at the very gates. ³⁴ Truly, I say to you, this generation will not pass away till all these things take place. ³⁵ Heaven and earth will pass away, but my words will not pass away."

THE ANTICIPATION OF THE *PAROUSIA*

For as long as I can remember I have been a Christian living in anticipation of the second coming of Christ. I have never believed anything but the Christian worldview and ethic, but the emphasis on end-time has always given the hue.

I was born of Christian parents. My father had been a young engineering student in Stockholm, Sweden, when at the age of 19, he became the recipient of a book that his father had gotten from a drunk who had rummaged it out of a garbage can. The book was *Bible Readings for the Home Circle*. It was a Seventh-day Adventist publication.

My mother was a second-generation Adventist—born of immigrant Norwegian parents in Battle Creek, Michigan. Her father, Christian A. Thorpe, was an editor at Adventist publishing houses, including the Review and Herald and Pacific Press, for fifty years. His editorial contributions were punctuated with the notion that Christ would come soon—even in his day. As a young Norwegian he had accepted the Adventist message and hope, and never wavered in his trust that he would live to witness the event—even to the day of his death.

My parents dedicated their adult lives to the work of the church's publishing institutions. On several occasions, I asked my father why he had given up his early ambitions in exchange for the lower-paying longer hours at the Adventist institutions (though I really thought I knew already). He would simply remark, "I believe Jesus is coming soon. I want to help spread the knowledge, and I want to live at a place where my sons can acquire a Christian education." My brother and I did receive a Christian education. Today we are both ordained ministers.

Why this personal background? Simply this—I think I understand what it means to spend a lifetime in anticipation of the *parousia* hope of Christ's imminent return. That hope motivated the home in which I grew up. It has been a motivating factor in my life. In my home Christ was coming soon. And the emphasis was always on "soon."

THE IMPORTANCE OF TIME

To understand my heritage, one must understand this emphasis on time. The denomination has always been sensitive to what was time oriented. The movement was born in the time-setting obsessions of nineteenth century New England.

Jesus taught that his disciples should ever be watching and making ready for his *parousia*. However, I have felt at times that I was both offender and offended because of inordinate emphasis on time—as though the counsel to beware of false messages about time did not exist, whether the form was that of a highly-charged offering appeal, a call for commitment to some individual's program, or simply a misplaced emphasis.

I still witness people victimizing and being victimized by the special interest causes rooted in the concept that time is short. It is not unusual, for example, for students to call me up in the middle of the night, or to approach me in my office and say, "Why should I waste my time studying when Jesus may come any day? I should be out there working!" When I suggest that they could be doing that kind of "work" right there in the dormitory while they are going to school they act somewhat surprised. The thrill and excitement of the "shortness of time" seemed to have overshadowed the fact that God called them to a work of witnessing to people.

All my life I have attended camp meetings and youth or church-wide conferences of various sorts. More times than not, the aberrant views being propagated on mimeographed sheets were time oriented. Warnings handed out by well-intentioned people regarding the leadership of the church or the waywardness of the schools as new signs of the nearness of Christ's return are anything but new.

Nevertheless, this is not meant to denigrate the importance of the times. This is simply to underscore the seriousness with which we view them, and the tendency we must emphasize it. Living in anticipation of the *parousia* is indeed a belief that is dear to the hearts of Christians. But we must often ask some introspective questions about our emphasis on time to control it and keep it in perspective.

When Jesus said we should watch and be ready[1] did he mean to emphasize watching more than being ready? When Jesus gave us signs of the end[2] was it his purpose that we should rejoice in those signs and perhaps even appear to gloat in the fact that we have recognized them as such or that we should take those signs as motivation to work all the harder to alleviate human suffering since the end was truly near?

When Jesus commissioned his church to preach the gospel was it his intention that we preach the *parousia* as though it were the gospel?

---

1. Matt 24:42, 44.
2. Matt 24:29, 32.

> [28] So Christ, having been offered once to bear the sins of many, will appear a second time, not to deal with sin but to save those who are eagerly waiting for him. (Hebrews 9:28)

That simple answer will provide a necessary perspective for any answers we may formulate to the above questions.

SOME BASIC DISTINCTIONS

Though this answer appears simple enough, its implications are complex and far-reaching, and they require the identification of some distinctions that are crucial for precisely addressing a generation that we believe will live to see the parousia. Seeking balance is a significant part of the Christian theologian's task, and making distinctions helps one to keep the tensions in the truth so that correct emphasis is maintained.

It should go without saying that once the pastor or evangelist, in his role as theologian, has seen balance for himself, and understands these distinctions, he will be able to communicate that balance more clearly.

Christian theology has historically seen the cruciality of order. Take for example, the theological notions conveyed in the Bible words "faith," "grace," "works," and "blood." To understand the plan of salvation it is important to put these words in the right order: Due to God's *grace*, he sent his Son to shed his *blood* in atonement, and by placing our *faith* in him we receive salvation which is evidenced through good *works*.

Getting these concepts in the right order reduces confusion and assures of the truth God is trying to communicate accurately. The same principle of order holds true in eschatology. Hence a look at some distinctions will be helpful here.

THE DISTINCTION BETWEEN TIME AND LOVE AS MOTIVATORS

Why do we witness? Because we believe Christ is coming soon? Or because we love humanity? Look at two reactions to the following situation: Imagine a devastating earthquake in Nicaragua. Thousands of people are killed or left homeless. A flood comes and wipes out others. The country is in turmoil. Disease strikes as the people are left to the mercy of the elements. The people are naked, sick, homeless, orphaned, penniless, and unable to help themselves. Pictures appear in the American press, and we watch the plight of these people on television.

Reaction A observes all of this and discovers in scripture: there will be famines, pestilences, and earthquakes—all this must happen before the coming of Christ. A look at the newspaper and the screen brings a shake of the head. Yes, it is clear now that the *parousia* is around the corner.

Reaction A finds a neighbor and proclaims, Look! Prophecy is being fulfilled—famine, heartache, homelessness, orphans, pain, suffering, hunger, disease—this proves it, neighbor—Christ is coming—get ready to meet your maker—anytime now the sky will open up as a scroll and Christ will descend through the open place in Orion and appear before us! Repent, for his coming draws nigh!

Reaction B also sees this but discovers other texts in scripture: Jesus said—clothe the naked, feed the hungry, heal the sick, give homes to the orphans. The heart is touched by the news of sheer human suffering. Reaction B runs to the bank, draws out some money, and writes a check to relief societies or contacts aid and welfare groups to find out what aid can be brought to alleviate human suffering.

Reaction B should not rule out Reaction A—there is an important time element to be seen in the events of the last days. But time is not the purest motivator, and a message that overlooks the reality of suffering or one that is not in the first instance sensitive to human pain, needs some re-evaluation.

This distinction is like the teachers who are asked, what do you teach? One answers, "mathematics;" another answers, "Bible;" and a third answers "students." Love and respect will forever be superior motivators to time.

THE DISTINCTION BETWEEN THE CHURCH AND THE INSTITUTION

Many Christians recognize contemporary attacks on the church as a sign of the end, and such attacks are to be expected. Scripture has made it clear that such hostility will ever be experienced by God's people in an evil age. The message of salvation will be criticized and misrepresented as antichrist "and friends" attack the foundations of God's government.

Is the church under more attack today than ever before? That question can only be adequately answered after we have defined the term "church." Church has always been under attack in this world because the principles of Jesus Christ are enemies of the sinful mind. Roman Catholicism has traditionally identified church with the institution as one in the same. Yet this is not the Protestant understanding of church in the New Testament. Thus, a new seed bed for eschatological confusion can develop if a careful distinction is not made here.

Many Christians have not historically taught that institution and church are the same. This fact is reflected in the notion that there are still many true believers in all churches of Christendom. Evangelism seeks to find those members of the church of Christ.

Many Christians interpret the New Testament more closely to that of the Reformers who held to the notion of a visible and an invisible church, although some versions have been expressed as "the remnant church" and the "remnant." It was a distinction that aimed to preserve a balance between outward profession and the innermost motives of the heart. It also tended to mitigate the natural human propensity toward institutional pride such as that shown at the tower of Babel.

There is a human tendency to institutionalize despite God's warnings against it. Many Christians are not exempt from such tendencies. Yet the biblical principle is simple: God's church is the sum of those who have entered saving fellowship with Jesus Christ. Paul calls them "the saints,"[3] or those who have been set apart based on their acceptance of Christ's work for them. The "institution" is not the primary meaning of the biblical term "church." One does not obtain heaven, nor does one secure readiness for the *parousia* by being institutionalized.

The place of the institution is to expedite and facilitate the work of God on earth. This does not mean everything an institution does is the work of God, but it does mean that men and women agree on an objective: to allow God to work through them in the spreading of the gospel to this generation.

Undue emphasis on the institution may undermine the work of the gospel. Therefore, the eschatological distinction should ever be kept foremost in the mind of the pastor or evangelist. While he stresses the place of the institution as an instrument of God he emphasizes the work of Christ and its acceptance as the base of the church.

Church members too often lose this distinction and sink into disillusionment because they confuse church with institution. Somehow they

---

3. Acts 9:32.

think church leaders are other than human, perhaps angels or something else. And it becomes painful for them when they see in the church organization some of the same traits that characterize any human structure.

If this distinction is maintained one can find his disillusionment eroded because the perceived corruption of institution does not constitute a corruption in God's church.

Dietrich Bonhoeffer aptly described God's church.

> Christian brotherhood is not an ideal which we must realize; it is rather a reality created by God in Christ in which we may participate.[4]

In short we can see these two distinctions in the statement from the writer to the Hebrews: Christ will return (1) to receive those who love him—not those who are simply enamored with time; (2) to receive those who have had sin dealt with in their lives according to his plan, i.e., his church—not a biblical institution.

THE DISTINCTION BETWEEN ETHICS OF THE GOSPEL AND ITS CORE MESSAGE

C. H. Dodd has popularized this distinction of the New Testament.[5] Technically the terms are responsively *didache* ("teaching," i.e., response expected to the gospel message), and *kerygma* ("preaching," i.e., the essential elements of the apostles' preaching that constitute the gospel message).

This same distinction can be illustrated brilliantly in the Ten Commandments of Exodus 20. Unfortunately, we often start our children off to memorize the Ten Commandments with Exodus 20:3, when we should stress Exodus 20:2 if they are going to have the proper understanding.

> [1] And God spoke all these words, saying, [2] I am the LORD your God, *who brought you out of the land of* Egypt, out of the house of bondage. (Exodus 20:1–2. Emphasis supplied)

Putting on the preamble gives the proper perspective to the rest of the chapter for it gives the *kerygma* of the passage.

Kerygma is the essential saving message; it states what God does or has done. *Didache,* which is ethical teaching, tells rather how one is to respond

---

4. Bonhoeffer, *Life Together*, 30.
5. Drane, *Introducing the New Testament*, 99–100.

to what God has done. Preserving such a distinction guards against mixing the order of the message and therefore helps to avoid confusion.

I talked with a person who was commenting on the theological training in religious colleges. He said, "I wish you would simply teach these young men to preach the gospel." Why, I said, "That is exactly what we do." As he talked on, he suggested they should be men who preach the pure gospel: "the millennium, the soon coming of Christ, Daniel 2, the seven last plagues, Armageddon, the state of the dead, the Sabbath, etc."

Now it was clear that for him the term "gospel" meant something different than the term is commonly understood to mean in scripture. Rather than meaning the essential work of Christ for our salvation, work in which we have no part except to accept by faith, he was throwing in all the various nuances and elements of the church's message. Such a shoddy approach to biblical terminology is confusing for both the pulpit and the pew and intelligent communicators of the word should work hard to avoid it.

The message of the church is broad of which the *kerygma* must be at the core. The "gospel" means "good news." But not any "good news" constitutes the New Testament gospel. For example, I once flew west to visit my mother who was in her eighties. Any visit to my mother was good news to me but that didn't make my visit to see her "the gospel." If I was going to fulfill the gospel commission it meant I was going to preach "the gospel"—and of all the churches and denominations in Christendom I believe we should have the most sophisticated, the simplest, the clearest understanding of the New Testament gospel that there is.

There may even be elements in any Christian message that are terrifying without the gospel. Armageddon is not the gospel. Armageddon would seem to be a terrifying notion without a personal commitment to the gospel. To confuse Armageddon with the gospel would accentuate the motivators of fear, and thus could undermine love.

Yet Armageddon is gospel-related in that it tells me that those who accept the gospel of Jesus Christ need not fear the wrath of God for it will never touch those who have accepted the redemptive work of Christ. That's why we may preach about Armageddon but not until the distinction is clear.

The state of the dead can be a precious doctrine to us because it tells us that death because of Adam's sin is merely a temporary thing for those who accept the righteousness of Jesus Christ. But it should not be called "the gospel." And the distinction between the elements and the core of the saving message should be kept in mind.

This is even more crucial when dealing with doctrines of clear ethical response. It is natural for self-centered humans to conclude that when preachers call for response it is intended in some way to win God's favor. Ethical response is just that: response. It is not the cause of God's love; it is the result of it. Working from the essential core of the message will help to alleviate confusion and aid fledgling believers (as well as mature ones) to understand what "watching" and "being ready" mean.

PICKING UP THE REDEEMED

Jesus is returning, not to redeem anyone but to pick up the redeemed. He already performed the work of salvation when he was here before—there is nothing you or I can do to add to that. We have always taught that Jesus saves from the power of sin, the presence of sin and the penalty of sin. Because of this truth the second coming becomes "the blessed hope."[6]

Only for those who have accepted the work of Christ for them is this a blessed hope. Because of the gospel of God in Jesus Christ they may expect eternal life, freedom from death, deliverance from Armageddon, the breaking of sin's power and eternal fellowship with the Creator.

Christ is coming back because sin would never do as an alternative for God's plan. And there are people on this earth who are pleading for deliverance because they are in total agreement with God—he must get back to pick them up. Until that occurs we are to preach. And in our preaching we are to maintain the clearest presentation and expression of the message we can.

As we faithfully allow these distinctions to clear up our communication we will find the Spirit using our messages to reach people in such a way that there will be added to the number daily those who eagerly await his return.

---

6. Tim 2:13.

CHAPTER TWENTY-SEVEN

Who Sings Louder Than Angels?

> "Toil, feel, think hope; you will be sure to dream enough
> before you die, without arranging for it."
>
> —John Sterling

HEBREWS 2:1–18

¹ Therefore we must pay the closer attention to what we have heard, lest we drift away from it. ² For if the message declared by angels was valid and every transgression or disobedience received a just retribution, ³ how shall we escape if we neglect such a great salvation? It was declared at first by the Lord, and it was attested to us by those who heard him, ⁴ while God also bore witness by signs and wonders and various miracles and by gifts of the Holy Spirit distributed according to his own will.

⁵ For it was not to angels that God subjected the world to come, of which we are speaking. ⁶ It has been testified somewhere,

"What is man that thou art mindful of him,
or the son of man, that thou carest for him?
⁷ Thou didst make him for a little while lower than the angels,
thou hast crowned him with glory and honor,

⁸ putting everything in subjection under his feet."

Now in putting everything in subjection to him, he left nothing outside his control. As it is, we do not yet see everything in subjection to him. ⁹ But we see Jesus, who for a little while was made lower than the angels, crowned with glory and honor because of the suffering of death, so that by the grace of God he might taste death for every one.

¹⁰ For it was fitting that he, for whom and by whom all things exist, in bringing many sons to glory, should make the pioneer of their salvation perfect through suffering. ¹¹ For he who sanctifies and those who are sanctified have all one origin. That is why he is not ashamed to call them brethren, ¹² saying,

"I will proclaim thy name to my brethren,
in the midst of the congregation I will praise thee."

¹³ And again,

"I will put my trust in him."

And again,

"Here am I, and the children God has given me."

¹⁴ Since therefore the children share in flesh and blood, he himself likewise partook of the same nature, that through death he might destroy him who has the power of death, that is, the devil, ¹⁵ and deliver all those who through fear of death were subject to lifelong bondage. ¹⁶ For surely it is not with angels that he is concerned but with the descendants of Abraham. ¹⁷ Therefore he had to be made like his brethren in every respect, so that he might become a merciful and faithful high priest in the service of God, to make expiation for the sins of the people. ¹⁸ For because he himself has suffered and been tempted, he is able to help those who are tempted.

THE EVENING THREAT

Two Christian college girls, sisters I think, were attending a night class together at a downtown university. When class let out the sky was black outside—one of those no-moon nights. The sisters walked across the well-lit parking lot toward their car when suddenly they became aware that they were being followed. As they looked around they saw two young men trailing them, two guys who had the look of nothing good.

The girls stepped up their pace toward their car—and so did the boys. Finally, they were running—and so were the boys. They reached their car, unlocked the door, jumped inside, locked their doors, started the engine, and sped away barely ahead of the two young men catching up with them. To their relief the young men didn't follow.

With hearts beating out of their chests, they headed for home—terrified at what had just happened. They were hyperventilating. But as they calmed down they became aware that they had both been praying all the time they were in flight. And as they talked together on the seventeen miles trip back to their home college where they were village students, they began to wonder if they had been supernaturally delivered from that frightening situation.

Both were Christian girls. Both had gone to church all their lives. Both had learned their memory verses for class and some of the texts miraculously came back to them now—verses about angels.

> [14] Are they not all ministering spirits sent forth to serve, for the sake of those who are to obtain salvation? (Hebrews 1:14)

> [7] The angel of the LORD **encamps** around those who fear him, and delivers them. (Psalm 34:7)

> [11] For he will give his angels charge of you to guard you in all your ways. (Psalm 91:11)

When they arrived home, their brother was waiting to meet them. Knowing nothing about what had just happened he told them that he needed to charge the battery in their car. The car had been starting a little slow and clearly needed some attention. In fact, he was surprised that they had been able to start the car at all.

Now they *were* scared! They hadn't a clue that they might have trouble starting the car. For just a second both of them relived the terrifying moments they had just been through, thinking what might have happened had the car not started. And now they were sure they had been miraculously delivered by angels. Now the memory verses were making more sense.

Their brother opened the hood to charge the battery. And then he looked at them. "What's going on here? There's no battery in here." And he showed them the loose battery cables dangling next to the engine. Someone had stolen their car battery. "But you just saw us drive the car into the driveway," they replied. He said, "You can't drive a car without a battery! Try starting it up."

His sister fumbled for her keys. She was shaking like a leaf. She turned the key—nothing—dead as a door nail—not a murmur—not a whine—nothing! But nothing had changed—she had just driven it into the driveway ten minutes ago. Nobody had touched the car between their driving in and his opening the hood. And now the two girls knew they had been supernaturally delivered. Angels had encamped "around . . . and delivered them!"

STORIES ABOUT ANGELS

I have heard stories like this all my life. And I have come to accept them uncritically—I just wondered why nothing like that ever happens to me—although there are some stories sort of like that that I could share from my life.

Of course, there are angels. I have been taught that and believed that all my conscious life. And as a child I knew there were angels who could do things beyond my comprehension. How many stories have you heard at camp meeting or general meetings of the church or read in bedtime stories, or church papers, where someone helped the storyteller supernaturally and when he turned to thank the person—the person was gone—like the Lone Ranger; only no one was riding off in the dust chanting, "Hi-ho Silver!"

Of course, these angels care about God's people—they are, after all, messengers on God's mission. As a kid I heard angel stories almost every week. Stories like this one about the girls—a man would help someone out of a jam and when the person turned to thank him he was gone. Like the Lone Ranger radio show—just as a person turned to thank the masked man, he was galloping over the hill with Tonto.

THIS GENRE OF ANGEL STORIES IS NOT UNUSUAL

When I was growing up I met a lot of people who believed if you couldn't understand something that was unexplainable, it was probably the work of evil angels sent here by Satan to confuse or deceive us. The Chinese acrobats—impossible what they did, must be working by the devil. Magic show—can't understand, must be the devil. Some insisted that surely Houdini was of the devil. But there were some good things that happened, and those things were caused by good angels, who God occasionally sent to help us out of trouble.

As Christians we were compelled to believe the story about the girls with their disappearing battery. I remember how I thrilled when I heard this story. While I didn't know the girls, I heard they were students at the college where I was teaching at the time and I didn't hear anyone question the story.

Every set of lips had an "Amen" attached. It was told by a member of my seminar class where people were invited to share their answered prayers for the previous week. And this was one of the most impressive stories. That's the way angels apparently worked and that's what angels were for—and that was before the TV hit shows, "Touched by an Angel," or "Highway to Heaven."

I'm sorry to tell you, the story I just related to you is not true. The girls made it up. They were so anxious to testify to the protecting power of God that they made up that story. It never happened. But even now, even though you know that you might be saying: "but it could have happened. That's the way angels work. They have the power to do things like that."

BELIEVING IN ANGELS DOESN'T MAKE YOU A CHRISTIAN

Most religions have angels, or something equivalent. And most of those angels may be like your Christian view of angels. In the religions around the Hebrews the angels were female. But among the Hebrews the angels were male. Perhaps you think of angels as neither because of Jesus' statement that angels neither marry nor are given in marriage.

> [30] For in the resurrection they neither marry nor are given in marriage but are like angels in heaven. (Matthew 22:30)

So, Christianity shares some things in common and teaches some things differently. From scripture we accept by faith some of the descriptions given.

First, Angels are not human—but a separate order of beings.

> [7] Thou didst make him for a little while lower than the angels, thou hast crowned him with glory and honor. (Hebrews 2:7)

In the future, believers will judge the angels, presumably the *evil* angels.

> [3] Do you not know that we are to judge angels? How much more, matters pertaining to this life! (1 Corinthians 6:3)

Angels don't have material bodies. That doesn't necessarily make them present everywhere but it complicates things when it comes to knowing where they are or seeing them. They are referred to as winds or spirits.

> [14] Are they not all ministering spirits sent forth to serve, for the sake of those who are to obtain salvation? (Hebrews 1:14)

Paul says, about the evil angels, we do not struggle against flesh and blood but against spiritual forces of wickedness.

> [12] For we are not contending against flesh and blood, but against the principalities, against the powers, against the world rulers of this present darkness, against the spiritual hosts of wickedness in the heavenly places. (Ephesians 6:12)

Angels are presented in the Bible as a company or host of people rather than a race of people. Occasionally they appear as men in the Bible. So, they have that *disguising* capability.

> [4] While they were perplexed about this, behold, two men stood by them in dazzling apparel. (Luke 24:4)

Angels are greater in knowledge than human beings are, but they do not know everything. There are fallen angels and there are holy angels.

> [34] Ah! What have you to do with us, Jesus of Nazareth? Have you come to destroy us? I know who you are, the Holy One of God. (Luke 4:34)

> [1] And a great portent appeared in heaven, a woman clothed with the sun, with the moon under her feet, and on her head a crown of twelve stars; [2] she was with child and she cried out in her pangs of birth, in anguish for delivery. [3] And another portent appeared in heaven; behold, a great red dragon, with seven heads and ten horns, and seven diadems upon his heads.
> [4] His tail swept down a third of the stars of heaven, and cast them to the earth. And the dragon stood before the woman who was about to bear a child, that he might devour her child when she brought it forth; [5] she brought forth a male child, one who is to rule all the nations with a rod of iron, but her child was caught up to God and to his throne, [6] and the woman fled into the wilderness, where she has a place prepared by God, in which to be nourished for one thousand two hundred and sixty days.
> [7] Now war arose in heaven, Michael and his angels fighting against the dragon; and the dragon and his angels fought,

⁸ but they were defeated and there was no longer any place for them in heaven. ⁹ And the great dragon was thrown down, that ancient serpent, who is called the Devil and Satan, the deceiver of the whole world—he was thrown down to the earth, and his angels were thrown down with him.

¹⁰ And I heard a loud voice in heaven, saying, "Now the salvation and the power and the kingdom of our God and the authority of his Christ have come, for the accuser of our brethren has been thrown down, who accuses them day and night before our God.

¹¹ And they have conquered him by the blood of the Lamb and by the word of their testimony, for they loved not their lives even unto death. ¹² Rejoice then, O heaven and you that dwell therein! But woe to you, O earth and sea, for the devil has come down to you in great wrath, because he knows that his time is short!"

¹³ And when the dragon saw that he had been thrown down to the earth, he pursued the woman who had borne the male child. ¹⁴ But the woman was given the two wings of the great eagle that she might fly from the serpent into the wilderness, to the place where she is to be nourished for a time, and times, and half a time.

¹⁵ The serpent poured water like a river out of his mouth after the woman, to sweep her away with the flood. ¹⁶ But the earth came to the help of the woman, and the earth opened its mouth and swallowed the river which the dragon had poured from his mouth. ¹⁷ Then the dragon was angry with the woman, and went off to make war on the rest of her offspring, on those who keep the commandments of God and bear testimony to Jesus. And he stood on the sand of the sea. (Revelation 12:1–17)

There are *holy* angels.

²¹ In the presence of God and of Christ Jesus and of the elect angels I charge you to keep these rules without favor, doing nothing from partiality. (1 Timothy 5:21)

They both have knowledge beyond the natural knowledge available to us, at least in our present state. They play the part of the "messenger."

Finally, they are stronger than human beings, but they are not all powerful. They are limited in their strength.

⁷ Now war arose in heaven, Michael and his angels fighting against the dragon; and the dragon and his angels fought. (Revelation 12:7)

An order of creation that has all these characteristics is going to become the subject of a lot of speculation and legend. I don't know how many of the stories that I heard as a kid were factual. I'm sure that those who told the stories believed them. I surely did.

The Bible does talk of angels. We were made a "little lower than the angels" but we have reason to believe that was a probationary period, which we failed, by the way, and so they are God's helpers to get us through the rough spots on our road.

ANGELS ARE NOT DISNEY CHARACTERS

Look at the main text again, beginning with the book of Hebrews.

> [14] Are they not all ministering spirits sent forth to serve, for the sake of those who are to obtain salvation? (Hebrews 1:14)

> [1] Therefore we must pay the closer attention to what we have heard, lest we drift away from it. [2] For if the message declared by angels was valid and every transgression or disobedience received a just retribution, [3] how shall we escape if we neglect such a great salvation? It was declared at first by the Lord, and it was attested to us by those who heard him, [4] while God also bore witness by signs and wonders and various miracles and by gifts of the Holy Spirit distributed according to his own will.
>
> [5] For it was not to angels that God subjected the world to come, of which we are speaking. [6] It has been testified somewhere,
> "What is man that thou art mindful of him,
>   or the son of man, that thou carest for him?
> [7] Thou didst make him for a little while lower than the angels,
>   thou hast crowned him with glory and honor,
> [8] putting everything in subjection under his feet."
> Now in putting everything in subjection to him, he left nothing outside his control. As it is, we do not yet see everything in subjection to him. [9] But we see Jesus, who for a little while was made lower than the angels, crowned with glory and honor because of the suffering of death, so that by the grace of God he might taste death for every one. (Hebrews 2:1–8)

There are key words and phrases here that help us understand why the redeemed sing a new song in heaven that the angels cannot sing.

> [10] For it was fitting that he, for whom and by whom all things exist, in bringing many sons to glory, should make the pioneer of their salvation perfect through suffering. (Hebrews 2:10)

Jesus is the pioneer of our salvation. The word means *source, first trail blazer*. He is taking us with him. The word means the first to go in and take someone with him. Notice what that involves. He is not ashamed to call us brethren.

> [11] For he who sanctifies and those who are sanctified have all one origin. That is why he is not ashamed to call them brethren. (Hebrews 2:11)

> [16] For surely it is not with angels that he is concerned but with the descendants of Abraham. (Hebrews 2:16)

He is not concerned about the angels; he is concerned about the human race. He shared in humanity.

> [14] Since therefore the children share in flesh and blood, he himself likewise partook of the same nature, that through death he might destroy him who has the power of death, that is, the devil. (Hebrews 2:14)

We have no evidence from the Bible that God became an angel. But we have clear testimony that God became a human being. He has ended our estrangement with God.

> [14] Since therefore the children share in flesh and blood, he himself likewise partook of the same nature, that through death he might destroy him who has the power of death, that is, the devil. (Hebrews 2:14)

The person who cuts off connection with God will in that estrangement die. I was working on my computer one day and everything went dead. I discovered my cat under the desk playing with a switch and she had turned everything off. I lost part of my document, but until I turned on the switch everything remained dead.

Being connected with God is being connected with life. Turn off your surge switch and your whole human computer goes dead. Life is not something we have inherently, innately, naturally. It is the Christian confession that life does not just happen. It is a gift from God. So, Christ, as pioneer of our salvation didn't just live to show God was fair in his expectations of created morally capable people. He also made up for their estrangement.

¹⁶ For surely it is not with angels that he is concerned but with the descendants of Abraham. ¹⁷ Therefore he had to be made like his brethren in every respect, so that he might become a merciful and faithful high priest in the service of God, to make expiation for the sins of the people. ¹⁸ For because he himself has suffered and been tempted, he is able to help those who are tempted. (Hebrews 2:16–18)

THEY SANG A NEW SONG

Is it any wonder then that when we have pictures of the saints in heaven they are singing their own song? The Bible tells us that "it is a *new* song"—a song of victory and redemption. No angel can sing that song because no angel has experienced what it was to be without hope until Jesus Christ mended the estrangement.

> ³ And they *sing a new song* before the throne and before the four living creatures and before the elders. No one could learn that song except the hundred and forty-four thousand who had been redeemed from the earth. (Revelation 14:3. Emphasis supplied)

In college our men's chorus sang about the angels and salvation.

> There is singing up in heaven such as we have never known,
> Where the angels sing the praises of the Lamb upon the throne,
> Their sweet harps are ever tuneful and their voices always clear,
> O that we might be more like them while we serve the Master here!
> Holy, holy, is what the angels sing.
> And I expect to help them make the courts of heaven ring;
> But when I sing redemption's story, they will fold their wings.
> *For angels never felt the joy that our salvation brings.*[1]

---

1. John R. Sweney (1837–1899) and Johnson Oatman, Jr. (1856–1922). "Holy Is What the Angels Sing."

CHAPTER TWENTY-EIGHT

SOME THOUGHTS ON FORGIVENESS

> "He that cannot forgive others, breaks the bridge over which he must pass himself; for every man has need to be forgiven."
>
> —LORD HERBERT

HEBREWS 13:1–10

¹³ Let brotherly love continue. ² Do not neglect to show hospitality to strangers, for thereby some have entertained angels unawares. ³ Remember those who are in prison, as though in prison with them; and those who are ill-treated, since you also are in the body. ⁴ Let marriage be held in honor among all, and let the marriage bed be undefiled; for God will judge the immoral and adulterous. ⁵ Keep your life free from love of money, and be content with what you have; for he has said, "I will never fail you nor forsake you." ⁶ Hence we can confidently say,
"The Lord is my helper,
 I will not be afraid;
  what can man do to me?"
⁷ Remember your leaders, those who spoke to you the word of God; consider the outcome of their life, and imitate their faith. ⁸ Jesus Christ is the same yesterday and today and for ever.

> [9] Do not be led away by diverse and strange teachings; for it is well that the heart be strengthened by grace, not by foods, which have not benefited their adherents. [10] We have an altar from which those who serve the tent have no right to eat.

IN THE EXPERIENCE OF FLYING

"The Lord is my helper, I will not be afraid; what can man do to me?"[1] What does that mean? Maybe the question is too general. Rephrase: What does that text mean to you in the context of flying?

Read it again—and this time notice a couple of the verses in the setting of *flying*—to the relatives for Christmas or summer of some special assignment.

> [6] God has said: "I will never fail you nor forsake you." So, we can confidently say, "The Lord is my helper, I will not be afraid; what can man do to me?" (Hebrews 13:6)

Do you believe that when you fly? Can you accept that? I want to recount the last airplane flight of an average conscientious young college Christian girl as she flew home for Christmas break. She received her plane ticket from her parents. She was excited—the thrill of getting away from school for a few days—the anticipation of seeing her friends at home again—the nervousness of riding in a plane.

She got to the airport in ample time—after what seemed like days she got through security and the invasive searches—she wanted a seat by the window. She got by the window—she was close to the screen. Every plane seemed to be different, but she didn't fly that much so she just took what they gave her.

Up to this point she had remained quite active—but now she had to sit and wait—the guy in the waiting area near her was reading a newspaper—the headline read: "225 Souls Die in DC-10 Crash." She was not flying on a DC-10. She could hardly wait to see her mother—but the plane stood between her and seeing her mother. The headline reminded her that planes occasionally don't make it, and her conscience reminded her that perhaps she wasn't ready to go yet.

The flight number was called. She started down the long tube to the plane—suddenly it resembled a cattle-chute. She found her seat; she

---

1. Heb 13:6.

was the first one there. She sat down; it was a bit tight on those economy flights. Fortunately, the two seats next to her were still vacant and she entertained the momentary thought that perhaps she would have all three places to herself. If these seats did fill up, she thought, things would get a bit claustrophobic right now.

But she was wasting time. Now was the time. Right now, she better get it done before she might be caught doing it. Acting like she was looking out the window, staring at an engine she couldn't see, she leaned her eyes on her hand like she was adjusting a contact and shot a quick silent prayer to heaven. "Dear Lord, I am sorry I haven't taken you more seriously. Please forgive me of all my sins and if this plane crashes save me in your kingdom. Amen."

LEARNING FROM THIS SCENARIO

First, if you can stop judging this young, conscientious Christian girl, you might even be able to identify with her in some ways. Have you ever thought what this little act says about our assumptions of *God and forgiveness*?

When we go through this little ritual are we suggesting that between the time we commit a sin and the time we ask forgiveness for it we are lost? If something should happen to us, something that proves to be fatal for us, would we be lost? But that's not all, are we suggesting that somehow the act of confession and the request for forgiveness secures the desired forgiveness? Does this mean that it makes up for the sin? Or we don't have forgiveness until we ask?

Now those assumptions are perhaps false or based on questionable theology. But think of them as suspect and there may be a dimension about forgiveness that you as a conscientious Christian, young or old, tend to forget.

FORGIVENESS IS GIVEN BY GOD, NOT SOMETHING WE BUY

While we have texts in scripture we have memorized at one time or other like:

> [9] If we confess our sins, he is faithful and just, and will forgive our sins and cleanse us from all unrighteousness. (1 John 1:9)

We also have texts like this one:

⁵ Keep your life free from love of money, and be content with what you have; for he has said, "I will never fail you nor forsake you." ⁶ Hence we can confidently say, "The Lord is my helper, I will not be afraid; what can man do to me?" (Hebrews 13:5-6)

We ought always to read these two texts together.

I question whether asking God "to forgive all my sins" has much to do with 1 John 1:9. I spent a week in Honduras speaking at a camp meeting several years ago. As we would drive out through the countryside we would occasionally cross a river—and there would be ladies washing their clothes in the river. They would take each item and wash it in the water, pound it with rocks, and whatever else you do when you don't have a Maytag. In my week in Honduras I never once saw any of these ladies take a great bag of clothes, dip it once in the water, and take it home thinking all the clothes in that bag were clean. In some respects that would be like saying, "Please forgive all my sins"—as though the words were magic and demanded no more out of us than to utter them.

There is no relationship around that could possibly exist on the basis described in this little story. Think, for example, of your parents—how much they put up with—with you! Or, maybe you would find it easier to think of what you put up with—with them.

As a college sophomore I wanted to go to my girlfriend's home for Christmas. She invited me; her parents invited me. But my father threw a fit—absolutely not!—eight hours on a bus together? Without supervision? Dad—what can you do on a bus? No supervision? There are forty people on the bus. I had an answer for every objection. He finally said, "No." I said, "Yes." And on it went for a week. Then I began to see him wavering and I knew I had won. My! What I had to put up with—with my dad!

But despite what I put up with he was still my dad. He is dead now and I often think of the times we had together. Times when we didn't agree and times when we did. Good times and rough times—misunderstandings and times when I didn't think he trusted me. Then I remember times when he must have trusted me because he wasn't naïve. I can remember trips we took—he took off work just for me. I remember that he made up for it by working around the clock the next day. There is no question that I inherited my fight of faith from my dad, who stuck with me no matter what happened.

No matter how many discussions, arguments, misunderstandings, good times, or rough goes—no matter if I hurt him knowingly or inadvertently—I always had the assurance of one thing: He was my dad. He could have written Hebrews 13:5: "I will never fail you nor forsake you." When I confessed my sin to dad, it was not my confessing that secured his forgiveness—my confessing only showed my acceptance of his forgiveness.

When my dad and I were on the outs I still knew that I was loved. The heat in my room was not turned off, the food on the table didn't cease to be there, the tuition bill did not quit being paid, the car didn't quit being offered (well, I take it back about the car). But my point is that my relationship did not end between confessions. I like the way Christ depicted our relationship to God—to convince an estranged race of people—humanity—that his love and forgiveness is constant and not reliant upon anything in our lives. He pictures us as branches on a vine.

For the girl in the plane—or better, for those who think that between sin and confession one is lost, the vine and the branches would not be a good illustration. Again, a father and a son—a spendthrift who seeks to escape his father's love. It was not the father who spurned the son—God does not spurn you. Again, a favorite New Testament illustration is adoption. A baby has no home—a family takes that baby and becomes its legal parents. Adoption illustrates the solid foundation on which a relationship with God is built.

Adoption is like another illustration—marriage. I have occasionally heard young people say, what is a piece of paper? If we love each other who needs that document? That is, of course, an immature and naïve question. You have a unique relationship with your spouse because of that piece of paper. That piece of paper represents your good name, your commitment, your willingness to devote yourself to this relationship.

Just like I have a unique relationship with the finance company with respect to my house and my car. That piece of paper protects me. That piece of paper protects my finance company. As a human being, I need protection and as a sinner others need protection from me. Adoption is God's pledge of faithfulness. It is a biblical picture that testifies you were born estranged due to circumstances beyond your control. When you accept Christ, you recognize that he has adopted humans and you say I want a part in this relationship. You are accepted and there are certain benefits you don't lose just because things don't always go right.

THE PLACE OF CONFESSION

So why confess sins? Because that's part of a true relationship with any living person. A young man came to me and wept over a hurt he believed he had caused me. I didn't expect it, I didn't force it, I was really surprised. But our relationship deepened because of it. It didn't begin our relationship. What he had done to me had not ended our relationship. But his confession caused me to know that he cared about our friendship.

If your relationship with God is simply one that says, I want everything this world offers without God and next time I get in a pinch I will plead to God, so I can have eternity with God—I suggest that you ought to look at God again. And at that relationship again. Eternity with God would be hell for those who care nothing about him here.

But if you genuinely care—then know this—God cares infinitely more—God's forgiveness is constant; you need not worry about that. But he does ask you to accept it—to enter a relationship where he is a serious part of your life. To enter a forgiving relationship with God is to realize that forgiveness is an attitude of God—not simply an isolated action.

In an insightful moment, my friend Max Phillips (d. 2014), as a college student, penned these words which he entitled, "God of the Desert."

> I
> On the burning sand I walked toward the cool oasis;
> > I had a map.
> So when God came by and offered me His,
> > I laughed and said, "I don't need it."
>
> But he wouldn't stop bothering me;
> > Every time I looked around He was following.
> When I stopped among the rocks to look for water once,
> > He caught up.
>
> II
> Holding out a canteen of water he said,
> > "If you drink this, you will never thirst again."
> Knowing this was unreasonable
> > I said, "Over the hill is a spring."
>
> But the water I found was foul;
> > Around it human bones were bleaching in the sun.
> Exhausted I fell beside the pool,
> > Defiant, trying to rest; I couldn't.

III

When God caught up, he said,
   "If you want shelter, I have a tent."
"I don't need it," I lied;
   He ignored my lie, said nothing.

Suddenly, leaping to my feet,
   I raced across the sand, my eyes fixed.
I threw away my map
   There it was! The oasis.

IV

Tired, bleeding, but triumphant, I looked over my shoulder;
   He was running after.
He ran with a pack on his back:
   Water, medicines, bandages—I scorned them.

"Leave me alone, God!"
   He slowed, then stopped.
Far in the distance the oasis was shining in the sun!
   I would show him!

V

I stumbled on a long, long time
   Before I knew the oasis was a mirage.
All around, the night turned black;
   I was thirsty, bleeding, tired; the desert was cold.

I stopped and sat down on a rock,
   My head in my hands; I was lost.
But I heard a sound behind me;
   And when I looked around me, there was God.[2]

[5] He has said, "I will never fail you nor forsake you." [6] Hence we can confidently say, "The Lord is my helper, I will not be afraid; what can man do to me?" (Hebrews 13:5–6)

---

2. Phillips, "God of the Desert," *Inscriptions*.

CHAPTER TWENTY-NINE

COMMUNICATION, INTEGRITY AND MORAL CONFLICT[1]

"Never let your sense of morals prevent you from doing what is right."

—Isaac Asimov

JOHN 3:16-17

[16] For God so loved the world that he gave his only Son, that whoever believes in him should not perish but have eternal life. [17] For God sent the Son into the world, not to condemn the world, but that the world might be saved through him.

THE WOLF AND THE LAMB

Once upon a time there was a wolf and lamb.[2] They chanced to meet when the lamb had accidently strayed from the sheepfold and could not find his way home. When the wolf saw the lamb, he recognized his next meal—a defenseless, easy catch, ready for the supper plate.

---

1. This chapter was an address given by the present writer before medical personnel (largely physicians and nurses) at Loma Linda University in Southern California.
2. Aesop, *Aesop's Fables*, 127–28.

However, being a wolf with a conscience of sorts, he set about to justify himself for making the lamb his supper.

"Good evening," said the wolf in as polite a tone as possible, so as not to throw the lamb into a panic.

"Last year you grossly insulted me and because of that I will be having you as my supper. Do forgive me, but that is the way things are, vengeance must be gotten for that insult. Wolves cannot afford to take such treatment from lambs for they would have no credibility left in all the vast woods. But I would like to be as compassionate as possible as I devour you for supper."

"But sire," bleated the lamb in a mournful tone of voice, "I was not yet born a year ago—I am very young and not old enough to have been the one who grossly insulted you last year."

So, the wolf replied, "But you have been stealing food from my pasture—I saw you grazing in the buttercups and the succulent grasses. That is trespassing and a crime against my ownership. For that reason, I must have you as my supper—no one would respect my authority if I continued to allow such behavior."

"No, good sire," the nervous lamb answered. "I have never tasted grass or buttercups. I am too young to eat anything but my mother's milk. It was not me you saw stealing from your field."

Again, the wolf argued: "Young lamb, you have been drinking of the waters of my artesian wells and for that you must become my supper."

"But I beg to differ, kind wolf," answered the lamb, nearly petrified with fright because he could see the line of reasoning. "But my mother's milk is both food and drink to me. I have not yet tasted water either."

With that the wolf, exasperated that his authority was being challenged at every turn, grabbed the lamb and quickly ate him up. And while he chewed talked and he said, "Well! I will not remain supperless, even though you refute every one of my charges."

Moral: *The tyrant will always find a pretext for his tyranny.*

THE NATURE OF TYRANNY

People have told me that is their favorite of all of Aesop's fables, and I have never met anyone who did not see himself in the story—as the lamb. Two people sat in my home and poured out their tale of woe about the raw deal they had just endured in the church organization. They were through

COMMUNICATION, INTEGRITY AND MORAL CONFLICT

with the church—it was over—they saw no more involvement at all. The tyrant had found a pretext for his tyranny. They were the lambs and the church was the wolf.

I once heard a man in high places in the church state publicly that every church worker could expect to experience at least four raw deals from "the brethren" in his career.

While I do not plan to spend this chapter doing exegesis on a fable, I use this story because it illustrates some important points about communication, integrity, and moral conflict. I am not a physician or a nurse and will not pretend to understand the challenges to your integrity that your profession dumps upon you. But I do share the common interest in professional Christian service with you. And I do have several close friends who are physicians, and we talk. And I do have big ears and a deep interest in growing in my sensitivity of all forms of moral dilemma that we face together.

For this reason, I found the request in the recent phone call to me to be challenging. Scary. This is not a theological topic and the best I may be able to do is demonstrate a desire to share some of what I have learned as a person who works in a highly political structure. A structure is really any organization in which people attempt to cooperate and make a corporate contribution to society.

When we talk about truth-telling and integrity in such an organization we must recognize some factors that go far beyond the lay perception of "total unity in God's church." As a child I enjoyed for a time the naïve belief that walking into a church in La Sierra, Collegedale, or Berrien Springs would be the same as walking into a church in Cairo, Copenhagen or Cooranbang. Everyone believed the same and all had hearts formed by faithful adherence to the victorious life and we were simply in a holding pattern as the Holy Spirit held back the winds of strife in the hopes that a few more people would repent.

That dream was shattered by my senior pastor when I interned in Southern California in the mid-1960s. He was one of the hardest workers I had ever known and in his first six months we tracked down virtually every name on our 600-membership roll. And many a time at the end of a hard day of many miles and many visits he would look at me and say, "Okay, Ed, if you were the Holy Spirit and you were going to start 'the latter rain' today in the homes you have just seen—in which home would you start?"

You could only fully appreciate that if you had been with us, listened to the people, watched them, and then connected that experience with my idealism and vision of what the church was or should be or could be. All those elements must be included, or I will sound judgmental, which I am not attempting to sound.

I will be the first to suggest that you plug in 150% of your mental relational capacity because the experiences I use may be like what you face only by contrast. As a religion professor talking to physicians and nurses it takes little insight to suggest that you have available far more potential independence than I do. Hence I am fighting the temptation to be envious of you in a day of declining demand for religion professors and obvious meaninglessness to the term "tenure" in our school system. I am discovering that with each passing year my age places my career increasingly at the mercy of the boss—however you may view him, wolf, lamb, etc. My career is very much dependent on skills of survival—skills I apparently have failed to keep in shape or maybe even develop at all.

POLITICS AND INTEGRITY

On the other hand, lest you take all of this as an apology for pursuing this topic, I watched my father-in-law seek an early retirement from a well-established and highly credible anesthesiology practice because of both internal political pressures at his hospital as well as the crunch of the soaring insurance rates. So, if I haven't been exactly where you are I sometimes wish I were and at other times am glad I'm not. At any rate, we can communicate on the plane of need to understand the political setting or our profession and idealism.

Finally, I want to define a couple of terms. I will use the term "political" not to denote corruption but to denote cooperation and the attempt to accomplish an objective corporately. When I have suggested I am not a very good politician to some of my bosses I don't think they understood me that way. So here communication has not been served very well. I trust you will accept my definition of this term and recognize that any blight that may be put on the term will have to have been put there by your mind, not as part of my intention.

Furthermore, why not admit politics into our thinking, even in the church organization, when everybody else knows it exists. It's like one administrator said to me when he was mercilessly attacked for hiring and defending his friends, "Who am I supposed to hire—my enemies?" Friends or enemies—both were admissions of the presence of politics. It is perhaps a dangerous term to use—but it does keep your attention.

I go by the straight *Oxford English Dictionary* meaning when I speak of integrity. It means *the whole man*. We could almost use equilibrium as a synonym except that term does not serve as well in its moral connotations. Integrity is that condition of having no part or element taken away or wanting—it is an undivided or unbroken state of material wholeness, completeness, and unimpaired freedom from moral corruption. Innocence? Sort of. Sinlessness? Only in eternal goal. But it does denote that state where sound moral principle reigns—adherence to, honesty through, sincerity of. The wise man wrote,

> [1] Better is a poor man who walks in his integrity than a man who is perverse in speech, and is a fool. (Proverbs 19:1)

I have a text—one that is basic to what I consider to be an adequate Christian ethic on integrity as it relates to truth-telling: perhaps the most familiar text in the Bible:

> [16] For God so loved the world that he gave his only Son, that whoever believes in him should not perish but have eternal life. [17] For God sent the Son into the world, not to condemn the world, but that the world might be saved through him. (John 3:16-17)

First, some brief observations on the text and then some brief observations on integrity, truth-telling and moral conflict. There is a bit of a dilemma built into this text, for which we make immediate mental adjustments because of semantics.

God loved the world, but we are not to. He was able to love it in a different way than we find ourselves inclined to love it. If, on the other hand, we are to love it in the same way as he loves it we could love it just as much as he did. We need to learn to love it that way and if we did we would find it easier to refrain from criticizing it as we usually do: from the standpoint of envy, or hatred.

A recent *Insight* article by Dan Fahrbach, the former editor, revealed that teenagers when they were with their families spent 17% of their time watching TV, but when they were with their friends spent only 3% of their time watching it. Dan goes on to suggest that their findings of this latest research would suggest that TV is an escape from boredom for most teenagers and if they had constructive relational activities they wouldn't watch it at all.

Hence all the ranting and raving we have participated in from the pulpits against the low morality of TV, and the degradation of the actors, etc., would have no relevance and could be dispensed with. But what would we preachers talk about? Judging and criticizing TV is such a convenient whipping post!

In forming any kind of adequate ethic on integrity it seems crucial that we learn to love the world *in the way God loves it.* The reason for this will become apparent as we proceed. That means this world is his creation and he is not anxious or willing to give it up no matter how much sin has done to it. And there are certain characteristics of that creation that have no parallel in heaven.

Earth is different from heaven. Our goal should not be to be angels but to be the most *human* beings around! God loves us as human beings. And yet for how many centuries have Christians left the impression that the greatest thing in this world would be to get out of this world? The greatest thing about being human is *not* to be human—to have wings, to be sexless, to do things none of us want to do in this life. How many of us are taking harp lessons—or is that an ability God will simply inculcate us with instantaneously, and while he also gives us the desire to play one?

SAVING THE WORLD

A second observation: God came to save the world not to judge it. That does not mean that there is no judgement in salvation. But condemnation was not his overriding purpose for dealing with the sin problem.

As a teacher of adolescents, I sit on a faculty that is made up of realists and pragmatists. Over the years you find practical realism creeping up on you—you are tired of the battles, you forget the changes you saw in other kids and each new case looks more and more incorrigible. The generations today are not like the generations before—you've heard it. We listen to case after case and the impression creeps in—eliminate this kid and my whole life will improve. So, you eliminate him and guess what?—you realize there are others waiting for the post he vacated!

It is generally easier to condemn than redeem. To approach a student body from a redemptive objective cuts across us even when we have the psychological theories in our head. I have studied adolescence in books—I now have two in a lab at home. I know many principles and I still find myself discarding them. Original sin cannot be overcome with paddles and tortures and punishments. I believe it, but I don't always live by it.

John 3:16 should never be read without John 3:17. I think integrity, in other words, is not our natural bent. Jesus stood firm to save—he did not come down here to condemn. He would not have had to come down here to condemn—that he could have done up there; just send down a comet!

In forming any kind of adequate ethic on integrity it seems crucial that we learn not only that this is God's world, and we can love it just as much as God loves it, but that we can love it in the *same way* he loves it, i.e., *redemptively*.

GROWING UP WITH BIAS

I grew up in a blue-collar home—neither of my parents finished college though they were supportive of my brother and me in our educational pursuits. Somewhere I inherited a strange kind of discrimination against the rich and the professions which I probably self-righteously embellished. Such an attitude is not that rare among college theology majors, as some of you former pre-meds will be only too willing to agree with.

At any rate when I began dating a physician's daughter from Los Angeles there were certain marks of degeneracy that I was anxious to make sure she was not guilty of. For a while I observed in silence. When her parents drove to the college I silently observed what kind of car they drove because that could surely be a symbol of sin. It was a very plain looking Oldsmobile station wagon—somewhat more extravagant than our seven-year-old Plymouth, but nevertheless not the mark of materialistic depravity I might have expected of such a profession.

It was at that point that my idealism led me to feel safe in revealing to this young girl my deepest religious convictions on material affluence, its degrading effects on the remnant church, and the thrilling news that she had passed the first test of what might lead to her arriving at a plane high enough to be considered for wifedom. My words were less than tactful but since when do the unrelentingly pious find it affordable to be such?

"I want you to know how much I respect your parents for not driving a Cadillac," I proceeded, expecting her to be overwhelmed with my progressive acceptance. She smiled. In my perfection I only *saw* the smile; I did not *discern* the smile. Hidden in that smile was the second car, parked at home, with its fins sticking out in the street.

Completely naïve of this fact was I that the family had been driving Cadillacs for a decade or more before this new critic had entered upon the scene. I suppose I should have suspected it. But they were so nice—they just didn't fit my stereotype.

To make a long story short, I met the other member of the family when they deemed it safe for me to—when I had drunk so much at the families "wine vats" that the dilemma would cause me to consider very carefully what I was giving up in rejecting the eighteen-foot 1960 Cadillac with fins that could impale you.

When I finally saw it, and sat in it, and rode in it, and drove it, I admitted (only to myself) something very curious. Virtually all my conviction, I decided, had been rooted in envy—not religious faith. It was both scary and relieving.

To become *redemptive* is often like that. It means giving up a judgementalism that is a form of security but at the same time is reinstating God to his role as the one who ultimately knows best.

In summary, to love the world as much *as God loves it* for the reasons he loves it and in the way he loves it must be at the base of integrity. I believe it will also form the base of truth-telling.

DISCUSSIONS OF TRUTH

No philosopher would admit that a discussion of truth is easy. Pilate symbolized its elusiveness simply by evading Jesus' presence in the sand-in-the-face comment: "What is truth?"[3] That was his philosophical way of avoiding Jesus' personal invitation.

For Christians truth resides in Christ. Any attack on him is an attack on truth. And some may be tempted to suggest that because we have truth as it is in Jesus we need not worry about truth-telling in corporate enterprises such as churches and hospitals and practices and classrooms.

Christian history is dotted with incidents where people need not be told through truth if it could advance the gospel. Christian ethics have been criticized for this. I will let you decide whether that is justified or not.

Two modern thinkers—one a *behavioral scientist* the other a *social theologian*—can give some perspective here.

The first was Lawrence Kohlberg, (1927–1987) a professor at Harvard, a Jew not a Christian. Kohlberg built his view of value-development

---

3. John 18:38.

on the child psychology of Jean Piaget and through decades of observation, formulated his theory that moral development was a cognitive phenomenon. He believed that the mind had the capacity to bring behavior into line. You may judge that any way you wish at this point but don't get bogged down there for now.

In his six-stage development, a progression we all go through sequentially, though not necessarily always at the same ages, Kohlberg saw the human being developing from *premoral* where one acts simply on stimulus such as pain or pleasure, to stages of morality of the most infantile to most mature. A child learns at a point in life, when his brain structures allow it, that simple authority rules through punishment.

In the first stage, physical consequences decide one's morals. In stage two: "You scratch my back, and I'll scratch yours." In stage three being nice, pleasing-ness, approval, and the beginnings of conscience are present. Stage four represents the concept of law and order. It is rigid, and social order must be maintained for its own sake. Internalization of value is occurring. These four stages represent what Kohlberg called "preconventional" and "conventional" moral development. Many people never go beyond these four stages.

His last two stages he called "post-conventional"—and he would limit its acquisition to about twenty percent of the adult population—in their late twenties at least. Stage five—social contract is legalistic but based on individual rights and standards. Society agrees on what is moral. Laws can be changed provided it is for the good of society. Those in stage five understand this, grasp it and fight for it. Stage six is the stage of ethical principle. A person who has advanced to this stage of moral development will see universal principles that go beyond the conventional laws of society.

So, while the laws said that black people must ride in the back of the bus, the moral mind of Martin Luther King said—that may be the law but that is immoral. Society says harlots and publicans are the dregs of society. Jesus says harlots and publicans need friends too. Physicians do not treat *the well*—they work with *the sick*.

The second was Reinhold Niebuhr (1892–1971), who was a Reformed theologian and ethical professor at Union Theological Seminary. In his book *Moral Man and Immoral Society,* Niebuhr set forth his position that aggregate or corporate man has a moral blind spot. What happens is that an otherwise moral man will get together with other moral men and form a corporation—and the ultimate purpose of such a corporation does not matter—it can be a beer company or a church. However, moral humans aggregated find something curious occurring. While you might think that the morality will come out in increasing volumes, exactly the opposite occurs, said Niebuhr.

What Niebuhr was saying was that all organizations are human, and something happens to intensify the sinfulness of humanity when it becomes corporate. The propensity of societal collective political cooperation is immorality. The corporation becomes tyrannical, and the tyrant looks for a pretext to practice his tyranny.

Combining the moral philosophical observations of Niebuhr with the behavioral science of Kohlberg, and if both are basically sound in their conclusions, we can make the comparison that a creative, morally mature individual who may be operating in stage six is going to run into immediate conflict. Especially is this going to be inescapable if he does not develop survival fitness—he is going to run into immediate conflict with any organization. Because organizations tend to operate at about stage two: "You scratch my back and I'll scratch yours." Stage six people are not back scratchers. Yet if you didn't have stage six people, humanity would make no moral advance corporately.

Before you dismiss this out of hand, observe it for a bit. And before you accept it as a hopelessly predetermined failure on the part of sinful human society look at Niebuhr's solution. The only way to keep society/organization/aggregate man honest says Niebuhr, is to build into your organization checks and balances.

Physicians have such with the AMA. Labor has such with labor unions. Teachers, nurses, with professional associations, etc. These are ways that society has done what is necessary and what recognizes Niebuhr's observations to be sound. To allow for sensitivity at all levels of organization—sensitivity to God's creation, the creative mind is a gift of God—part of that human gift that gives society hope of integrity.

BEYOND SIMPLE ANALYSIS

I want to apply these observations now to a simple ethic of truth-telling which will not solve all the problems you face that have never even been revealed to me yet but bring all of this together. When you were a kid truth-telling was quite easy. Mom and Dad said, "Tell us everything." And you did. If you didn't you lied. Lies were definable. Truth was definable. Then you met your first friends—outside the home—not too much different because they were peers.

Then you went to school. Now you had not only parents but teachers. Pretty soon you had bosses. Then you had patients and they had families. And you had a spouse and children.

Professional societies, corporations, "aggregate man," federal agencies, insurance companies, tax returns, investors, and on *ad infinitum*. No longer was it simple. And the more complicated it got, the more complex; the more people you answered to, to more people wanting to hear a version of your story that pleased their ears. And the more you felt like Tevye, the milkman in "Fiddler on the Roof," who uttered those exasperating words after his first daughter has married a Jew of *her* own choosing, and his second daughter has announced a husband of *her* own choosing. Now his third daughter is marrying a *non-Jew*. And in his exasperation Tevye cries out: "How can I bend before I break?"

Suddenly truth-telling is no longer easily defined. What is truth to one is error to another. Because physicians and nurses are always on the firing line of responsibility and decision-making you cannot just get away all that often.

Here is where there is a central principle for the Christian communicator taken from the insights gained in John 3:16–17. God's model is to *love the world*—he entered the world, created life takes priority with God. With God *living* takes priority over *saying*. *Words* were for *creating life*. *Words* were for *living*. Truth is found in your relationship to people before truth is found in your words.

Think back when you were a kid—you had to tell your parents the whole truth, but they didn't have to tell you the whole truth. They told you what they wanted you to hear. There is a principle there—and be careful how far it is pushed. The principle is that we communicate intelligently when we communicate differently depending on the situation: parent/child, husband/wife, friend/friend, teacher/student, government/subject, friend/foe.

Dietrich Bonhoeffer illustrates this in his *Ethics*.[4] A schoolboy goes to school and his teacher asks him in front of the class, "Jimmy, is your father a drunkard?" Now Jimmy has two laws at work. He must be *true to his teacher*. To do this he should say, "Yes, teacher, daddy is a drunkard." But he also must be *true to his family*. The family does not need this added pressure. So, he *lies* to his teacher and remains *true* to his family. Here Bonhoeffer is suggesting that the child lacks the experience and the

---

4. Bonhoeffer, *Ethics*, 367.

tools to handle this situation. "No" is materially untrue, but the boy is *true* to his family. *Relationship* is prior to *words*.

Bonhoeffer also suggests that only the cynical fanatic would hold to the position that truth in words must be maintained under every and all circumstances. Such a person wounds shame, desecrates mystery, breaks confidence, betrays the community in which he lives, and laughs arrogantly at the devastation he has wrought. It is this person who sits in judgment on God's world, it is he who does not love the world as God loves it, in the way that God loves it, and for the reasons God loves it. Instead, he judges the world out of envy and hatred. And in the final analysis he "serves Satan."

LOVING THE WORLD AS GOD LOVES IT

Several years ago, a student wrote an article in an Expository Writing class in college. It was a parable, and it was to be submitted to a denominational youth journal. But in those days the paper didn't print parables because they were considered to be fiction.

However, her teacher was so impressed with the article that he decided to submit it anyway. To both his and her surprise the article won a prize, and she received a letter from the editor informing her something to the effect that though the journal did not usually print material of this kind they were going out on a limb. They would print it.

The article won immediate acclaim from youth around the nation. It is still being read and plays have been written off it. It also drew a great deal of criticism. But it demonstrated one thing in the minds of a great many people in the church. Just because it was a parable did not mean it was a lie. *Just because it never happened it still was the truth.*

Words are not the only vehicles of lies. Looks, silence, gestures, demeanor, deliberate omissions. These are all ways to lie. But a person who has learned to love the world *as God loves it;* a person who has learned a redemptive approach to life because of God's model of love; perhaps that is the person God has in mind when he describes the new earth as a place where there are no liars.

> [7] He who conquers shall have this heritage, and I will be his God and he shall be my son. [8] But as for the cowardly, the faithless, the polluted, as for murderers, fornicators, sorcerers, idolaters, and *all liars*, their lot shall be in the lake that burns with fire

and sulphur, which is the second death." (Revelation 21:7–8. Emphasis supplied)

In his poem, "The Fools Prayer,"[5] Edward Rowland Still (1841–1887), depicts a court jester called upon by the king to entertain the delighted guests with the words, "Sir fool, kneel now, and make for us a prayer!" With that he obliges—but the prayer takes a different turn than the king expects, as in the moment of inspired genius he prays.

> These clumsy feet, still in the mire,
>   Go crushing blossoms without end;
> These hard, well-meaning hands we thrust
>   Among the heart-strings of a friend.
>
> The ill-timed truth we might have kept—
>   Who knows how sharp it pierced and stung?
> The word we had not sense to say—
>   Who knows how grandly it had rung?
>
> Our faults no tenderness should ask,
>   The chastening stripes must cleanse them all;
> But for our blunders—oh, in shame
>   Before the eyes of heaven we fall.
>
> Earth bears no balsam for mistakes;
>   Men crown the knave, and scourge the tool
> That did his will; but Thou, O Lord,
>   Be merciful to me, a fool!

If we struggle and care to tell the truth perhaps that is evidence that we are learning to love the world as God loved it. Truth is not just something we tell, it is not just something we have, it is not just something we do. *Truth is something we are.* To be true to that is the beginning of integrity, a wholeness that offsets all our propensities in the aggregate, political organizations that, despite their faults, bring great blessing to God's creation.[6]

---

5. Edward Still, "The Fool's Prayer," in T. R. Lounsbury (ed.). *Yale Book of American Verse.*

6. For further reading on this notion see Edwin Zackrison, *For the Love of the World.*

CHAPTER THIRTY

Beware of False Teachers

"The greatest truths are the simplest; and so are the greatest men."
—Julius C. Hare

2 Peter 1:1–10

¹ Simeon Peter, a servant and apostle of Jesus Christ, to those who have obtained a faith of equal standing with ours in the righteousness of our God and Savior Jesus Christ: ² May grace and peace be multiplied to you in the knowledge of God and of Jesus our Lord.

³ His divine power has granted to us all things that pertain to life and godliness, through the knowledge of him who called us to his own glory and excellence, ⁴ by which he has granted to us his precious and very great promises, that through these you may escape from the corruption that is in the world because of passion, and become partakers of the divine nature.

⁵ For this very reason make every effort to supplement your faith with virtue, and virtue with knowledge, ⁶ and knowledge with self-control, and self-control with steadfastness, and steadfastness with godliness, ⁷ and godliness with brotherly affection, and brotherly affection with love. ⁸ For if these things are yours and abound, they keep you from being ineffective or unfruitful in the knowledge of our Lord Jesus Christ. ⁹ For whoever lacks these things is blind and shortsighted and has forgotten that he

was cleansed from his old sins. ¹⁰ Therefore, brethren, be the more zealous to confirm your call and election, for if you do this you will never fall.

RECOGNIZING MORAL DILEMMAS

The second epistle of Peter is not an epistle given over to many moral dilemmas. In a moral dilemma you have a situation where you must choose between very close oral distinctions—often two rights; more often perhaps, between two wrongs.

For example, there is a classic moral dilemma of sacrificial adultery where a woman commits adultery with a guard in the office so that he will use his influence to release her husband from a German death camp.

Which is more important? To keep her husband alive? Or to keep herself chaste? Does faithfulness to him not include doing what she can to save his life? That's the dilemma. Theoretically you cannot have both her purity and his life. So, you must now choose between the two. That creates a *"moral* dilemma."

We can complicate the dilemma. Suppose the woman in the story gets pregnant through this encounter? When her husband is finally freed there is a baby in his home. Should she tell him where that baby came from? Or let him think this is a war orphan she picked up while he was in prison? If she tells the truth what should his response be? Should he accept the child as a constant reminder of his wife's love? Or shame?

Such stories are interesting, occasionally happen and are not always easy to solve. And we can learn principles of clarification regarding our own decision making as well as intensifying our conviction of right and wrong. However, we have little of this kind of thing in this epistle.

This tends to be a book of sweeping choices between blatant wrong and/or clear right. We have in strong admonitions and illustrative encouragements to remain faithful to God under all conditions, whether you find yourself in a Christian ghetto or surrounded by paganism. We have warnings and promises, depictions of God's attitude toward wickedness and the wicked, promises of God's faithfulness toward righteousness and the righteous.

We have reinforcement and reminding for any Christian who finds it convenient or tempting to forget that Christ is returning soon. "Remember" is neither a word nor a notion unknown to the author of this epistle. And his writing style seems calculated to fit our varied personalities. If we tend to be chronically forgetful and must be reminded with fearful examples of God's wrath to motivate us from dead center toward faithfulness, this epistle will oblige. Remember Sodom and Gomorrah, remember the sinful angels, and remember the wicked world of Noah's day. Insist on persisting and we will share their fate.

If on the other hand, we find the promises of God encouraging and satisfactory inducements to faithfulness—if we thrive on the power they bring us—Peter will provide us an ample supply to get us through. It was Peter who wrote that most comforting thought:

> [4] By which he has granted to us his precious and very great promises, that through these you may escape from the corruption that is in the world because of passion, and become partakers of the divine nature. (2 Peter 1:4)

So, here we see the concrete issues of right and wrong clearly spelled out and played out. Partly this is true because the enemy, though subtle, was rather clearly defined in the days when this epistle was written. And the epistle is aware of the enemy.

All true enemies have a subtle side, and the enemy of Gnosticism was no exception. You will find as you read here that this enemy was insidious, deceiving, and exploitative. So, it has the marks of a true enemy.

But on the other hand, a Christian should have no trouble condemning behavior that includes such things described here: greed, exploitation, lust, and licentiousness. Peter reminds us in certain terms what God thinks of things and people who would deceive. It is important that we remember this as we study about "false teachers."

BEWARE OF FALSE TEACHERS

There are some crucial implications in this warning. First, there are some "surface" implications: not all teachers are true, trustworthy, or sound. There is the suggestion that Christian wisdom requires discernment. There is even the suggestion that there may be a conspiracy afoot.

Second, there are some "below the surface" implications. It may be that even the teachers are deceived, yet they are in a position to teach. In such a case there may be no conspiracy afoot, just misunderstanding or development of thinking. There is the suggestion that we can evaluate what may or may not be a "false" teacher. Finally, there is the implication that time has little to do with this problem—it was prevalent in Peter's day and throughout the era of Christianity. What are the implications for us today?

NOT ALL TEACHERS ARE TRUE

One need not read the scriptures very far before a pattern becomes apparent. When God through his Holy Spirit moved upon holy men of old to write down what they were told or shown, *another spirit arose*—and that was to object to what God was doing. When the true prophet arose, a false prophet followed.

Things have not changed. With the presence of Christ truth has become more definable, but the opposition to truth has not lessened—if anything it has increased. If prophets are in disrepute today teachers will serve the purpose better. If you are attracted by the miraculous as it comes through prophets, then you can be susceptible to a false prophet and one may be used, if on the other hand you are a skeptic about the supernatural then a teacher will serve a far better purpose.

This was true in the days of the angels. God spoke, and Lucifer demeaned. Direct contradiction was his method. Not much moral dilemma there. *God* said—*I* say. It was that simple. The moral dilemma came when the angels had to choose between God the creator, and the beautiful creation of God. And that was undoubtedly tough.

This was true in the days of Noah. The prophet sets forth the future of the world—it will be destroyed. The false prophets arise and deny. They are false, they are untrustworthy, and they are not sound.

I don't see that you must read the text of 2 Peter 1:1–3 to see that they are "dishonest." A false prophet or teacher can be very honest. And we have perhaps overstepped the bounds of our own commission when we begin assigning motives. The false teacher is defined by his views not by his heart. He secretly brings in destructive heresies. He denies the master who bought him. He is licentious. He is greedy. He exploits with false words.

I'll admit that greed, exploitation, the secret introduction of destructive heresy could be clearly understood to be acts of the heart and very conscious attempts to deceive. But I would not like to categorize all false teachers as having a dishonest heart. For two reasons: (1) God has not given me the ability to read the heart, and (2) I could easily become a witch-hunter who is convinced that God has laid on me the task of cleaning up the church's act. To me witch-hunting is every bit as dangerous as false prophets because witch-hunting brings the same ultimate result in the church as the false prophet: moral and spiritual disillusionment, organizational chaos, and loss of sensitivity and love toward all.

There was a time when, by using some of these characteristics listed here as a standard, you could have called Paul a false teacher. There was a time when you could have called Paul a witch-hunter. The results were not much different in either case. But Paul's experience proves that a false teacher can be honest to his progressive understanding of God's truth. Paul's experience proves that some of whom we label "false teachers" are still teachable and can develop out of that position. Through divine intervention Paul was converted and became a true teacher.

What if the Christians had killed Paul before his conversion? What a loss that would have been to the church. The Christians did not concentrate on destroying Paul, they concentrated on sharing truth. There is an important principle with regard even to false teachers. I cannot see that Peter is encouraging us to begin a witch-hunting campaign against false teachers. But I can see where he is reminding us to be very aware, to be on guard, to be wise.

CHRISTIAN WISDOM INVOLVES DISCERNMENT

A frustration that any professional teacher faces is the ignorant and complacent student, the one who not only says, but lives, the attitude: "I don't know, and I don't care." Teachers spend hours of think-time trying to figure out how to motivate and help these students. In some cases, pupils grow out of it, but others seem fixated for life. This drives the conscientious teacher on to create situations in the classroom that will move his student off dead center.

Recently I expressed my frustration in class by reminding my class all that I had done for them. I ended my appeal to enter the thrilling life of learning by saying, "I am doing everything in my power to see that all of you get up to a C in this course." And in tragic innocence that was comical, one student looked at me from his back-row seat with a furrowed brow and blurted out, "Why?" He couldn't see why I should care if he passed *if he didn't*. He was saying to me, "What's it to *you*?" He was saying to me, "If I get a D I'm happy, why can't *you* be?"

This radical evaluation demonstrates some of the inadequacies the student suffers in his attempt to evaluate and understand teachers.

A few years ago, in the 1960s when student uprisings were frequent, and administrations were somewhat held in siege to allow more serious student voice in the running of campuses, it became popular and accepted for administrators to allow students to evaluate teachers. Such questions were asked as:

> Does the teacher get your homework back to you in a reasonable period?
>
> Does your teacher keep up to date on his lectures?
>
> Is your teacher on top of his discipline?

More recent approaches to these student evaluators however have shown that students were largely unqualified to evaluate a teacher in some major areas that originally came under their scrutiny. One of these areas had to do with the *discipline* of the teacher. The reason the student was taking the course in most cases was to get up to date or to learn about that field. What then qualifies a student to critique a teacher in his expertise?

Furthermore, students often evaluate a teacher on his personality, his looks, and his disposition. Hence, the evaluation tends to be too subjective and thus not helpful.

More recently evaluations have been largely limited to such questions as:

> Is he on time for class?
>
> Does she return tests when she says she will?
>
> Do you perceive him as fair?

These are questions that students could conceivably answer with a degree of validity.

Peter's inspired instruction regarding the detection of false teachers requires of a Christian wise and informed discernment. It implies that we be informed as to what Christianity really believes and teaches. Peter stood firmly on the scriptures as the test and insisted that scripture was not a matter of private interpretation. Rather it came through the Holy Spirit as he moved the Bible writers to write. To discern something as *heretical* because it constitutes something I have never heard before, or never understood that way before, or find hard to believe, or do not wish to accept it, is inadequate.

"Heresy" can be the Christian equivalent to yelling "fire!" in an auditorium crammed with nervous people. There is a kind of fervor built into the word itself. Hysteria is on the other side of the door and innocent people can be trampled to death in the effort to get away from the alleged lapping flames.

In Peter's case "heresy" probably referred to the teachings of the Gnostics who had an elaborate kind of *salvation by knowledge* system that gave lip service to the importance of Christ but practiced a kind of baptized Greek philosophy. It dichotomized God and evil, it did away with essential Jewish/Christian elements of God as the almighty creator, it undermined the view that Christ was very God and very man at the same time. Ultimately it ruined the whole Christian view of Christ's atonement as a necessary payment for man's sins. The outcome was an antinomianism in which man justified himself in his sins and confused sin with righteousness so that there was essentially no difference between the two.

Hence Peter warns: Watch out for those who deny that Christ *bought* you—the ultimately high price of your salvation must not be minimized. This heresy along with that of preaching there is no law to which you need to pay allegiance brings licentiousness, greed, and exploitation. Don't read their hearts, look at their teachings and the results in their lives—see for yourself what *heresy* is and where it leads.

Peter is not calling for a witch-hunt that is equally as destructive to the Christian evangelistic enterprise and mutual trust in the church as is heresy. He is calling for discernment based on the descriptions he gives: a religion that downplays the "ransom" of Christ and the necessity of moral accountability before God.

Accepting Peter's counsel should help toward neutralizing our natural interest in becoming embroiled in conspiracy theories and thus feel we are somehow preaching the gospel or doing the church a favor. Of course, there is a conspiracy—Satan is adequately unmasked as the great deceiver. But Christian McCarthyism is not the great commission. And I submit that when one takes on such a task one may be consigning oneself to the status of a new false teacher. None of us is beyond that possibility.

THE EVIL OF FALSE TEACHERS IS SEEN
IN WHAT IT DOES TO THE GOSPEL

The warnings of Peter were against conditions that existed in his day. But he was saying—this has existed in the past, it exists now, and it will continue to exist. In our propensity toward eschatological hysteria, it would be easy to spend our time hunting for falsehood to ferret it out. While this may be legitimate in some cases, it seems that a steady diet of this would make us very insensitive to the felt needs of those around us. Rather than looking for ways we could help we would spend our time evaluating people and their positions.

Our scripture passage[1] has a clear spiritual tone to it about the importance of people. People are of value because of "the Master who bought them."

> [1] But false prophets also arose among the people, just as there will be false teachers among you, who will secretly bring in destructive heresies, even denying the Master who bought them, bringing upon themselves swift destruction. (2 Peter 2:1)

Our worth stems from God's evaluation of us in the atonement. Hence the great evil of the false teacher is that, advertently or inadvertently, he exploits people, he destroys people's spirit, he introduces a new reason for living—rather than to glorify God they now view him as a guru. He brings disrepute to the cause of Christ because of the bickering and chaos that results, as well as the unchristian actions and attitudes.

God's own attitude toward this whole situation is very enlightening. The apostle Peter writes that God has a place reserved for these people in the judgment. But even while they live they will not really *enjoy* life for he keeps "the unrighteous under punishment until the day of judgment."[2] That primarily indicates anticipated destruction which provides its own kind of suffering.

So final judgment is sure, but he still works to save. A false teacher could be a true one tomorrow. And if we are indeed true teachers, we could be false tomorrow. A lot depends on the methods we use in dealing with these so-called false teachers. Are they locked into their false teaching? Or are they themselves searching for more truth?

---

1. 2 Pet 1:1–10.
2. 2 Pet 2:9.

GOD'S DIM VIEW

Peter made it clear that God takes a very dim view of false teachers. He consigned the evil angels—those who were finally confirmed in their evil, to *tartarus:* the lowest depths of hell. He destroyed the world with a flood—and those who chose to swim without God went with it. It was their final decision. He turned Sodom and Gomorrah into ashes. And some chose to enjoy the flames. That was their final decision.

Be aware, wrote Peter, where teachings will take you when they minimize the atonement of Christ—for that gives you a clear picture of your worth from a divine angle. Be aware, wrote Peter, where teachings will take you when they minimize the law of God—for that law was not given as a limit on your freedom but rather a ticket to liberty and happiness.

Finally, but not by any means the least important, remember, wrote Peter, that God is a *saving* God. Even in the angels he found some who were true. Even in the world of Noah he found eight. Even in Sodom and Gomorrah he found Lot and his family.

When you have remembered that, use it as a model. That will bring you out of whatever false teaching you are doing or have done, and that will bring others to heavenly Canaan. Our passage of study closes on the optimistic and blessed note:

> [9] Then the Lord knows how to rescue the godly from trial, and to keep the unrighteous under punishment until the day of judgment, [10] and especially those who indulge in the lust of defiling passion and despise authority. (2 Peter 2:9–10)

CHAPTER THIRTY-ONE

I Have the Joy Down in My Heart

> "Joy is the life of man's life."
> —Benjamin Whichcote

JOHN 16:20-24, 32-33

[20] Truly, truly, I say to you, you will weep and lament, but the world will rejoice; you will be sorrowful, but your sorrow will turn into joy. [21] When a woman is in travail she has sorrow, because her hour has come; but when she is delivered of the child, she no longer remembers the anguish, for joy that a child is born into the world.

[22] So you have sorrow now, but I will see you again and your hearts will rejoice, and no one will take your joy from you. [23] In that day you will ask nothing of me. Truly, truly, I say to you, if you ask anything of the Father, he will give it to you in my name. [24] Hitherto you have asked nothing in my name; ask, and you will receive, that your joy may be full. . . .

[32] The hour is coming, indeed it has come, when you will be scattered, every man to his home, and will leave me alone; yet I am not alone, for the Father is with me. [33] I have said this to you, that in me you may have peace. In the world you have tribulation; but be of good cheer, I have overcome the world.

THE FABLE OF A GARDEN

When Bob handed me the seeds I had no idea what I was in for. Okra seeds are so unassuming. In my primitive, idealistic and somewhat naïve religion I had moved to the country where I could be *closer to the earth*. In fact, as a city pastor I had prayed that our next place of labor could be in a rural atmosphere where our children could grow and develop in a surrounding "free" from worldly influences. Such a setting required the growing of a garden.

When winter began to melt into spring I hired a man to plow up my backyard. I talked to Bob, who had an historical reputation for great gardens, and he gave me advice—rich advice. I bought a rototiller.

My wife also committed herself to this refreshing spurt of spirituality and added her energy as we sought to turn our red Tennessee clay into earth that resembled anything I had noticed in California. She would put the children down for their naps and pull weeds or bring them out from their naps to play in the clay while we sought to tame the wild land.

We planted the usual fare—radishes, green beans, corn, watermelons. As I think back on it now, I read no books about gardening, though I was open to suggestions from those who knew. Becoming a farmer did not enter into this venture—growing a garden was the goal. The children made friends so their interest in the garden waned. My wife spotted a green snake slithering down a furrow one day while she was weeding and that was the last time she ever stepped foot in the garden. So, I was left to enhance my spirituality alone.

As the only one in my family left who apparently still wished to go to heaven, I set about to raise my crop. But I found that as the summer progressed, my interest became thwarted by my battle with the elements—particularly the weeds. Another curse was the rain. While rain eliminated the need for irrigation it increased the likelihood of rot—and it seemed to me in my uninformed mind that my watermelons might have made it if they hadn't rotted on the vine.

With the combination of the weeds, the elements, my lagging interest, and the two weeks my rototiller was in the shop being fixed after hitting a pipe, I experienced near crop failure. I did provide sanctuary for gophers, field mice and other rodents, worms, birds, and snakes. What I produced was an outdoor terrarium that fortunately existed far enough from the house as to provide some beauty from our second story family room window. But when you got close to it, it became a virtual jungle teaming with frightful residents.

THE TALE OF THE OKRA SEEDS

Despite it all, one element in this story stands out above all the rest—the okra seeds. When Bob gave the okra seeds he made it clear that these were the best seeds I would ever have—a handful of seeds would produce a year's supply of okra for a family of four. And he was right. None of us had ever eaten okra but after sampling some, it became clear that one pod of Tennessee okra was a year's supply for my family of four.

I am ahead of my story—if you lived in the South you had to eat okra—so we set out to grow *the best*. Two rows of okra went in and were a smashing success—this was the only crop the worms stayed away from, the birds would not touch, the gophers let alone, and the insects avoided. That should have been a clue.

The day came when I picked my first bushel of okra—two rows had produced a bushel. After picking it I developed a strange itch, but it went away in about an hour. My wife boiled up some okra for supper and learned that you do not boil okra. That summer we applied every "tried-and-true way" to fix okra. Since boiling produces a kettle of what resembles slimy mucous, you must do other things to okra—like mixing tomatoes with it. Or you fry it in corn meal. However, I think okra's doom was sealed with that first evening when we saw that pot of boiled okra.

From that day I think I remember my two rows of okra producing a bushel a day. At first I picked it faithfully, for my religion included the thought that I should waste nothing. Each day we tried a new recipe. After a week it was clear things were not going to change. We appealed to friends who gladly took it. Each day I itched for an hour until finally I opened a "U-Pick" arrangement in the backyard with my neighbors—"U-Pick and U-Take and U-Eat."

The summer ended, people had their fill of okra and the pods were left to grow—and they grew. A normal palatable pod of okra is around 3–5 inches. When we quit picking these pods grew to 6–7 inches—then 10–12—and finally 15–16 inches (probably hyperbole). Then they reproduced and dropped their seeds.

Sorrowfully, I close the curtain on my experience—I plowed up the rotten stuff, and I pulled up the okra stalks and burned them. I leveled out the garden plot and I threw some grass seed out there and I covered the whole garden area with straw. If you were to go back there today you would not be able to tell that a garden ever grew there. The gardening period of my life became history.

BE OF GOOD CHEER

The instruction from God's word may seem remote to this story, but do not worry about that.

> [33] I have said this to you, that in me you may have peace. In the world you have tribulation; but be of good cheer, I have overcome the world. (John 16:33)

Jesus continually told us to take courage, be strong, stay faithful, rejoice and be of good cheer. Here John wrote about the work of the Holy Spirit—the representative that Jesus will send when he is gone. This instruction was given shortly before he was going away.

Life is like a woman in labor[1]—she experiences pain or sorrow, but when the child is born she does not go around talking about the labor—she rejoices that she has a child. Life is like the persecutor—he laughs when you cry. He ridicules while you weep. Life is filled with pain and heartache—but that will all be removed when the Spirit comes.

For some the Spirit has come, but you still have sorrow, so be careful not to draw any conclusions yet. What is disconcerting about life, even for Christians, is that we develop expectations that do not happen. Especially is that true for young people. Never in our stages of existence do we have such exciting, idealistic views of life as when we are seventeen. And we have built those up for those first seventeen years until we are ready for the great fall into disillusionment precipitated by reality.

I couldn't wait to get that garden going. I knew it would be easy to do. I knew people who were a lot dumber than me, I thought, who grew showcase gardens. I knew with my IQ that I would have no problem.

A major problem with the seventeen-year-old is that she is working with the information we have tried to give her. But she is also working with idealism that is like baby-fat.

In eighth grade I weighed 140 pounds and my mirror told me I was fat. In tenth grade I weighed 140 pounds and was skinny. What was the difference? In eighth grade I was 5 foot 4, in tenth grade I was six foot one. I had lost much of my baby fat by the tenth grade.

Now when we are seventeen we have lost little of our mental baby fat; we still look at the world very idealistically. So, we have expectations—we trust people and we are oblivious to many of the hard realities of life which we will learn by experience in the years to come.

---

1. John 16:21.

It is good not to lose all our idealism, but it is also naïve to preserve our baby-fat idealism. When that snake came through the garden it ended gardening for members of my family, even though there were still some good things we could learn from the garden. So, the Spirit comes into your baby-fat idealism, and you have certain expectations. You read somewhere that Jesus died, the apostles were persecuted, and great people lost their jobs or their lives for the cause of Christ. Somehow that is a showcase garden somewhere.

Have you ever given thought to how the Old Testament sanctuary is presented? We talk of the *beauty* of the sanctuary—its *glorious cloth* and its *fine fragrances*, and its lovely things—*the gold* and the *fine woods*. But if you think about the sanctuary without your baby-fat mind, it was more like a slaughterhouse. Of course, they needed incense—it helped to cover the smell. What would your kitchen look like if you slaughtered a dozen sheep on your stove every day?

You've seen the butchers at the grocery store with their blood covered aprons on; how many times a day do they change those aprons? The priests wore aprons and outer garments. But the picture books speak to our baby-fat minds. They encourage us to think of the *beautiful truths* of the sanctuary. The truths may be beautiful, but the sanctuary was not a pretty sight. If you have ever had to put a dog or a cat to sleep you know what I mean.

So, the Spirit has come, we think, but the pain and the sorrow are still here, and our life is unfulfilled, and we lose our children, or death takes our loved ones, or divorce destroys the harmony of our planned existence. And we wonder—what of those "beautiful truths"—what has happened to our garden?

The seventeen-year-old defines "joy" differently than the adult. If I walk into my classroom and exclaim, "We are going to have *fun* today!" I meet a barrage of excited questions: Are we watching a movie? Are we playing a game? Are we ordering out for pizza? I say, "No! None of the above! We are going to learn a thrilling new technique of memorizing!!" And the whole room becomes a chorus of groans. "Fun" is a relative term.

So it is with "joy." Joy has a special meaning for me. I cannot hear the word or think of the word "joy" without two things coming to mind. One is Christmas; because in first grade we had a Christmas pageant based on the theme, "Joy to the World," and "Hark the Herald Angels Sing," and Mrs. Groome our teacher dressed us up like angels and we danced (walked with vigor) around the tree, and sang, and opened presents and had cake and milk!

DEALING WITH BABY FAT RELIGION

The other is connected to camp meeting. Years ago, we had camp meeting on the college campus where I lived, and I used to love that. My grandpa would take me by the hand, and we would walk to camp meeting. Grandpa always had a pocket full of lemon-drops.

I went to the kindergarten division and we sang, "I've got the Joy, Joy, Joy, Joy, Down in My Heart." And I sat next to Bonnie. I had a five-year-old's crush on Bonnie. And that song became associated with my crush and that was a good feeling. I never forgot that song. I would sing it—with gusto. And somehow that whole situation created a baby-fat idealism about joy.

In dealing with our baby-fat religion, we must deal with our baby-fat *ideas*.

There are Christian adolescent psychologists and experts in the field of developmental psychology who would suggest that a young person's maturity, regarding religious experiential development, is at the point of the songs he sings. Kindergarten songs can indicate kindergarten development. Camp songs indicate that point.

I sat in a church service at a college recently in which I listened to *college-age students* requesting songs like "If you're happy and you know it clap your hands," and "I am in the Lord's infantry" as they stood and jumped and sat and marched and shot, and so on. When do we normally shed our baby-fat ideals? How can a joy be so far down in our hearts that it sustains us through everything life throws at us? And how can we shed the baby-fat in such a way that joy becomes a principle in our lives rather than just a fleeting feeling?

I'll take you back to my garden. I had so complete a baby-fat mentality about gardening that I threw it all away. I don't really care if I ever try to grow a garden again. It wasn't until I had attempted and failed at growing that I suddenly realized most of the things I planted I didn't even like to eat. The corn was fine, but how many radishes can you eat?

I did have visions of having so many watermelons that I could tear out the hearts and throw the rest away, but okra was never on my list of favorites, and I have never been particularly fond of yellow, green, brown, or black squash, all of which I planted. But the important thing is that because of that experience I became disillusioned with gardening.

How many Christians who believed the Holy Spirit had come had so many baby-fat ideas about God and life that they threw it all out when the sorrow came? They heard the part about joy from the pulpit, but you had to *read* about the *sorrow* part in the word. And they had seldom, if ever picked up the *word*. You pick up a paper, or a magazine, or some literature, but you don't pick up the *word:* because baby-fat idealism already *has* the answers to life. Why pick up *the word?*

The word would have emphasized the *suffering* of Christ, it would have pointed out the *sorrow* of life, it would have informed us of the *ugliness* of sin as reflected in the *bloodiness and horror* of the sanctuary. Baby-fat doesn't like that. Baby-fat likes fairy tales. Seventeen-year-olds like romances not painful realities. And that's normal for seventeen-year-olds. But it does not sustain in the realities of life.

Jesus carefully instructed that we would have pain just like the lady in labor.

> [22] So you have sorrow now, but I will see you again and your hearts will rejoice, and no one will take your joy from you. (John 16:22)

JOY AND FUN

"Joy" should have a different meaning to us than it has to a person of the world—to a person who does not know Jesus Christ. "We're going to have *fun* today" may not mean we are going to watch a movie today or play a game today. It may have an *eternal* meaning. I don't think Jesus would ever suggest that a trial itself is going to be *fun*. In all the New Testament I never see Jesus or any of the apostles suggesting that we should be joyful *because* we have it hard. That may be a baby-fat ideal too. I do see the instruction to rejoice *under* trial. I do not see the instruction to rejoice *over* trial.

You must admit that many people believe the caricature of the Christian with the long face—at least many people around seventeen. You've all heard the jokes: I saw a mule, he's looking just like your saintly aunt; the pastor went in for a portrait, the photographer upon hearing he was a minister said, "and you will want a portrait that depicts solemnity?" The workman walked by a church and remarked, "I've seen hundreds go in there, but I haven't seen anyone with a smile." And on and on.

Is that true? Or is that baby fat? Is dedication solemnity? My cousin tells of visits to grandma's house. "All I remember," he said, "is that we had to sit on a stool from Friday sundown to Saturday sundown and we couldn't drink Coca Cola."

As you watch TV this week try to define *joy* and where you can find it according to the descriptions given there, because if you have only a baby-fat idealism about the Christian's source of joy (or even definition of joy) you will slowly buy some of that worldly propaganda: money buys joy, power represents joy. The bar drowns sorrow and by implication brings joy. Music, amusement, in fact, basically any self-seeking pleasure will give a *spot of joy*.

THE CONSTANCY OF JOY

Here we come to the crux of the matter—the constancy of joy. One of the baby-fat characteristics of joy is that *it is a spot in time.* Seldom if ever does the baby-fat idealism allow for *a joy that is constant.* At Disneyland I may stand in line for an hour for that two-minute *spot* of joy. But somehow it was worth it. I cannot *sustain* that spot of joy, but I can go back for more.

If *eating* is my joy I can come close to constancy if I eat all the time, but then I suffer in other ways and those ways tend to deplete the benefits of my so-called joy: bigger clothes, new furniture to replace the old as it collapses under my enlarging frame, the sneers, and snide remarks from onlookers. These all take their toll as I seek to indulge my gluttonous joy.

It was Christ's contention that we can have *true joy* even in a world of tribulation. That joy is constant, it is deep in the heart just as a seed is deep in the ground. It is a *fruit of the Spirit.* Yet even though it is down in the heart it is not *rooted* in the feelings. It is based in faith—that God oversees this life of ours and even if we lose this present life he has done what is needed to insure our eternal welfare. And *that is joy*—down in my heart.

It is a part of Christ's religion that *true joy* bursts forth as a person recognizes his justified standing before God.

> [1] After this I saw another angel coming down from heaven, having great authority; and the earth was made bright with his splendor. (Revelation 18:1)

The saints go on to praise God for *his judgment!* What judgment? The judgment that they are saved. The teaching here is that God is giving reasons why we should be saved—not why we should be left out (an idea so many of us grew up with). When the day comes that you can honestly say, "Because of Jesus Christ and his work, aside and apart from me, I am declared righteous in his sight, and am assured a place in his kingdom!" Then you truly have that joy down in your heart—that joy that will sustain and keep you through whatever you may have to face.

A mistake all made in our baby-fat idealism was to confuse the fact that because our joy is down in our heart it was somehow *produced* down in our heart. Joy is a fruit of the Spirit—it is a *result* not a *cause*. It is like *happiness*. Happiness is something you reach *on the way* to some other place; it is not an end or a goal.

We can look at the okra again. I was only successful in growing one kind of vegetable, and that was the okra. I found out later that my soil was miserably suited to grow anything I tried to grow except okra. Had I created the right situation—added the right nutrients to the soil, ventilated the squashes and the watermelons, hung the peas and the beans correctly—I could have had a genuinely nice garden like my next-door-neighbor had. If I didn't like the results I could at least sell some of the stuff and get some of my outlay of cash restored. But instead, I only got fruit I didn't like because the conditions were only right for that. The conditions were also right for rodents, snakes, insects, worms, bugs, and weeds. And I got all of these.

> [22] But the fruit of the Spirit is love, *joy*, peace, patience, kindness, goodness, faithfulness. (Galatians 5:22. Emphasis supplied)

Baby-fat idealism does not produce the *joy* Jesus spoke of because it is not mature. It does not read life through the dictionary of the gospel to discover the real meanings there.

WEARING THE CROWN

I have the joy down in my heart: because Jesus has done something for me that was accomplished totally apart from me. I am not responsible for one thing he has done for me; I am not responsible for producing my salvation; I am his child and have the authority to control my attitudes; because of all this I have the *right* to be joyful! We can all ask for the courage to re-examine those baby-fat ideals we have and allow that joy to happen.

One time I was studying, and my two-year-old daughter came to the door with a yellow mixing bowl on her head. "Look daddy, I'm wearing a crown!" she exclaimed with excitement. In Christ we have the *anticipation* of a crown; in Christ we have *assurance* of a crown; in Christ persecution takes new perspective; in Christ sorrow is defeated; in Christ joy is constant not a spot in time. In Christ we have the joy down in our hearts that will give a renewed strength to erode that baby-fat idealism that causes us spotty and constant disillusionment.

> [33] I have said this to you, that in me you may have peace. In the world you have tribulation; but be of good cheer, I have overcome the world. (John 16:33)

CHAPTER THIRTY-TWO

Marked for Eternity

> "The mind's the standard of the man."
> —Isaac Watts

1 JOHN 2:4-5

> ⁴ He who says "I know him" but disobeys his commandments is a liar, and the truth is not in him; ⁵ but whoever keeps his word, in him truly love for God is perfected. By this we may be sure that we are in him.

THE ANGELS' MESSAGES OF REVELATION

In the "first angel's message" we hear the call to repentance.

> ⁶ Then I saw another angel flying in midheaven, with an eternal gospel to proclaim to those who dwell on earth, to every nation and tribe and tongue and people; ⁷ and he said with a loud voice, "Fear God and give him glory, for the hour of his judgment has come." (Revelation 14:6–7)

In this message we hear God's evaluation of "Babylon," "the beast" (the greatest representation of the misuse of religious authority that this world has ever seen).

> ⁸ Another angel, a second, followed, saying, "Fallen, fallen is Babylon the great, she who made all nations drink the wine of her impure passion." (Revelation 14:8)

Finally, in the third angel's message we hear the judgment of God on those who either follow or reject the claims of this Babylon.

> ⁹ And another angel, a third, followed them, saying with a loud voice, "If any one worships the beast and its image, and receives a mark on his forehead or on his hand, ¹⁰ he also shall drink the wine of God's wrath, poured unmixed into the cup of his anger, and he shall be tormented with fire and sulphur in the presence of the holy angels and in the presence of the Lamb. ¹¹ And the smoke of their torment goes up for ever and ever; and they have no rest, day or night, these worshipers of the beast and its image, and whoever receives the mark of its name."
> ¹² Here is a call for the endurance of the saints, those who keep the commandments of God and the faith of Jesus. (Revelation 14:9–12)

A DESCRIPTION OF DISLOYALTY

When the sword of judgment falls it cuts two ways. It judges some to be "righteous" and others to be "unrighteous." The "mark" and the "seal" are symbolic ways of referring to final decisions—those made by the worshipers themselves.

This message teaches the importance of final decisions. If we continue to be fascinated with the ways of the world we will receive the mark of the world. This eternal principle has an eschatological perspective: by beholding the beast we will at last be irreversibly changed into the likeness of the beast.

In this case, the "beast" represents all the evil the world can muster—everything that was originally good has fully now been perverted and used totally against God and his faithful. The contrast is clear: Satan vs. God, the false vs. the true, the synagogue of Satan vs. the church of God.

The disloyal are characterized by their total enamorment (Gr. *proskuneo*—to worship, to show obeisance, lit. "to kiss toward") with the ways of the beast and any manifestation of his principles. The Greek *eikon*, "image," indicates more than just a resemblance, but rather a perfect reproduction. The beast-worshipers are marked in the head and the hand; they have internalized (*the head*) the principles of the beast and practice (*the hand*) his ways. And they follow the world with a thoroughly religious fervor.

THE RESULT OF DISLOYALTY

All those alive on earth at the end of time face the consequences of their decision.

> [10] He also shall drink the wine of God's wrath, poured unmixed into the cup of his anger, and he shall be tormented with fire and sulphur in the presence of the holy angels and in the presence of the Lamb. [11] And the smoke of their torment goes up for ever and ever; and they have no rest, day or night, these worshipers of the beast and its image, and whoever receives the mark of its name. (Revelation 14:10–11)

On the one hand, they may seal their decision to worship God. Should they choose to do this, they suffer the force of the universal economic boycott.

> [16] Also it causes all, both small and great, both rich and poor, both free and slave, to be marked on the right hand or the forehead, [17] so that no one can buy or sell unless he has the mark, that is, the name of the beast or the number of its name. [18] This calls for wisdom: let him who has understanding reckon the number of the beast, for it is a human number, its number is six hundred and sixty-six. (Revelation 13:16–18)

On the other hand, they may mark themselves as worshipers of the beast and his image. With this decision they suffer the unmitigated wrath of God. The warning to those who would choose the experience of the beast's rule could not be stated in more fearful or emphatic language than that of the text:

> [10] He also shall drink the wine of God's wrath, poured unmixed into the cup of his anger, and he shall be tormented with fire and sulphur in the presence of the holy angels and in the presence of the Lamb. [11] And the smoke of their torment goes up for ever and ever; and they have no rest, day or night, these worshipers of the beast and its image, and whoever receives the mark of its name. [12] Here is a call for the endurance of the saints, those who keep the commandments of God and the faith of Jesus. (Revelation 14:10–12)

The Jews believed that punishment in God's presence increased the emotional suffering of the convicted.

In New Testament Greek, "wrath" is expressed two ways: either as *orge* or *thumos*. As *orge*, wrath disconnects from emotion to demonstrate a settled indignation based on careful and clear thinking. As *thumos*, wrath becomes a vehement fury very much involved with emotion and feeling. As *orge*, the wrath of God suggests a surgeon who carefully extracts the cancer from the dying victim to save his life. As *thumos* the wrath of God implies a volcanic tumult of terror and finality. The New Testament writers most often employ *orge* to describe the wrath of God, but in this passage John uses both *orge* and *thumos* to express the fearsome fury of God's final treatment of sin.

In Bible times it was customary to mix wine with water and spices. The language here suggests that this wine retains the spice mixture but not the watering down, implying the strong effects—an allusion to the book of Psalms.

> ⁶ For not from the east or from the west
>   and not from the wilderness comes lifting up;
> ⁷ but it is God who executes judgment,
>   putting down one and lifting up another.
> ⁸ For in the hand of the Lord there is a cup,
>   with foaming wine, well mixed;
>   and he will pour a draught from it,
>   and all the wicked of the earth
>   shall drain it down to the dregs. (Psalm 75:6–8)

The "wine that is God's wrath" is poured *unmixed*; (lit. "mixed unmixed") upon the disloyal.

> ¹⁰ He also shall drink the wine of God's wrath, poured unmixed into the cup of his anger, and he shall be tormented with fire and sulphur in the presence of the holy angels and in the presence of the Lamb. (Revelation 14:10)

Thus, the terribleness of the divine alternative to grace is apparent.

A DESCRIPTION OF THE LOYAL

Finally, John describes those who God judges to be "saints"—those "set apart" through their choice to be faithful to God in the face of the great fury of the beast.

> [12] Here is a call for the endurance of the *saints, those who keep the commandments of God and the faith of Jesus.* (Revelation 14:12. Emphasis supplied)

Christ calls for steadfast endurance and those who demonstrate this persistent loyalty are characterized by two qualifications: obedience and faith.

This is nothing new. These two qualities have always defined the faithful. Those who claim "to know Christ" but openly deny the power of Christ in their lives are sadly deceived.

Wherever the saints appear in the book of Revelation they are described: as "servants of God."

> [3] Do not harm the earth or the sea or the trees, till we have sealed *the servants of our God* upon their foreheads. (Revelation 7:3. Emphasis supplied)

As "undefiled," "chaste," having "no lie" in them, "spotless," and "conquerors."

> [4] It is these who have *not defiled themselves* with women, for *they are chaste;* it is these who follow the Lamb wherever he goes; these have been redeemed from mankind as first fruits for God and the Lamb, [5] and in their mouth no lie was found, for *they are spotless.* (Revelation 14:4–5. Emphasis supplied)

> [2] And I saw what appeared to be a sea of glass mingled with fire, and *those who had conquered the beast and its image* and the number of its name, standing beside the sea of glass with harps of God in their hands. (Revelation 15:2. Emphasis supplied)

But lest we be tempted to think that some merit goes to them or that they have somehow *earned* such a status we must always recognize how this status is achieved. They are always "clothed in white robes."

> [9] After this I looked, and behold, a great multitude which no man could number, from every nation, from all tribes and peoples and tongues, standing before the throne and before the Lamb, *clothed in white robes,* with palm branches in their hands.... [12] Saying, "Amen! Blessing and glory and wisdom and thanksgiving and honor and power and might be to our God for ever and ever! Amen." (Revelation 7:9, 12. Emphasis supplied)

And they are in robes made white in the blood of the lamb.

> [14] I said to him, "Sir, you know." And he said to me, "These are they who have come out of the great tribulation; they have

washed their robes and made them *white in the blood of the Lamb*." (Revelation 7:14. Emphasis supplied)

And they have been "redeemed"—a work done outside and apart from them.

> ³ And they sing a new song before the throne and before the four living creatures and before the elders. No one could learn that song except the hundred and forty-four thousand who had been redeemed from the earth. ⁴ It is these who have not defiled themselves with women, for they are chaste; it is these who follow the Lamb wherever he goes; *these have been redeemed from mankind as first fruits for God and the Lamb.* (Revelation 14:3–4. Emphasis supplied)

They have a constant song.

> ¹⁰ And crying out with a loud voice, "Salvation belongs to our God who sits upon the throne, and to the Lamb!" (Revelation 7:10)

The saints have no misgivings that whatever obedience they have given has been in response to their salvation, not to gain it. Indeed, the perfect obedience of Christ, imputed to them by faith, has been their salvation. Keeping God's law is the natural response of those who have faith in Jesus.

How is one numbered with the faithful? The principle is the same at all ages and will not change at the end. Through faith in the atoning work of Christ one responds to God's directions. Indeed, the great contrast is simple: either one pays obeisance to the ways of the world, here personified in the symbol of "the beast," or one worships God through faith. And this is demonstrated through a consistent desire and effort to obey God.

ABOUT THE AUTHOR

EDWIN HARRY ZACKRISON (1941—) was born in Hinsdale, Illinois, into a family of printers, educators, musicians, artists, writers, and editors. He was ordained to the Christian ministry in 1969. He received his Bachelor of Arts degree (1963) from Loma Linda University, his Master of Arts (1964) and Bachelor of Divinity (1966) from Adventist Theological Seminary, and in 1984 his Doctor of Philosophy from Andrews University in Theological Studies and Developmental Psychology.

After pastoring for seven years in Southern California, he became Professor of Religion at Southern Adventist University (1972) in Collegedale, TN. Moving to Southern California in 1984 he served as chair of the Religion and Drama Departments, La Sierra Academy, Riverside, CA, where he extended this education by taking classes at Lamb's Players Theatre, Willow Creek Community Church, Fuller Theological Seminary, University of Utah, and University of Las Vegas for training in dramatic arts. He taught drama and directed the La Sierra Academy Performing

Arts Society and founded *Expressions Drama Company,* and *Destination Players,*which traveled to Europe and Australia. He ran the PAS for ten years, directing and producing fifteen Broadway musicals, funding an orchestra for the academy and performing hundreds of drama sketches.

In 1987 he joined the School of Religion at Loma Linda University and La Sierra University where he served as Professor of Theology and Ministry. In 1996 he joined the faculty of Mt. Sierra College (Monrovia, CA) and University of Phoenix (Ontario, CA) teaching philosophy, humanities, ethics, social sciences and theatre arts. He was ordained to the clergy of the Christian Church (Disciples of Christ) and pastored the First Christian Church, Garden Grove, CA, and State Street Christian Church, Redlands, CA, for the next five years.

In 2001 he received his Master of Business Administration from DeVry University, Keller Graduate School of Management, in Pomona, CA. The next year he moved to Ringgold, GA, where he was Administrator of Ringgold Therapy Group and Associated Psychological Services, joined the faculty of Miller-Motte College, in Chattanooga, TN., teaching Humanities, Social Sciences, and Business Administration. He retired in 2014 after serving on the faculty of University of Phoenix for fourteen years in the Department of Humanities.

Dr. Zackrison writes from Corona, CA, where he lives in retirement. He is author of twelve books and many published articles.

BIBLIOGRAPHY

Aesop. *Aesop's Fables*. New York: Lancer, 1968.
Aquinas, St. Thomas. "Knowing and Naming God." *Summa Theologiae*, vol. 3.
Bradford, Gamaliel. "Exit God." *Shadow Verses*. New Haven: Yale University, 1920.
Bonhoeffer, Dietrich. *Ethics*. New York: Macmillan, 1975.
———. *Life Together*. San Francisco: Harper & Row, 1954.
Buckley, Jack. "Paul, Women and the Church: How Fifteen Modern Interpreters Understood Five Key Passages." *Eternity*, 31, 1980.
Bunch, Taylor G. *The Seven Epistles of Christ*. Washington: Review and Herald, 1947.
Campbell, Melvin and Edwin Zackrison. "Improving Your Church's Responsive Readings and Scripture Readings." *Worship Leader*, July-August 1994.
———, and Edwin Zackrison. *Interpretive Readings for Christian Worship*. New York: iUniverse, 2003.
———, and Edwin Zackrison. "Nicodemus at Night." *Readers Theatre for Christian Worship*. New York: iUniverse, 2003.
Donne, John. "Meditation XVII." *Devotions upon Emergent Occasions*, 1624.
Drane, John. *Introducing the New Testament*. San Francisco: Harper & Row, 1986.
Elkind, David. *All Grown Up and No Place to Go*. Reading, MA: Perseus, 1998.
Ellul, Jacques. *Apocalypse: The Book of Revelation*. New York: Seabury, 1977.
Furniss, John. *The Sight of Hell*. Dublin: James Duffy, 1872.
Gabriel, Charles H. "The Glory Song." Hall, J. H. *Biography of Gospel Song and Hymn Writers*. New York: Revell, 1914.
Hartford Institute for Religion Research. Harford, CT: Hartford Institute.
Herschel, Abraham Joshua. *The Sabbath*. New York: Farrar, Status, and Giroux, 1951.
Highet, Gilbert. *The Art of Teaching*. New York: Vintage, 1950.
Howe, Margaret. "The Positive Case for the Ordination of Women." Kantzer, K.S. and Stanley N. Gundry, eds. Grand Rapids: Baker, 1979.
Idle, Eric. "*Life of Brian*." Nashville: BMG Rights Management US, 1979.
Köberle, Adolf. *The Quest for Holiness: A Biblical Historical and Systematic Investigation*. Minneapolis: Augsburg, 1964.
Miall, William. *Can It Be True? An Inquiry as to the Endlessness of Future Punishment*. London: Elliot Stock, 62, Paternoster Row, 1868.

Mickelson, Berkely and Alera. "Does Male Dominance Tarnish Our Translations?" *Christian Today,* October 5, 1979.

Morris, Leon. *Christianity Today,* June 4, 1976.

Murdoch, W. G. C. "Edward Heppenstall." Vern Carner and Gary Stanhiser, *The Stature of Christ: Essays in Honor of Edward Heppenstall.* Loma Linda, CA: Vern Carner and Gary Stanhiser, 1970.

Neff, LaVonne. "The Ordination of Women." *Adventist Review,* August 5, 1976.

Neufeld, Don F. *Seventh-day Adventist Encyclopedia,* rev. ed. Washington: Review and Herald, 1976.

Pease, Norvel F. "Edward Heppenstall: A Person Tribute." Vern Carner and Gary Stanhiser, *The Stature of Christ: Essays in Honor of Edward Heppenstall.* Loma Linda, CA: Vern Carner and Gary Stanhiser, 1970.

Phillips, Max Gordon. "God of the Desert." *Inscriptions.* Mountain View: Pacific, 1970.

Pliny the Younger. *Letters.* New York: Penguin, 1963.

Richards, Lawrence O. *A Theology of Christian Education.* Grand Rapids: Zondervan, 1975.

Riles, Wilson. "Foreword to the Second Edition." Earl V. Pullias, *A Teacher is Many Things* (Bloomington, IN: Indiana University, 1977.

Spurgeon, Charles H. *All of Grace: An Earnest Word with Those Who Are Seeking Salvation.* Chicago: Moody, 2010.

Steinbeck, John. *East of Eden.* New York: Viking, 1952.

———. *Journal of a Novel: The East of Eden Letters.* New York: Penguin, 1990.

Still, Edward Rowland. "The Fool's Prayer." Lounsbury, Thomas R., ed. *Yale Book of American Verse.* New Haven: Yale University, 1912.

Stinnet, Nick, James Walters and Evelyn Kaye. *Relationships on Marriage and the Family.* New York: Macmillan, 1984.

Storrs, George. *Six Sermons on the Inquiry: Is there Immortality in Sin and Suffering?* New York: Bible Examiner, 1955.

Stott, John R. W. *The Epistles of John.* Grand Rapids: Eerdmans, 1964.

Sweeting, George. "Is the Church Unfair to Women." *Moody Monthly,* March 1980.

Sweney, John and Johnson Oatman, Jr. "Holy, Holy Is What the Angels Sing." *Seventh-day Adventist Hymnal.* Washington: Review and Herald, 1985.

Toffler, Alvin. *Future Shock.* New York: Random, 1970.

Thouless, Robert H. *Introduction to the Psychology of Religion,* 3d ed. New York: Cambridge University, 1971.

Walvoord, John. *The Revelation of Jesus Christ.* Chicago: Moody, 1966.

Wenham, John. *The Goodness of God.* (Downers Grove: InterVarsity, 1974.

Zackrison, Edwin. "Edward Heppenstall: Influence as A Teacher." Andrews Society of Religious Studies, November 17, 1989.

———. *For the Love of the World: For God So Loved.* Eugene, OR: Resource Publications: An Imprint of Wipf and Stock, 2021.

———. "Inclusive Redemption." Habada, Patricia A. and Rebecca Frost Brillhart. *The Welcome Table—Setting a Place for Ordained Women.* Langley Park, MD: TEAM, 1995.

www.ingramcontent.com/pod-product-compliance
Lightning Source LLC
Chambersburg PA
CBHW050347230426
43663CB00010B/2027